UNTIED KNOTS

Tales of Travel
and
Back at Home

James M. Flammang

TK Press
(division of Tirekicking Today; est. 1993)
Elk Grove Village, IL 60007

UNTIED KNOTS:
Tales of Travel and Back at Home

Copyright © 2023 by James M. Flammang

Cover design by James M. Flammang
Cover image source: Adobe Stock (104945343)

All rights reserved. No part of this book may be used or reproduced in any manner whatsoever without written permission, except in the case of brief quotations embodied in critical articles and reviews.

Print and electronic editions published by TK Press
(a division of Tirekicking Today), Elk Grove Village, IL 60007
First Printing: February 2023

Publisher's Cataloging-in-Publication data

Names: Flammang, James M., author.
Title: Untied knots : tales of travel and back at home / by James M. Flammang.
Description: Elk Grove Village, IL: TK Press: a division of Tirekicking Today, 2023.
Identifiers: LCCN: 2022951721 | ISBN: 978-0-9911263-4-7
Subjects: LCSH Mexico--Description and travel--Fiction. | Mexico--Fiction. | Travel--Fiction. | Chicago (Ill.)--Fiction. | Autobiographical fiction. | Short stories. | BISAC FICTION / Short Stories (single author)
Classification: LCC PS3606.L3545 U58 2023 | DDC 813.6

CONTENTS

Tales of Travel

Introduction. v
1. Night Bus from Memphis. 1
2. Night Train Out of Querétaro.. 6
3. Heading South. 16
4. Christmas in the Port. 27
5. An Old Man at Cannes.. 38
6. Entry Point. 46
7. Queasy Crossing. 51
8. Hostility in the Hostel. 55
9. Discomfort Zones.. 60
10. Highland Freeze. 77
11. Ready? Go!. 83
12. Roadworthy. 91
13. Get It While It's Hot. 98
14. Smitten.. 106

Back at Home

15. Desk Duty. 113
16. Bad Sports. 118
17. Hotel Del Rey.. 126
18. Wakeup Time.. 131
19. Winding Down.. 136
20. Scandal in the Dayroom.. 142
21. Slipping Into Stupid.. 149
22. Inhuman Relations.. 155
23. Mail Call. 164
24. Whites Only '59.. 168

From the Archive

25. The Last (Debt-)Free Man. 179
26. Slow Getaway. 198
27. Guzzler Gulch. 210
28. Crazyhouse.. 224
29. A Bad Time for Crime. 232
30. Sunday Morning Blues.. 245
31. Our Biggest Job Yet.. 260
32. Score One.. 271
33. The Courage of Kenneth. 291

About the Author. 297

Introduction

Countless writers of factual material turn to fiction at some point in their careers. Just about every copywriter, journalist or editor seems to have a manuscript for a novel or two tucked away somewhere. Or, perhaps more likely, partly finished and then stuffed into a drawer or file cabinet, just in case the urge ever strikes again.

Even though I've been a full-time writer for my entire adult life, I'm not one of those hopeful novelists. Oh, every now and then I've turned out a short story or essay. But nearly every time, a string of rejections from magazine and newspaper publishers brought that deviation from my regular quasi-literary life to an abrupt halt.

Before long, I'd return to what I did best. For more than 40 years, it was writing about automobiles and the car business. I functioned as a historian as well as a journalist, publishing some 30 books, half of them chronicling the history of the automobile.

Can an elder journalist/author who's concentrated on factual material for most of his life make a sudden switch to fiction? If you're reading this page, I guess the answer has to be Yes.

Some of these stories were written within the past decade. Others were developed many years ago – even *decades* ago – but never published. Quite a few were finally completed long after the first words were committed to paper. Or, for more recent pieces, to the laptop's innards.

Literary antiquities, you might say. Tales from the past – tossed aside long ago, but filed away for possible future use.

Stories are split into three categories: "Tales of Travel" and "Back at Home," followed by a set of early fictional pieces taken from my Archive.

Inspiration for the travel tales stems from real-life journeys, undertaken as far back as the mid-1970s. Those stories are close to factual, stemming from my own experiences. Or, in most cases, what my wife/editor, Marianne, and I encountered on foreign trips and during periods when we traveled or resided in Mexico.

Home-based stories are more strictly fictional, though most often with a factual foundation or undertone. Nothing new about that. Most authors rely, at least in part, upon actual events, observations, and thoughts from their previous (non-literary) lives.

Let's consider all of them to be fact-based fiction. Or, more specifically, autobiographical fiction.

But why fictionalize reality? For one thing, you don't have to worry about total accuracy, relying on memory that's likely elusive – rarely, if ever, fully reliable. In addition, you can omit or ease past incidents that add nothing of consequence to the narrative.

Our travels rarely resembled a holiday getaway, but generally felt more purposeful. When feasible, we've strived to avoid Americans, along with touristy locales or pastimes. Now and then, I must admit, we've come up with a small falsehood, claiming to be Canadians.

As quiet, unassuming people, we've often had difficulty establishing easy relationships with people along the way – but some that happened were beautifully memorable. On a train in Holland long ago, in a compartment shared with three young people, each from a different country, one of them expressed surprise that we were Americans. Why? Because we were quiet.

Living simply throughout our daily lives never turned us into backpacker types. Yet, we've differed sharply from typical holiday and vacation visitors, seeing the world through what might be considered a more analytical, observational lens than most, and shunning luxury. We invariably view ourselves as more traveler and observer than tourist.

My travel on business over a quarter-century put me into a wealth of lavish accommodations and multiple-star restaurants; but

Introduction

the lodgings that I remember most fondly were near the bottom of the price scale.

Several stories are about long-term stays, but with a bit of a twist. We didn't always know where, when, or if we'd be returning – or if we had a home to return to.

Characters described in these pages often resemble ourselves, at least to an extent. Whether real or fictional, they tend to be offbeat, different, distinctive – outliers, in today's parlance, or non-conformist in yesterday's idiom. Likely troubled in some way, but principled. Few are ordinary, boring, or dull. At least, I hope not.

"Back at Home" stories try to maintain a comparable working-class sensibility, including a greater kinship to labor than to bosses. Like those based on travel, they may come closer to the countercultural fringe of the 1960s and 1970s than to modern, sanitized versions of the world. People and places may be unfamiliar to many contemporary readers, but their hopes and regrets should ring a few bells here and there.

My attraction to passenger trains should be obvious in several of these tales. Ships, too. Some of the most memorable days of my life have been spent riding on rails or enjoying the breezes on the open sea. Public transit is another personal preference, especially when traveling in Mexico or Europe. Despite my professional relationship to automobiles, when traveling, I've been content to let someone else do the driving.

James M. Flammang
February 2023

Tales of Travel

Largely based upon offbeat travel experiences by the author, James M. Flammang – usually accompanied by his wife, Marianne – these tales blend fact with fiction in varying degrees. Most of the personal travel took place in Mexico, but the author also has been a frequent traveler to events connected with his work as an independent journalist.

1

Night Bus From Memphis

She eased aboard just after midnight, at the Memphis bus station. Young. A lot younger than me, so I shouldn't have been looking in her direction at all. Yet, something about her forced my attention, drew my reluctant but willing eyes toward her. Again and again, every few seconds.

Blonde. Shoulder-length and lustrous, but not the kind that suggested periodic chemical treatment. Natural, most likely.

Slim enough, but not starved-looking – though a heavy but loose-fitting jacket helped conceal her shape.

Pretty, too, in a gentle way. Not a beauty, but possessing an earthy innocence that suggested awareness – perhaps even wisdom – beyond her years. Or, could it be simple, middle-aged lust rearing its salivating, wolflike head? Try as I might, I couldn't quite rule out that possibility.

Settling gracefully yet firmly into her seat, nearly halfway back in the bus on the driver's side, she appeared to be alone. No one sat next to her, at any rate. And none of the boarding passengers asked her to let them climb past, to get at the window seat.

She occupied the aisle position as if born to reside there, moving little, appearing neither bored nor impatient. Just waiting, accepting that the coming night-hours, while likely uneventful, would pass steadily: minutes ticking off like flies that became suddenly bored and flew hurriedly away, on the edge of annoyance.

I was two rows behind her, on the aisle but at the right-hand side. I'd been on this bus since Chicago, and got off to take advantage of the brief rest stop in Memphis, en route all the way to New Orleans. A quick hot dog was the only available sustenance in the curtailed time frame.

"Five minutes!" the driver had called out while I was stuffing down that dog. I'd ridden enough buses to know that straying away for six could be taking a chance on being left behind. Most often, that five minutes would actually be ten or more before the driver slowly climbed back into his seat; but you could never be sure.

Feeling besieged by guilt and embarrassment, even though no one knew my thoughts, I wondered what it might be like to ask her permission, then wiggle past her into that unoccupied window seat. Idiot! I chastised myself. Maybe naked lust is all it is, after all. But then, the word "naked" began to prompt yet another series of wicked fantasies before I shut down my thoughts, pulling out a newspaper to occupy my momentarily-unclean mind.

I wanted to give her a name, since I had no idea of her real one. But that seemed a little too intimate. Too bold, too confident. Best to be anonymous in circumstances like this. Wouldn't hurt to imagine there was a cop somewhere on the bus, capable of reading my mind. Just to be on the safe side, keep any lascivious imaginings from gaining a foothold.

She wasn't "jail bait" young. At least, I didn't think she was. So, an encounter wouldn't draw the attention of the authorities. Still, she was of a different generation. Even when I'd been her age, I'd found it difficult to talk to young women. Now? She'd just laugh. Or scoff in disbelief. Or maybe look up in alarm, with the startled face of an assault victim ready to yell for assistance.

Or would she?

Far better to keep this blossoming relationship solely in the head. Few dangers present there. No chance for humiliation, unless you insist on doing it to yourself. No regret, either – or perhaps more frightful yet, acceptance. What would I do if she nodded yes? Was I ready for a real-life encounter with a young stranger, in the middle of a trip I was taking to try and begin a new life in the storied South?

Because this new hoped-for life was mine alone, I was traveling south by myself. Not that anyone I knew would have had any interest in accompanying me. Back in Chicago, I'd had a few acquaintances: at work, in the corner diner, leftovers from college. But no real friends.

Women? My last romance – and it was a stretch to call it that – ended months ago. Should have ceased sooner, to tell the truth. Things had been good at first. We were alike in a lot of ways; two loners, really. We'd come together for a while, but then it was time to go our separate ways. From the start, we'd both known that's how it would end. For me, that's pretty much how it always ended.

Probably for her, too, though Elaine never talked all that much about herself, about her private life, her growing-up years. In fact, it was as if she appeared out of nowhere one day, at the next table in the diner, as I was finishing yet another unexciting, but sufficiently filling, dinner. Probably perch. That was the Friday special. Every Friday. Cheapest plate on the menu.

Elaine wasn't anything like this bus girl. Bus woman? Not sure which was correct in this case. She looked so young, yet so mature at the same time. More mature than me, most likely. That wouldn't take much, to be honest.

No wonder I'd let my hungry eyes stray in her direction. Up until that moment, my life had been nothing but dull. Ordinary. Not worth mentioning at all. Time just passing; taking up space, waiting for something to happen that never did.

Twenty years out of college, and I'd done nothing. I mean, seriously, zero. Excitement? Adventure? That was for other people, real people – like the characters found in books and movies. No, I was the guy in the background, who not only never got the girl, but wasn't even noticed by anyone at the party. If I'd been invited there in the first place.

Would bus girl be exciting? Would she have thrilling stories to tell, exotic affairs to recount, intense trysts to recall? Or, despite her casual posture, her alluring silhouette, was she more like me than she appeared, underneath?

Though I couldn't see her face in the darkened bus, particularly since we both faced forward, I had no real idea what she looked like. My fantasies took over from reality, giving her the alluring eyes of a nubile young temptress, a gently curved little nose ending in a tantalizing tip, unpainted lips spread ever so slightly apart in a gesture of wonderment.

Then, I'd abruptly snap back into reality, all too aware that she probably looked like a thousand other young women. More like an overlooked waitress at the end of her shift than a reincarnated Delilah.

All through that long night, hearing only the bus tires humming their endless, droning cadence on the pavement below, my mind alternated between the edges of carnality and far more gentle imaginings. Not lust, exactly. Not quite. Rather than fantasizing a vigorous coupling of naked bodies, I pictured a gentle embrace, a thoughtful kiss with lips that barely touch; or at most, a bashful hand reaching toward the circumference of her breast, before retreating in embarrassment.

For part of that quiet night, I was in love. For the rest of the time, I chided myself for my foolishness and struggled to think of other things. Mundane things. The job interview that was coming up. Where I might live when I got to New Orleans. Each time, I failed to keep the yearnings from resuming their pathway directly into my consciousness.

She got off at Jackson, early in the morning. About six, I think. Hard to be sure, because my watch had stopped; but dawn was climbing into the sky.

Not that it mattered. I failed to follow her, as I knew I would not. Obviously, the right thing to do. Or not do. Still, what if the complex dynamic created in our brains could eventually ease into reality, and private fantasies could suddenly become real? Just in case it's possible, perhaps we'd better give more thought to our imaginings. Maybe this young blonde enchantress had a fresh life waiting for her in Jackson that could have been mine as well. Who can say? Who will ever know?

2

Night Train Out of Querétaro

That morning, we boarded the southbound train at San Luis Potosí. It was winter in the Mexican highlands, and that city had been frightfully cold throughout our three-week stay. We'd even seen snow on the ground. Scattered in white blotches at random spots, but actual snow.

Our dirt-cheap room had a private bath, but rarely any hot water. No heat, either. Nearly every day, we'd trudged downtown to sit a while in a grand restaurant that had electric heaters positioned along the lower walls. Good *comida* (food), too, but that was secondary to the cozy warmth emanating from those orange-glowing heaters. We'd have been pleased to sit there for hours.

People hadn't been too friendly in San Luis Potosí. Not nearly as much as they'd appeared to be when we'd first seen the place a few years earlier. So, we weren't unhappy to be leaving. We'd only stayed there so long because we had to wait for a tourist-card extension to arrive in the mail. *Lista de Correos*. General Delivery. Once it arrived, we were packed and ready to head for warmer days.

We enjoyed a relaxing journey through the Mexican mountains, aiming roughly south. The train was going all the way to Mexico City, but we planned to get off in Querétaro, about halfway down. There, we would wait for a train heading toward Guadalajara. By the next morning, we'd be there – the second biggest city in Mexico – if all went well. That little detail always had to be considered. This was Mexico, after all, in 1981. Anything could happen.

On our trip north to San Luis, for instance, we'd been ready to enjoy a leisurely nine-hour journey. We loved these old American rail cars, which had seen U.S. service in the 1950s and eventually made their way south of the border for another life. They even kept the dining cars, which served surprisingly satisfying Mexican "classic" meals. Tortillas and *frijoles* – beans – came with every order.

As things turned out, that trip got a lot more leisurely than we had in mind. Hours after we were supposed to have reached San Luis, in the dark of night, I woke with a start to see that we were sitting motionless on a siding. Who knew where? Nobody seemed to know what had happened. Not the conductor, not the other passengers, who had sat buzzing in conversation through most of the evening, at the other end of our First Class coach.

Now, all was subdued. Silent. Minutes passed. Hours. By the time the sun rose, shedding its first shards of illumination on the arid desert floor, the train was moving again. Slowly at first. Then, little by little, getting close to normal speed as even more hours passed.

When we finally pulled into a city, I asked someone: "Is this San Luis Potosí?" No, he said. Aguascalientes.

I was mystified. By my recollection of the Mexican map, Aguascalientes was far from San Luis, in the wrong direction.

Several hours later, we finally reached San Luis, but it looked more like an entry point into hell. Way before we neared the station, hordes of young Mexican boys were running toward the moving train, climbing aboard – through the windows.

Was this some weird form of banditry? No, we soon realized. These were members of families that had been waiting for the long-delayed train. When they learned that it was getting close, each family sent its most fleet-footed young fellow to climb aboard prematurely and quickly claim seats for the family.

By the time we reached the station, the aisles were jammed to immovability. How can we ever get out? we wondered. Somehow, after plenty of pushing and shoving, we managed to squeeze ourselves and our luggage past the new arrivals and out to the platform. Our nine-hour trip had taken 37 hours. The reason? As we learned later, an explosion in a tunnel along the route had required diversion of the train in a completely different direction.

Now, heading back south again three weeks later, the mood was far more relaxed. Out in the fields, the *campesinos* were busy at their agrarian tasks: lifting, pulling, digging, straining. Our own physical exertions were no more taxing than lifting a fork or a cup. We were right in the middle of a four-month stay in Mexico, remaining a couple of weeks at each stop before climbing aboard yet another American-made coach car, left over from the past and given new life south of the border.

This was the 1980s, and trains still crisscrossed the country. Rail transport had been a vital part of the 1910 Revolution; but by now, their popularity had seriously waned. Buses were the preferred mode of transport for nearly every Mexican: rich or poor, urban or rural. They were also the choice of most foreigners visiting (or residing) in this lovely and vibrant, but inevitably-troubled, nation.

An incident on a cross-country VIA Rail train in Canada, a couple of years later, demonstrated a stark difference in passenger behavior. Two young gentlemen from Newfoundland, often dubbed "Newfies" by their compatriots, were frightfully drunk after midnight. So intoxicated that they sprawled along the aisle of our train car, preventing other passengers from getting by without stepping on one or both of them.

In Mexico, virtually all train riders we encountered, at least in First Class, were polite and reserved, civilized and quiet. Ordinarily, Canadians are perceived as particularly well-behaved in public. At least two "Newfies" apparently served as exceptions to that rule.

Because no trains went directly from San Luis Potosí to Guadalajara, we had to make a transfer in Querétaro – a midsize metropolis, some four hours northwest of Mexico City. This time, we hoped for an arrival time closer to the schedule. Not that any of the stations *had* schedules, either posted or printed. Nor did any of the passengers. We weren't even sure the employees on the train had them.

In the smaller towns and cities, at least, the most you'd find would be a chalkboard with figures scrawled on it to indicate that a train was scheduled at a particular time. Did it run every day? Were there any details passengers should know about? No one could say. You just took your chances.

Except in the bigger cities, too, there was often no one to ask. Train employees were seldom seen – and if spotted, tended to be involved in completely different duties, oblivious to the fate of any waiting passengers.

Back in Chicago, at the main public library, in a fortuitous bit of foresight before leaving for Mexico, I'd photocopied a batch of schedules from an international rail guide. As a result, I may have been the only person on the whole system who possessed a sheet of paper stating when our train was due to arrive in Querétaro.

Time tended to be somewhat flexible in Mexico, compared to the U.S. To our surprise, our southbound train was just about on time, reaching Querétaro at 5 o'clock. So far, so good. Our next train wasn't due to arrive until 11:00 p.m., so we had quite a long wait ahead of us. Still, no reason that should be a problem.

Even though the train platform was long, the waiting room was small. Little more than a good-sized storefront, maybe 20 feet square. A few hard benches, *sanitarios* – public toilets – and a chalkboard that dispensed no useful information at all. A ticket window, shuttered, with no indication of when – or if – an agent might appear.

Although we'd had a filling lunch on the southbound train that afternoon, hunger began to gnaw a bit, an hour or so into our wait. We'd acquired no information about eating places in the area, but Mexican neighborhoods are invariably jam-packed with taquerías, typically tiny storefront purveyors of edibles. Leaving my wife to guard the suitcases, I walked a couple of blocks in one direction. Then another, and another.

After the fourth such trek, I returned to the waiting room to report that this portion of Querétaro was the exception: there appeared to be no restaurants within a two-block radius that looked satisfactory. Because both of us were prone to stomach upsets when traveling in the country, we had to exercise a bit of caution about what and where we ate. But I'd been unable to spot any establishment that looked even a little bit promising.

Much later, we learned that had I gone just a block farther in one of those directions, I'd have reached the apex of a slight hill and could have seen the sprawl of Querétaro dead-ahead. An abundance of tantalizing cafés, hotels, and full-service restaurants lay scattered through the historic center of the city. Instead, we made do with leftover crackers and nuts, vowing to get an abundant breakfast in Guadalajara when we arrived shortly after dawn the next morning.

Every now and then, someone walked into the station and took a seat on one of those unwelcoming benches. Another passenger waiting for the 11 o'clock to Guadalajara? Maybe. Often as not, though, that new arrival would sit for a time, then stand up, look around, and leave the waiting room. Eventually, we realized that the station, which at least provided a place to sit, was a temporary resting spot for people in the area.

Or sometimes, a more permanent rest stop. After three hours or so, a seemingly heavy-set man, wrapped in ponchos and blankets, eased into the waiting room and plopped down on one of the benches. Within seconds, it became obvious that he was a homeless street person – mainly because of the penetrating stench that he emitted. Urine. Plenty of it, from the smell of things. Evidently, he didn't bother with the barely-hygienic but clearly available public rest room, which was a few steps away, but used his own garb as a private toilet.

Though he sat there quietly, he stole periodic glances in our direction. Clearly, gringos were not a common sight in this waiting room. Neither he nor anyone in the passing parade of temporary visitors said a word, or gave any indication of hostility. Yet, it was clear that we were regarded as a curiosity, a rare vision.

Each passing minute brought an additional dose of uncertainty, gnawing at our increasingly frenzied minds. For long periods, we hardly said a word to each other. I couldn't help but ask myself the obvious question: What if the train doesn't come? Were we waiting for a mechanized Godot, illusory and ambiguous, destined never to appear? Or, could our steel-wheeled escape carriage be trusted to arrive at the appointed hour, ready to sweep us away from the desert highlands and into the gardenlike beauty of Guadalajara.

Like many public toilets in Mexico, outside the major tourist areas, the *sanitario* in this tiny station was not something to look forward to using. Strictly for urgent needs. While occupying a stall during a sudden bodily emergency, I glanced downward to observe what looked like a prehistoric little creature crawling up from the sewer grate. A lizard of some sort, no doubt; but despite its diminutive size, it looked like it belonged back with the dinosaurs.

Back on the bench in the waiting room, we watched a well-dressed couple come in and sit. But not for long. They soon departed. Were they troubled by the crudity of the station? Mistaken about where they were? Stepped into the wrong doorway? *Quién sabe?* Who knows?

Tiring of waiting, I walked out onto the station platform a little before dusk. Strolling slowly alongside the tracks, I came upon a fellow wearing a campesino-style sombrero. Immediately, he began to address me in Spanish. Despite my efforts to learn the language enough to converse with a person, I couldn't understand him. Embarrassed, I admitted that fact. All he could do was nod, then look away into the distance, at nothing in particular. Was he also waiting for the Guadalajara train? I could have at least asked him that much. What kept me from putting together those few words of inquiry?

Simple fear, of course. Fear that he would answer back with words that entered my ear, got lost inside my language-feeble brain, and exited out the other side – having made no impression at all. Some gringos could just wade into a conversation in another language, somehow making themselves understood and grasping the gist of what others were saying. I admired them. And at the same time, sad to admit, almost detested them.

My Spanish in those days was shaky, if usually adequate to get us from one place to another, and taken care of once there. Still, ordinary conversations taxed my unconfident abilities, and I foolishly tried to avoid them whenever possible. Wrong move, I knew. But fear and unease often make a person shy away from situations that could ultimately be beneficial – and even memorable. After all, some of our most cherished encounters had taken place after exchanging a few words in Spanish with a passing stranger.

Just as darkness began to overtake the station, a man who seemed to be a railroad employee strolled past. Finally, I thought. Now we're getting somewhere. He disappeared inside the "employees only" area, into an office farther down the platform. Gone. Never seen again. Obviously, he wasn't the station agent, but some other functionary of the railroad. In any case, his presence had evaporated.

Soon, the darkness outside and dimness inside the room began to grow eerie, almost frightening. Now, we could hear faint sounds of liveliness from far off. Couldn't even tell which direction the sounds came from.

As 9 o'clock made its way toward 10, the seconds passing with painful sluggishness, the minutes seemingly endless, worry seemed to be enveloping my entire being. What would we do if the train failed to arrive at 11:00, as my precious paper schedule promised? How long would we wait before giving up? Then, where could we go? Could we find a place to eat? What was going to happen next?

Most worrisome, where would we go if the station closed up completely, later into the night?

Ridiculous, I told myself. This isn't deep Africa or rural Asia, it's Mexico. Close to home. Only the language differs.

No, came my immediate answer to myself. This was truly a different culture, and for these few hours, we were feeling lost within it.

Just before 11:00, the sound of a far-off whistle eased into the waiting room. Could it be? As the shrill cry of a locomotive grew louder, then louder yet, I had my answer. I dashed out to the platform's edge, to stare northward down the tracks. Yes, the light from the engine was clearly visible, growing brighter and bolder as the train approached the Querétaro station.

Mere moments after the scheduled hour, the eight-car procession wheezed to a halt. As I turned to rush back into the station, my wife was coming out the door, dragging our two suitcases along.

Once aboard, with our luggage safely stored in the overhead rack, we picked out a pair of good coach seats. The trip to Guadalajara was supposed to take eight hours, so a comfortable seat would be most welcome.

This being Mexico, nothing was perfect. At first, we didn't notice anything amiss. Then, gradually, a distressing stink began to fill the air of our coach car. Could it be the toilet? I got up and walked toward the end of the car, but turned back before I got there. Twenty feet away from the toilet, the stench became practically unbearable. Thankfully, our seats were far enough away to make the trip tolerable. Good thing we'd used the primitive but passable facility back in the station, because the thought of having to enter the one in our car was too much to bear.

Through the night, we both dozed sporadically. At one point, I awoke to see what appeared to be an inferno, smoke and flames reaching toward the sky, right outside our moving window. Was it a mine? An oil refinery? Some kind of sprawling factory? I never did find out.

Early the next morning, as dawn began to break, the train pulled into Guadalajara. No more infernos. Just lovely patches of grassy parks and neatly-manicured trees, almost forming a welcoming pathway into the city.

Guadalajara was a lushly beautiful metropolis, even in the hectic bus-station area at the edge of downtown, where we'd be residing for a couple of weeks. Then, we would be stepping aboard yet another Mexican train, heading north toward the U.S. by way of the Pacific coast to experience different views of this ominous, yet indisputably romantic country.

Meanwhile, Guadalajara was a great city for walking. Good thing, too, because we were compelled to walk everywhere. Never, not once, at any time of day, did we see a city bus that didn't have passengers hanging out the entry and exit doors, unable to make their way to the interior for their ride.

Needless to say, being less than agile ourselves, we decided it was far easier to walk leisurely, taking in the sunny ambience, than to make the attempt to cram our way inside any bus. Taxis were the only alternative, and we preferred to avoid them whenever possible.

Unpleasant visions came to mind of being well within the interior of a city bus in Mexico City, feeling a sudden, urgent need to vomit. I'd reacted swiftly on that occasion, calling out "Puerta!" (door) as loudly as I could – no small matter for a shy introvert. Amazingly, a path between the bodies cleared in an instant, providing a direct route to the outside, succumbing to nature's call the moment we stepped out of the doorway onto the pavement.

Today, four decades later, trains are long gone – erased during a frenzy of privatization in the 1990s. So are most of the stations. Last time I saw Veracruz, on the Gulf coast, its handsome terminal stood idle and neglected, chained shut. The station in Puebla had been transformed into a railroad museum. Hardly anyone seems to remember where Mexico City's massive Buenavista station was – or still is – located, no longer a mecca for cross-country passenger travel. Only a short-run commuter train has made any recent use of this once-glorious monument to Mexico's railway past.

Not only privatization, but lack of ridership, took its toll. Apart from the touristy Copper Canyon run between the northern city of Chihuahua and Los Mochis on the western coast, long-distance Mexican trains appear to be gone for good.

After Andres Manuel Lopez Obrador was elected president in 2017, he revealed a proposal to revive rail travel, initially carrying visitors into the Yucatan. Promises of a high-speed railway network have been made, but few would gamble on that ever happening. Financial and environmental issues brought early progress to a halt. Even if it does become reality one day, the experience won't be the same as it was in the 1980s and before. Not even close.

Who can say what that little station in Querétaro is now. A taco stand? Parking garage? Rows of retail *tiendas*? Whatever it may be, it's not likely to be the site of anything comparable to the quiet adventure of waiting patiently into the night for a train that might – or might not – ever arrive.

3

Heading South

When we left our home in rural Wisconsin that morning, taking a taxi to the bus station, we were carrying two large suitcases. Nothing unusual about that. With one exception, that is. Inside those two non-wheelie carriers were packed all our worldly goods.

After five years in a rented, hundred-year-old farmhouse just past the outskirts of town, we wouldn't be coming back.

We'd sold or given away nearly all of our possessions. Only a few boxes remained, containing personal documents and a handful of keepsakes. Those would be stored in the basement of my mother's apartment, in Chicago.

This wouldn't be a quick trip. Not a vacation, either. We intended to be gone for six months, if not longer. More importantly, we had no plans for the future, after our eventual return. We had no idea where we might be going, or staying, after crossing the border back into the U.S.

We had severed all our local connections, quitting our jobs and saying good-bye to friends and family. I abandoned the clients I'd accumulated as a freelance copywriter, working from home. What might I be doing – or trying to do – a year from now? And where? No idea.

Some good fortune had come our way, in the form of a small inheritance. Suddenly, after living paycheck to paycheck like millions of others, we had enough money to buy ourselves some time in a new place, with a fresh attitude and no tangible prospects.

All we knew was that we wanted a complete change in our lives, and the opportunity to forge ahead. Making a destination decision was easy. We would head south, into Mexico. No discussion needed.

We weren't kids. Certainly not twenty-somethings embarked upon a casual excursion to somewhere, perhaps promising beaches and booze, before returning to "real" life that would include career and family. Both of us were 40ish at the time. Urbanites. I'd grown up in working-class Chicago and lived there most of my life, until this five-year stretch in Wisconsin – a move prompted by a growing distaste for the big city.

Marianne, my wife for the previous six years, hailed from a smaller city in central Illinois: Peoria, to be specific. In those days, Peoria was best known as the headquarters of the Caterpillar corporation. It was also a test market for just about all of the fast-food restaurants and Kmart-style chain stores in the nation. Plenty of Americans flocked to those cookie-cutter establishments that had increasingly dotted – and to many eyes, darkened and threatened – the American landscape over the previous couple of decades.

We were not among them. Ours had been a simple life, owning little, unruled by money. To not only continue but expand upon that goal of simplicity, Mexico looked just right to us.

No one would call us adventurers. Yet, a few short-term acquaintances – folks we met on trains, in particular – did exactly that. Evidently, we looked like largely stay-at-home types: the sort who, when leaving home on holiday, remained strictly within U.S. borders. Even Canada was considered rather exotic by a lot of Americans, whereas our closest friends were Canadian and we visited them every year or so.

We'd actually met them several years earlier, in Mexico. They were traveling through Mexico, en route to South America, and took a lengthy break in the town where we resided at the time. It would be the biggest journey of their lives by far. All four of us were taking Spanish classes at a language school in the town. We quickly became fast friends and remain so to this day, decades later, now that we're all senior citizens.

Every few years, we also flew to London to visit relatives. All told, though we had no experience trekking through exotic lands, we were comfortable with on-our-own travel beyond U.S. borders.

We'd been to Mexico for the first time on a three-week honeymoon. Then, a year later, having fallen for the laid-back life we'd experienced briefly in the colonial city of San Miguel de Allende, we returned for a much longer stay: almost five months. Would have been longer yet, but Marianne took a nasty fall while walking in the hills outside San Miguel, resulting in a compound fracture that required orthopedic surgery in Mexico City.

Now, it was 1980. Autumn. We'd planned our trip so we would be on our way south, out of the country, right on Election Day.

Ronald Reagan ran for president that year. In response, I'd given up voting as a personal protest against a country that would nominate such a man for the top office, much less actually put him in the White House. Obviously, most Americans disagreed. Emphatically.

Our journey might be called "Southbound, Interrupted." Rather than head directly south toward the Mexican border, we planned to pass through three countries in one sequential bus trip. Focusing on Greyhound and its rivals for the U.S. leg, we could pick from a choice of long-distance, First Class bus lines once we crossed the Mexican border. Or better yet, we could look into taking the train for the long trek from Ciudad Juarez to Mexico City.

We'd already made some tentative plans for other Mexican train journeys, later in our itinerary. Train travel in that country was one of our main goals for the entire trip.

Such a trip would be easy to undertake just about anywhere in Europe, with its expansive networks of trains and buses. Not so much in the U.S. In addition to Amtrak, we would wind up taking a series of buses – all the way from Montana to the Mexican border, then onward toward Mexico City.

Eager to get some distance away from our previous home in central Wisconsin as quickly as possible, we departed the area by bus, but soon switched to an Amtrak train for the initial leg of our planned journey.

Established only half a dozen years earlier, Amtrak was already showing signs of shrinkage in coverage of the country. We'd always loved trains, enjoying not only the gradually-flowing scenery but the peaceful, cocooned ride. That joyful reaction to train travel would escalate substantially once we boarded the Mexican version.

Before long, we would be headed directly south – but not yet. Though our ultimate destination was Mexico City, we wanted to visit our closest friends, who were Canadian farmers, to relax and reminisce a bit about our weeks together in central Mexico.

At this particular time, they worked at regular jobs: he as a math teacher, she a visiting nurse. Before turning southbound, then, we began our trip by traveling northwest, aiming for the Canadian border above North Dakota.

At dinnertime in the train's dining car, we sat across from a clergyman. The Reverend and his wife were quite taken with the description of our anticipated journey, which lay ahead. They considered it quite an adventure, impressed that we had taken such a bold move – in effect, leaving our previous lives behind with no specific plans for the future beyond our several-month stay in Mexico.

Before starting our southbound journey, we wanted to rest up and give ourselves a peaceful transition from our prior lives, contemplating what might lie ahead. Therefore, a few days before the U.S. election, we stepped off the train at Minot, North Dakota. An hour later, we were crossing into Canada. Our friends lived a couple of miles outside of a tiny town in southwest Manitoba, not far from the U.S. border.

Untied Knots

Thankfully, our border crossing into Canada was mostly uneventful, though the same could not be said about border confrontations in later years. Customs/immigration officials weren't quite as rigorous and suspicious in 1980 as they would become later. Even so, a visitor might be eyed with mistrust, interrogated intently, and even pulled aside for more penetrating – even humiliating – investigation.

What, we wondered, would our crossing into Mexico be like? Lax? Tight? Easygoing or unpleasant? We'd find out soon enough. Our previous trips to Mexico had been taken on airplanes, arriving at Mexico City's airport, which had presented no problem.

Reached by local bus from Winnipeg, our friends' town was even more rural than our previous residence in Wisconsin, in a rented farmhouse near a city of 40,000 people. And like another world, compared to Chicago – my birthplace and growing-up locale. A week or so in this petite Canadian outpost sounded like the perfect spot to start making our transition into Mexican life.

Re-crossing the border into North Dakota after our visit, we checked into a pleasant hotel in downtown Minot. Friendly and somewhat classy it was, as well as sparkling clean,, yet inexpensive.

After supper in the hotel's dining room, we settled into our room, ready for a leisurely evening of political TV viewing. We were prepared to spend a long night watching the election returns pour in. Or trickle in.

Instead, soon after we sat down in the room, newscasters began calling it for Reagan. After absorbing those distressing election results, we were even more eager to depart North Dakota – and the U.S. – as promptly as possible.

Back on the westbound Amtrak train, this time we would travel a shorter distance: just 303 miles, to Malta, Montana, where we could board a bus headed south. After a single night in the state of Montana, we were finally pointed in the right direction.

While waiting for our southbound bus, I spent a lazy hour or so watching a UPS worker tossing packages into his truck, making sure each one rose into the air and came down on the truck floor with a hard thump. Was he angry at the parcels, I wondered. Their recipients. Or his job.

For a while after our bus got on the road, there was some doubt about its ability to get us to our next destination: Denver. Mile after mile, the driver appeared to be practically wrestling with the gearshift lever when trying to get the bus rolling along the highway at suitable speed. That was exactly what happened, he told me at the end of this segment of our journey.

Late in the evening, the bus halted for a rest stop, in front of a hotel in Cheyenne, Wyoming. Is there any other city name that sounds as purely western as Cheyenne?

Well after midnight, another rest stop promised time to visit a restaurant across the street, apparently open late each night – perhaps 24 hours a day – to accept bus-riding transients. Everything was dark in this small town, which I'd like to have seen in daylight. Could it be even more western in tone than Cheyenne?

Like so many far-from-fancy eateries throughout the country, the all-night diner existed to fill some basic needs, not to provide a memorable culinary experience. Basically, it was one of a near-infinity of food purveyors that stretched from coast to coast, and from the Canadian border to the Mexican frontier. As such, it was part of an America that was already beginning to disappear. Most likely, like its countless cousins, it was doomed to imminent or at least eventual extinction, especially decades later when the digitized world began to blossom (or, arguably, to deaden).

We pulled into Denver at dawn, heading right downtown. Most bus and train stations had not yet made the move to locations outside the city limits, away from the central business district.

Right across the street from the bus station was our next short-term residence: an old cattleman's hotel with high ceilings and doors, paneled with once-rich wood, practically oozing history and character. We expected to see cowpokes and ranchers striding bowlegged but confidently down each corridor, and were almost disappointed to find the hallways empty most of the time. After a bit of rest, we spent the day walking around the mile-high city.

Next stop: Santa Fe, New Mexico, not long after passing through Taos. Half a block away from our classy, highly-regarded hotel was the lively and busy central plaza, or square – often called the *Zócalo* in Mexican cities and towns. Both the colorful hotel decor and the atmospheric ambience of daily life within the plaza presented a welcome, advance taste of Old Mexico. Who wouldn't look forward to crossing that border as soon as possible.

Our final U.S. stop was El Paso, Texas, checking into an ordinary room in an older, low-budget hotel in the central area – practically steps away from the border. This would be helpful preparation for the basic accommodations we expected to occupy, once below the border. Soon, we'd be crossing into Ciudad Juarez, just across the Rio Grande. From here on, our lodgings would be Mexican hotels that were way more basic: the ones frequented not by affluent gringo tourists, but by Mexican families and low-budget business travelers.

Evidence of the presence of migrants and daily visitors from Mexico was easy to spot. Trash filled nearly every square foot of a small park near the border crossing.

Looking more closely, nearly all of the rubbish turned out to be wrapping paper, boxes, and bags. Like Mexicans in other border cities, residents of Ciudad Juarez as well as those hailing from farther south made the crossing regularly, to buy merchandise that would cost considerably more in Mexico. Striving to conceal the origin of at least some of those newly-purchased items, all wrappings that signaled their brand-new status were ripped off and discarded.

After crossing the U.S.-Mexico bridge the next morning, we walked quite a way to the Juarez train station to make inquiries about departures. Initially, we'd considered taking the Aztec Eagle – the best-known passenger train in Mexico – but that train left from Nuevo Laredo, some 600 miles to the southeast.

As in many good-size cities, a degree of wariness seemed prudent during our walk into Ciudad Juarez. However, it was nothing remotely like the Juarez of the 21st century, when news reports would regularly warn about the rise to power of the drug cartels, along with the fate of distressed migrants, mostly from Central America, seeking asylum in the U.S.

Inquiries at the railroad station produced the news that we'd have to wait a day or two for the next train to Mexico City. After a quick consultation, we decided to take a bus instead. That way, we could leave almost immediately. Early that evening, we boarded the Mexican bus on the Texas side of the border. The first leg of our journey took only a couple of minutes, as the bus stopped at the customs/immigration station on the Ciudad Juarez side of the Rio Grande. May as well have walked over the bridge, we realized later, and boarded the bus on the Mexican side instead.

Immigration officials had the authority to ask about entrants' funds, to make sure they had enough money to cover the length of their planned stay in Mexico. Rather than travelers' checks or credit cards, we crossed the border with $3,000 in cash, hidden within our underwear. As a result, we had to partially disrobe so the officer could meticulously count our dollars. He declared our bankroll to be insufficient, stamping our tourist cards for a 90-day stay instead of the 180 days we planned to be in the country.

A second customs inspection took place 12 miles south. Nothing was said to us as an officer strolled down the aisle of the bus. Rather than turning our great getaway into an early disaster, we'd escaped with our lives and finances intact, silently applauding the honesty of the border inspectors – though not their estimate of our living costs over the next six months.

We didn't plan to stay long in Chihuahua, the first major city on the Mexican segment of our trip. Just one night, most likely. After a quick meal at the bus station, we ambled across the street and into an economy-priced hotel. Cavelike rooms lacked windows, but the restaurant right next door promised a satisfying *cena* (dinner).

Among the patrons that evening was a group of unusually tall Black men. Overhearing their conversation, it became clear that they were players in an American basketball team, probably semi-pro, in Mexico to participate in a game. "How do you say breast in Spanish?" one of them asked a teammate after taking a good look at the approaching waitress. Now, what could he have had in mind? We deduced that he wasn't planning to ask about the composition of the chicken dinner on the menu.

The final leg of our southbound journey was a long one: some 895 miles by bus, all the way to Mexico City. A stunningly beautiful blonde woman occupied one of the seats. She could have been a movie star.

(That wasn't necessarily a fantasy. In Mexico, even affluent people might be seen on an intercity bus.)

In the dark of night, at the edge of a town, the bus rolled to a lumpy stop. Flat tire. As soon as the driver announced the problem, each and every man piled out of the bus to "help." (Their assistance appeared to consist of ceaseless chatting about the situation, rather than any physical assistance for the young driver who was changing the tire alone.) During and after this long once-in-a-lifetime trip, we've observed this gender-based phenomenon more than once.

Years later, while riding a bus between Oaxaca and Mexico City, a small SUV suddenly veered in front of a double-length Coca-Cola trailer-truck in the adjacent lane. Despite struggling to maintain control, the driver lost the battle and, in seconds, the truck twisted 90 degrees and headed into the air, dropping down an embankment. Each man left the bus that time, too, but most of them dashed helter-skelter down that rock-strewn embankment, ready to help with an obvious disaster. Sadly, as made clear by the solemn expressions on their faces as they trudged back up the incline, the driver had failed to survive.

Arriving in Mexico City in early morning, we couldn't help but feel awed: filled with hope and anticipation, not unlike the deaf girl in a movie we'd seen, as she arrived, wide-eyed, in New York, the biggest city of them all. Later in the day, when entering the city's massive and magnificent central *Zócalo* for the first time, that sense of bedazzled delight was magnified considerably.

We'd stayed at our chosen accommodation, the Hotel Paris, once before. This time, we foresaw a three-week residency. Each morning we paid our room rent in cash: Mexican pesos, equivalent to about $13 (U.S.) per day. Weekly rates or discounts were rarities in lower-end hotels.

All of the rooms faced an inner courtyard rather than the outside world. Ours was situated in a separate alcove, lacking a window but comfortable enough. Quiet, too.

No matter. Step out the front door, past the check-in desk, and you were in the middle of a bustling downtown street, absolutely packed with humanity. The steadily-moving crowd often made it difficult to make one's way along some sidewalks, but it was invariably worth the effort.

Our plans would take us elsewhere in the country after three weeks, but what's often called D.F. (*Distrito Federal*) was almost sufficient in itself. Around nearly every corner, you could expect to encounter something interesting or different. Maybe exciting, or inspiring. Or yes, dangerous – but worth the modest risk.

Inconveniences and potential obstacles were inevitable in 1970s-1980s Mexico, from availability of safe drinking water to traffic-riddled downtown streets and taxi drivers of questionable repute. Bandits were still a concern in northern parts of the country, but worries about drug cartels and their violent behavior were several decades in the future.

On the other hand, revolutionary fervor seemed to be growing.

On a previous, shorter visit, we'd already seen signs of political unrest under President Luis Echeverría: often subtle, but unmistakable. At the same time, hints of possible danger and uncertainty about what lay ahead were part of the country's attraction to longer-term visitors.

Many years later, we had to accept the reality that a lengthy trip such as our 1980-81 trek might no longer be prudent. due to crime and danger in the north.

Later in our journey, on a train in Mexico, we encountered a group of smug-looking students, wearing familiar backpacks that suggested adventurous activities. They gazed disdainfully at our worn but conventional, suburban-American suitcases as we struggled to raise them onto the luggage rack. Little did they know that those three pieces of luggage contained nearly all our worldly goods. And that unlike nearly all tourist visitors to Mexico, we had no home in the U.S. to return to after our journey.

Meanwhile, could this be the start of a new life? If nothing else, it would provide a period of respite from the political and other disasters that we believed were in store north of the border. We were ready for as much of Mexican life as possible. We felt right at home.

4

Christmas in the Port

Monstrous. Shocking. What else could you call the zealous, seemingly rampaging crowd hurtling down the platform in Mexico City's monolithic Buenavista station when the train to Veracruz was called. To inexperienced gringo eyes, the frenzied mass of fast-moving, mostly Hispanic humanity breezing past us suggested certain old-master paintings depicting hell. Perhaps purgatory. Frightening almost, at least initially.

Christmas was only a week off, and urban Mexicans have long been fond of taking in-country holiday trips at that time of year. Rather than attempt to rush in tandem with the teeming crowd, we kept walking at a brisk yet moderate pace down the seemingly endless platform until the crowd began to thin out. At that point, we were approaching the sleeper cars (*dormitorios*) at the end of the train. By then, nearly all of the train's passengers had clambered aboard one of the coach cars, whether First or Second class.

We were lucky. I'd reserved a roomette (*camarín*) for two in the sleeper section, so we didn't have to join the scramble for regular, unreserved coach seats. Still, it was hard to resist rushing down the platform in a frenzy comparable to the horde of other passengers. How could we be sure that we weren't missing something important by not picking up our pedestrian pace.

I still couldn't believe how tiny the fare was for such a luxurious accommodation. Luxurious by our standards, that is. Ordinarily when riding the rails, Marianne and I would be in one of those coach cars; but this was a special trip for us, part of a four-month stint of traveling through Mexico – by train, whenever possible.

Prior to departure, we'd spent our final night in Mexico City in a modest hotel practically across the street from the station. Strolling the neighborhood that evening, I came across a large group of people in a park, listening avidly to a group of musicians. Even without lyrics, their melancholy song seemed to convey a sense of both urgency and restraint, suggesting a Mexico of the troubled past, faced with hope for a more benevolent future.

Or, maybe I was too influenced by several books on Mexican history and culture prior to our trip. Before long, in any case, I realized it was a gathering of the Communist Party – the second one I encountered during our trip.

Purchasing our tickets at the station was a breeze, barely taxing my still-subpar grasp of the Spanish language. Not so, the conversation I struggled through in the hotel lobby. A fellow guest started right off in Spanish, not switching to his superior fluency with English until several strained minutes had passed. He seemed to be testing my facility with the language, at which I clearly failed, despite having studied the subject for years. Decades, actually. In any foreign language, some folks just never quite seem to manage fluency beyond the bare minimum. I may as well have been named head of that constricted-fluency group.

Throughout the huge old train station, just a few miles north of the city's *centro historico*, it was just about cold enough to see one's breath. More than just chilly, it qualified as frigid. A session of snow wouldn't have been surprising, but even that would not have been a deterrent. We were headed east, to Veracruz city, on the Gulf coast. By the time we got there the next morning, all thoughts of cold and sleet and snow would have faded away, leaving only visions of semi-tropical, caressing warmth.

Back in the U.S., Ronald Reagan had just been elected president for the first time. A few years earlier, we'd spent our honeymoon in Mexico, followed the next year by a five-month stay in one of the historic colonial towns that dot the central highlands. This time, we'd fled below the border to travel between several tempting cities. Mainly, though, we had come to ride some of the Mexican trains that continued to offer low-priced, smooth transportation between most regions of the country. We may have missed the renowned Aztec Eagle, but there were plenty of other routes to tempt the passenger rail enthusiast.

This overnight train would roughly follow the route taken by Cortez when he led his not-so-merry band from Veracruz toward the Aztec city of Tenochtitlan (near modern-day Mexico City) back in 1519, long before railroads would be invented. More recently, trains had played a major role in the Mexican Revolution that burst into the world's view in 1910.

A sudden silence overtook us as we boarded the train. The sleeper car turned out to be not only comfortable, but blissfully quiet: a silence that was almost eerie, in stark contrast to all the racket on the platform.

Originally intended for use by a single person back in the day when our train car was new and in regular use north of the border, in Mexico our *camarín* (roomette) was billed as providing space for two. Even though both of us were a tad on the chubby side at that time, we managed to squeeze into the narrow single bunk, with virtually no space to spare. Yet, we spent a surprisingly comfortable night.

In early morning, just past dawn, immediately upon awakening, I raised the window shade and we were thunderstruck. We were rolling through the jungle of eastern Mexico. Neither of us had ever seen a jungle before, and the sight was mesmerizing. Indigenous women could be seen washing clothes in the river. Even if we couldn't quite make out any strange creatures traversing the jungle floor, scurrying through the brush, we just knew they were nearby.

As our train approached the station in Veracruz, we could clearly see several of the nearby buildings, blazing brilliant white in the early-morning sunlight: the kind of gleaming, unrepentant white brilliance that almost hurts one's eyes, signaling the viewer to look away after a second or two.

This was the tropics, after all. Our first experience in such exotic territory, having grown up in the American Midwest.

One quirk of Veracruz city became evident as soon as we began the stroll to our chosen hotel. Practically every sidewalk pothole – and there were plenty of them – was filled to the brim and beyond with trash, matted down as if it had been there practically forever.

Perhaps the deepest-buried globs of trash had been tossed onto the ground, centuries earlier, by the European *conquistadores* who'd landed at what became a prominent port city. We doubted that it fell from the hands of indigenous natives of the region. More likely, of course, the garbage could be attributed to the bad behavior of recent, careless tourists. Trash in the wrong places was far from unknown in other parts of Mexico, but here it seemed like a unique characteristic of the community.

Our downtown hotel, the Santillana, appeared to be a sensible low-budget choice. Basic, for sure, but wholly adequate for our needs. At the equivalent of $13 U.S. per day, the price was right, too. Still, a glance at the seatless toilet in our private bath jolted me to attention for a moment.

On the plus side, the location could hardly be beat. Veracruz's *Plaza de Armas* – the central square – was a short walk away. Restaurants of every price level and likely quality seemed to be everywhere. Right across the street from our room, the fish market was loaded with mini dining facilities, promising seafood delicacies that could hardly be fresher anywhere. After all, the *malecón* walkway, adjoining the Gulf of Mexico, was barely a block away.

In the 1948 movie version of B. Traven's novel, *The Treasure of the Sierra Madre*, Fred C. Dobbs (Humphrey Bogart) refers to his current location (Tampico) as "the port." True enough, but with its centuries-long history, Veracruz has been an even more vital port city on the Gulf. Cargo ships and their crews from around the world dock there, forming a broad, ever-changing backdrop for the *malecón*. As a result, Veracruz conveys an unmistakable sense of foreignness, but one that's considerably different from the aura that marks other Mexican cities.

Delightfully reminiscent of Mexico in the 1950s or 1960s, if not earlier, Veracruz exuded a semi-tropical aura. Lively and colorful, the city appeared to function at a leisurely pace. Wooden marimbas roamed the historic area of the city, centered on the shady *Plaza de Armas* with its string of open-air restaurants and welcoming hotels.

Not many Americans or Canadians visited Veracruz in the early 1980s. Those who did tended to gravitate toward a handful of luxury resorts, south of the city – just as they do today. That suited us nicely. In our view, a day in Mexico without encountering a *gringo* was a good day.

One Mexican fellow sitting near us in the Santillana's lobby started a conversation by proclaiming his syphilis affliction, in matter-of-fact words, almost proudly. In this instance, I almost wished my grasp of Spanish had been a little weaker. Even if I had never heard of that disease before, its symptoms would surely be emblazoned into my brain by his explicit description.

Most people in Veracruz turned out to be friendly and pleasant. One *señora* sitting on a bench near us started to converse in Spanish, soon stating that everyone should have *niños* (children). Evidently, that included us, and she declined to accept our explanation for being childless.

Our favorite conversation, though, was with a pair of young girls selling sandwiches in Boca del Río, a suburb of sorts, south of Veracruz. They seemed to delight in talking with us, making use of their knowledge of English as learned in grade school. Talking with children is easier than conversing with adults, though youngsters typically *expect* to understand your words, and see no reason why you should have any trouble with theirs.

Movie-viewing in Mexico wasn't quite the same as in other places we'd been. When the film snapped and the screen went blank at an outlying cinema one day, patrons instantly erupted into a near-frenzy. Their reaction was not unlike drivers stuck in heavy traffic who would lean hard on their horns, as if ear-splitting sounds would somehow impel the immobile cars and trucks to start moving again, despite the lack of space for them ahead on the road.

Veracruz has long been well known for its lively *carnaval*, but that wouldn't take place until February or March. Even so, impromptu performances on the street could be seen now and then. One day, an especially sexy woman stood in the cargo bed of a moving pickup truck. Though she barely moved at all, she delivered one of the most sensuous dance performances imaginable, as the truck rolled slowly down the street.

Sometimes, it doesn't take much motion to produce a strong impression. Her dance moves highlighted just an ordinary day in an always lively, colorful tropical metropolis that felt more like a small town.

Anyone looking for liveliness didn't have to go far. At least one guidebook has called the *Plaza de Armas*, Veracruz's version of the *zócalo*, the most boisterous and merry one in the country. Music could be heard from all around, culminating in full performances on many evenings. Most *zócalos* in Mexico are at least reasonably quiet and serene most of the time. Not here. Though not especially large, Veracruz's central square was among the prettiest, and busiest, that we'd encountered in Mexico.

Early one morning, we took a train to the city of Jalapa for a day trip. A sizable college town, Jalapa turned out be a pleasant place to spend a few hours, boasting lovely parks and a vibrant, youthful atmosphere. Regardless, my strongest memory from that day didn't involve book-hungry students or blissful picnickers. It was the recollection of a two-headed calf (deceased and stuffed), mounted prominently at the tiny train station.

Before departing that morning, we'd paid our daily hotel rent as usual; but evidently, that amount had not been recorded properly. So, officially, we were not on the books for that evening, as we learned abruptly after returning to the hotel following dinner. Asked by the night clerk if we'd paid a woman who was *gordita* (chubby), she used her hands to demonstrate her colleague's ample waistline. Sure enough, that was an accurate appraisal. She accepted our recollection of the day clerk's appearance as evidence that we were paid up in *pesos* for another day.

Strolling along the *malecón* one evening, we came across the Mexican Navy orchestra, in front of a naval headquarters building, playing a sequence of relaxing nightsongs. Impeccably uniformed in brilliant white, seated on a large patio, the musicians emitted an almost dreamlike haze over the admiring audience. It seemed as if we were indeed enjoying a performance on a warm December evening, and at the same time hovering above the assembled crowd. Looking back, it was one of the most pleasant evenings of our lives.

A 1993 made-for-TV movie called *The Wrong Man*, starring Rosanna Arquette and John Lithgow, features a lengthy scene in that very spot, featuring a performance by that Navy orchestra.

Beaches in and around Veracruz haven't been considered of the same caliber as those in other areas of Mexico, but they could be just as enjoyable for those who are less picky. Though I kept my feet dry during our visit to the beach, Marianne got those shoes and socks off in a hurry to savor a quick wade in the Gulf.

Because Marianne became ill during our three-week stay – a common occurrence in Mexico at that time – I had to go out and search for *tortas* (sandwiches) and light takeaway foods to bring back to our room. Ice cream, too, to ease the stomach as well as titillate the taste buds. An enjoyable task, because Mexican ice cream is among the best in the world, created in a cornucopia of flavors that aren't likely to be found elsewhere.

Directly across the street from our little room, with its slow-turning ceiling fan, was the city fish market. Like clockwork, at 6 a.m. each morning, the vertically-sliding, corrugated-panel safety doors that fronted each stall clanged open with a resounding series of metallic thuds. Thus ended everyone's sleep, except for the most exhausted Santillana residents: the ones who could doze through any sort of commotion or disturbance.

The sound was not unlike that of a sledgehammer striking the base at one of those carnival games. The big device that tests your strength, by revealing how far your hammer swing can send the indicator toward the top of the scale. No conventional alarm clock could possibly jolt a person awake with such a blast of impossible-to-ignore sound.

Rich, colorful seafood cocktails contained just about every creature that swam in the Gulf, from the expected shrimp and sundry saltwater fish to octopus and eel. So fresh, the sea creatures might have leaped out of the Gulf just a moment ago. We consumed those aquatic delights while sitting on stools, facing the counter.

Like many resident Mexicans, we enjoyed a *comida* (several-course luncheon meal) each afternoon, often at a little hideaway restaurant, slightly removed from the city center, whose daily lunch special included watery black-bean soup. Although Marianne tended to shun that particular soup, in favor of other choices, to me it was a delicacy to be savored and remembered.

On Sundays, we headed for a little café near the *zócalo* for a major gastronomic treat: *paella*. Made with the freshest possible seafood, taken right from the sea that lined the eastern edge of the city, this delicacy was common in Spain but not quite as prevalent in much of Mexico. The only seafood to match it in delectability, in our view, was *huachinango a la Veracruzana* (red snapper, Veracruz style), a specialty of the region. Best of all, of course, might be the fresh shrimp that could be purchased in packets right along the beach, having been harvested from the sea only minutes earlier, consumed right on the spot.

Christmas in the Port

For breakfast, we frequently indulged ourselves at the Gran Café del Portal, a sprawling, rather elegant establishment across the street from the lively *zócalo*. Highlight of the café was the service of coffee, a beverage taken mighty seriously in this part of the country. One waiter would deliver a glass that contained a modest amount of rich, dark-as-night coffee. Then, when ready to imbibe, you'd clink your glass with a spoon. Momentarily, a different fellow, the *lechero*, would appear. His job: to pour steaming milk into the glass, flowing acrobatically from a serving pitcher that he'd gracefully hoist far into the air as he poured.

A similar coffee experience could be enjoyed at the Gran Café de la Parroquia, a short distance away, along the *malecón*. The Parroquia was even older than the Gran Café del Portal, said to have been founded in 1808.

One recollection from Veracruz is less pleasant. Rather than bring us a menu, a waiter at the restaurant in the deluxe Gran Hotel hid behind a pillar, presumably to avoid serving us. This was one of several occasions where we went unserved at restaurants, in Mexico and elsewhere in the world, for unknown reasons.

Streetcars had disappeared from most American cities during the 1950s, if not before. In 1980, though, two distinct types could still be found in Veracruz. A classy, beautifully restored tourist trolley followed a short, winding loop route out of the *centro* (city center) and into a residential neighborhood.

Not many tourists or other visitors were likely to be found on the conventional streetcars, which had been familiar on U.S. streets for everyday transportation a couple of decades earlier. Only a handful remained on duty in Veracruz, still retaining a sizable helping of character, but their condition was best described as scrapyard-ready. Plate glass windows, for instance, were likely to be broken, with sharp edges waiting for the less careful, so wary passengers had to keep their distance. Safety advocates would likely faint away at the sight of one rolling slowly down its track. Just a few years later, those authentic if badly-worn streetcars would be gone for good.

Because we were in Veracruz as Christmas approached, we were treated to one of the traditional *posadas*, whose origin reaches back to pre-Hispanic times. Children walk through the streets carrying a simulated, decorated altar, chanting Christmas songs and asking for gifts, in a procession that recalls Mary and Joseph seeking lodging. Finally, knocking on one of the doors along the route produces a welcoming invitation from the host.

New Year's Eve was less celebratory, though foghorns sent out melodies from the big ships in the harbor, marking the occasion at midnight. Most revelers evidently preferred activities indoors, with friends and relatives, rather than boisterous outdoor activities.

Thirty-odd years later, when in Veracruz for a much shorter visit, at Carnival time, I stopped into the Hotel Santillana and asked to see a room upstairs. To my surprise, it hadn't changed a bit. Neither had the price, which was an even greater surprise. The number of pesos per day was far different, but the equivalent in U.S. dollars was unchanged: still $13.

Sadly, the train station was padlocked shut, Mexico's passenger railroad system having been eradicated in the 1990s. But one of the old cars could be glimpsed through the dirt-streaked window in the now-shuttered front door.

Just about every Mexican city or town, especially those with a prominent colonial heritage, exudes an exotic atmosphere, even if it's unabashedly modern on the surface. In Veracruz, the sensation of foreignness has always been compelling rather than threatening, as if this port city were functioning in a different, earlier era.

In recent times, danger has become the rule in Veracruz – both the city and the identically-named state. Our first visit, lasting three weeks, had taken place in a time of relative innocence and anticipation. In 1980, life in Veracruz seemed slow-paced, yet exciting – even a tad adventurous, at times. Merely going to a movie or a concert could turn into a memorable outing.

Decades later, when I saw in a newspaper that three dozen dead bodies had been tossed out of a truck near a bridge in Boca del Río, I realized that I had stood at that very same spot, waiting for a city bus, just a couple of weeks earlier.

5

An Old Man At Cannes

On the train edging out of Paris, he couldn't help but wonder if this trip was a mistake. Cannes? The French Riviera?

Gazing out at the Mediterranean sea through the window of his coach seat, he was both excited and hesitant. Even a bit worried. Truthfully, more than a bit. Could it really be possible that he was headed to such a fantasyland right now?

Maybe he should get off at the next stop, he thought. Turn around. Head right back to the anonymity, the sparkling lights of Paris, where he'd spent the previous three weeks working on a special international project for one of his American clients.

On the one hand, this was a lifetime dream come true. In and around Cannes, according to the guidebooks he'd devoured, along with oral reports from colleagues who'd been there, he would encounter a veritable sea of naked – or at least, *mostly* unclothed – female flesh. Suddenly, as fleeting images of unclad femininity raced past his brain, his head began to feel flushed, almost feverish.

What could possibly be more beautiful, more perfect? As a lifelong connoisseur of feminine pulchritude – now there's a word you never hear anymore – nearly always observed from afar, he was now traveling toward what might be considered the real-life version of his long-held fantasies.

What lay ahead, he wondered yet again. Not just movie stars flocking to the annual film festival, which had taken place several weeks earlier; but ordinary women. Pretty women. Some less so, of course; but each one enticing in her own distinctive way. All would be savoring the sun along the Mediterranean beachfront, wearing only skimpy thongs to cover the essential yet forbidden regions.

Topless, though. A sea of breasts – big, small, average; alluringly shapely or a bit less remarkable – stretching across the sand, toward the Mediterranean vastness. And he'd be able to observe them all, first from the safety of the promenade that ran along the beach, evidently stretching as far as the eye could see.

Sure, most of them would be be sunbathing some distance away. Not many close-ups, most likely. Still, they would be bare. Almost, anyway. Bare and beautiful, practically all of them.

Though he was hardly free of impure thoughts, his adoration of naked women was not lascivious in nature. Not much, anyway.

He certainly did not delude himself into thinking that any attractive woman, clothed or not, young or mature, would have the remotest interest in him. Even in his younger days, such fantasies never intruded. He'd always been content to look, to watch, to admire – never imagining that the sensual recipients of his sidelong gaze would ever know, or care, that he existed.

Having been a film buff all his life, he thought Cannes would be the ideal spot along the French Riviera for his final foray into feminine beauty. He knew this would be his last chance. He'd never be back in France, or anywhere in Europe. From now on, with retirement looming, it would be the dreaded rocking chair for him. Recliner, to be accurate, parked in front of the old TV with its ancient cathode ray tube that he refused to replace with a modern flat-screen, as long as it continued to work well. Which it did.

He'd been pleasantly obsessed with naked women and girls ever since he was a young boy. Maybe eight or nine years old. He'd managed to find some risque magazines of that day, which set the stage for a lifetime of gazing at the magnificence of endless bodies – and a lifetime of way-too-frequent self-abuse. Or, in kinder terms, self-stimulation. Personal amusement, perhaps.

Even at his advanced age, having participated in the act what seemed like millions of times, he couldn't bring himself to use the precise word. The "m" word. Throughout his youth, young adulthood, and even his marriage, what a fictional character in the novel *A Confederacy of Dunces* categorized as his "hobby" was a regular event. So were nearly-ceaseless fantasies of naked women prancing through his mind.

Funny. Naturally, he knew that virtually every man engaged in this self-abuse, coupled with rich fantasies, for most if not all of their lives. They even thought of it as self-amusement or self-stimulation. Yet, he felt as guilty about it now, at age 72, as he had when he was 10. Probably more so. Weeks before actually planning the trip to France, he'd started feeling a little fidgety about it.

He had picked out what sounded like a charming little hotel, near the train station and only a few blocks from the beach. Sometimes, those online descriptions and reviews fooled you, but he'd done considerable research. He didn't want to be unpleasantly surprised, discovering that the hotel wasn't as convenient as it appeared, or as well-kept, or that it lacked some basic comfort or other. You don't want a once-in-a-lifetime experience to be marred by trivial problems that could be avoided by careful advance planning.

Arriving late in the afternoon, he considered staying in his room and starting fresh in the morning, but quickly rethought that choice. Instead, he hurriedly paced the four blocks to the beach area. At least, he'd be able to answer one question that had been bothering him: would people look strangely at him because he was fully dressed, strolling a beach filled with people in various states of undress? Would a clothed old codger be welcome? Or glared at — even chastised. Maybe condemned, in harsh French.

That query was answered quickly. To his surprise, he noticed that the beach, though far from crowded, boasted a fair number of sunbathers — accompanied by onlookers wearing sweaters, jackets, even suitcoats and what appeared to be light overcoats. Most of the sunbathers wore ordinary swimsuits, though some bikinis were on the skimpy side. His concern about being mocked for wearing a jacket and hat was obviously unfounded.

He didn't ordinarily wear sunglasses, but had them on today. Not because of the sun, though it was bright and pleasantly warm, but strictly so he could gaze at bodies of particular interest without having anyone note his intense interest. Just a precaution against irritating a possessive boyfriend – or a tough, angry young lady, for that matter.

Practically every time he looked in a woman's direction, he recalled a movie he'd seen about tourists in Paris. That sadsack actor Steve Buscemi, playing a stereotypical uneasy tourist, was sitting on a bench in a Paris Metro station when a young couple on the opposite platform, evidently feeling frisky, began to "make out." Intently. Suddenly, though he'd been keeping his gaze averted as much as possible, the engaged fellow turned, saw him and sat up, yelling in a threatening voice what had to be the French equivalent of "What are you looking at, you old fart?" And he hadn't done more than glance at the couple, because there was nothing to see. Not yet, anyway.

That kind of attention, he did not need.

His heart had been thumping ever since he left the hotel, and now it speeded up even more. Though he couldn't see any topless ladies in the vicinity, some of the bikini-clad women were real beauties. Not all. More of them than he expected were middle-aged or older, and even some of the younger ones looked a bit plain – like ordinary people. He liked that, actually.

Within seconds, he was feeling overwhelmed by the sight of so many women, typically clad in swimwear of one sort or another. A breathtaking paradise of flesh, he described the scene to himself. Unimaginably alluring. Already, he felt like he never wanted to leave. Meanwhile, he was trying hard to store visual memories firmly in his mind, knowing that he'd never see anything like this again.

Well before his arrival at Cannes, he'd worried that he might suffer a heart attack while ogling beautiful, semi-clad young ladies. But he'd never had heart trouble, as far as he knew. Besides, what better way to go?

After reaching the far end of the beach, he turned back and made another slow stroll through the sand. Again, the views were stunning; but at the end of his round trip, he felt a trifle disappointed. Even though topless bathing was supposed to be acceptable everywhere in France, the only ladies he'd seen with their tops off were lying on their stomachs, revealing only a hint of what he'd hoped to observe freely. Few seemed to be wearing authentic thongs, either, so he discovered few memorable views of bare *derrières*.

When he got back to his hotel, he was still elated, but a trifle downcast. Next morning, he was up early. Skipping breakfast at the hotel, he headed directly to the beach, figuring that he'd get a *petit dejeuner* a little later. Or skip that light breakfast and go directly to lunch.

Oh, was he glad he had a second day to wander and observe! When he saw his first topless woman, lying quietly on her back with smallish breasts in full view, he started to feel faint. As he strolled slowly along the beach, struggling to maintain a cool demeanor, even more women without tops eased into view. Not a lot of them, but enough to cause his heart to race even more rapidly, as his breaths began to grow shaky, on the verge of gasping.

Most surprising, except for himself, glancing back and forth as surreptitiously as he could behind his dark glasses, nobody appeared to pay any attention to the topless ladies. To regular beachgoers, they seemed to be simply part of the scene, not worthy of any particular notice. He'd read that French people maintained that attitude; but still, it struck him as startling when he actually witnessed the phenomenon.

Throughout his life, he couldn't help considering erotic images as "guilty displeasures," never able to suppress the intense guilt he felt when viewing anything of a sexual nature. Even the tamest DVD or men's magazine.

Despite his leaning toward visual lust since early childhood, he'd never admitted that failing to anyone. Not even to a doctor, or a psychiatrist – and he'd seen several of the latter during his life. For once, here in Cannes, he had an opportunity to see some of those delectable fantasy ladies in reality, not just in sexy videos and pictures – though it still ranked as "just looking."

Or was he merely one more dirty old man? A worn-down codger, hoping to leer at young beauties in a state of natural bareness. There was no way he could justify his urges in his own mind.

Bad habit? That's exactly what it was, he realized: leering at ladies on the beach, whether it was at Cannes or the local beach back home. Or on any street, in any park. He knew it. Never pretended it wasn't happening.

Whether anyone else considered him nothing more than a dirty old man didn't matter. That's what he considered himself, even when his eyes were aimed at nothing of consequence.

A long time had passed since he'd experienced the "real thing." His marriage ended decades earlier. Last time he went out with a woman was so far back, he could hardly remember it. Nothing much had happened, anyway.

Now, despite being male, he was practically an honorary virgin. Like that pudgy character George Costanza predicted about himself on one episode of the old *Seinfeld* show, he would spend 24 hours a day watching girlie films and videos on the Internet, given the opportunity.

He enjoyed peeking at *derrières* as the ladies walked away – only momentarily, so he couldn't be accused of leering. Or staring. When walking the streets, at home or away, he'd become quite adept at scanning the horizon ahead for hints of see-thru apparel, or the delightful jiggle of curvaceous (or pointed) breasts. He had intense visions of topless girls playing volleyball on the Cannes beach, as vividly described by a colleague who'd been there years earlier.

Then there was the constant struggle to keep his eyes from wandering where they didn't belong – gazing down the necklines of blouses or into loose shoulder openings of sleeveless dresses.

Or, maybe French gentlemen were just good at keeping their eyes focused straight ahead, while managing to observe all that could be seen along the sand: left, right, and, if you're lucky, straight ahead and nearby.

He'd read about the all-nude beach, too, and desperately wanted to see it. But that was a few miles out of town, reachable only by bus, and he figured he'd be so nervous by the time he got there that he'd be in serious danger of a stroke. Besides, he was just too timid and shy to "go all the way" like that. He certainly didn't want to create a stir, while in Cannes for only a couple of days.

One of those news stories he'd read noted that attitudes might be changing. Women were becoming less inclined to show their breasts in public, much less anything else. Evidently, a growing proportion of the French population now decreed any sort of display of bare skin to be "vulgar" – whatever the best French word might be – just as they typically did back in the U.S.

Was nudity on the beach really crude or tawdry, as those surveyed French persons apparently insisted nowadays? How could that be, when the female body – with or without clothes – was so darn beautiful? Even the ordinary-looking ladies are beautiful, especially when attired in a bikini or thong. Or less.

Surely, if anyone appreciated that possibility, it had to be the French. Not anymore, evidently. Not when a hefty percentage of the population now considered *any* sort of display of bare skin to be tawdry.

Each and every day, every morning, for his entire week-long stay in Cannes, he made his way to the promenade and onto the beach itself, trying to look as inconspicuous as possible. By lunchtime, he'd had enough. Not really *enough*, of course; that would be impossible. But his discomfort would overcome his desire after an hour or so.

On top of that basic guilt, he couldn't help feeling tacky about viewing the ladies surreptitiously, from a distance. He knew it was wrong. He worried about violating each young lady's privacy. Yet, he couldn't keep himself from doing it again the next morning.

At least, he hadn't spent each day taking pictures of the sunbathers from afar, much less close up. He'd shot only half a dozen or so, which turned out a bit fuzzy. Probably for the best, though he couldn't quite bring himself to delete them from his camera.

By week's end, he realized – and almost accepted – what he'd truly known all along. He *was* a dirty old man, albeit one who harmed no one. Not really. Not when he knew that thousands, millions, of forlorn males engaged in similar pursuits day in and day out.

Besides, no real, flesh-and-blood woman was ever going to gaze in his direction again. Not even an older one. Yet, the urges would surely continue to dominate his mind. They wouldn't disappear, or even recede into insignificance. So, what choice did he have.

By the time he got on the return train to Paris, he was glad to leave Cannes and the Mediterranean Coast behind. He'd gotten the most intense desire out of his system, at least to a point. But he headed home with no joyful memories from the week. In the end, it wasn't much fun.

6

Entry Point

It was 1980. November. Shortly after the election of Ronald Reagan as U.S. president.

Marianne and I were leaving the country largely – or at least partly – as a silent protest against his nomination and, at the point of initially planning the trip, only possible election.

We'd decided to cross the border into Mexico at El Paso, Texas, across the Rio Grande from Juarez. Practically all of our worldly goods were in our possession, tucked into a pair of suitcases.

Like the renowned Canadian author and long-term resident of Mexico, Malcolm Lowry, I hated and dreaded border crossings. Unease would be inevitable. Hesitation and uncertainty also were likely to impede our entry into Mexico. Some of that fear might have been eased if we'd chosen to fly to Mexico City. But on this trip, we wanted to experience some of Mexico's intercity buses and, especially, trains.

Unlike nearly all persons crossing into Mexico, we would be dealing with border officials while carrying $3,000 in cash, hidden within our clothing. That was quite a healthy sum in 1980, neatly sewn into several tiny fabric parcels (*bolsitas*), safety-pinned into briefs and panties. (Such a practice was wholly legitimate, but uncommon to say the least.)

No ill-gotten gains were involved; no drug money or anything illicit. That stash was simply our life's savings, augmented by some of the proceeds from a small inheritance.

Our funds were cash only: no traveler's checks, no credit cards.

Entry Point

I'd foolishly given up my FirstCard (a precursor to Visa plastic) in protest against one of its policies, and I detested traveler's checks.

Many entrants whisked through the entry process with little or no difficulty. Others were given a hard time. The counterculture era was over, but border officials could still be suspicious as well as officious. We knew we might be asked to show all our cash, all our dollars. Not only would that be awkward and embarrassing, but potentially dangerous. Corrupt officials were hardly a rarity in 1980s Mexico, just as they'd been for decades.

We planned to stay six months in Mexico. Because we'd been south before, we knew we had enough to last that long, since we were accustomed to modest living. But not enough to live at the typical American/gringo tourist level.

On our two previous visits, just a few years earlier, we'd remained in the same town – San Miguel de Allende – for almost our entire stay. During the previous decade or two, San Miguel had turned into a haven for American retirees, as well as both real and aspiring artists and writers.

This time, we'd be traveling, but staying a week or two, maybe longer, in a succession of places. We fully expected to have some cash left over at the end, for use when we decided where we wanted to go at that time, after returning to the U.S.

That was one big way we differed from the usual. We no longer had a permanent home; not even a temporary one. Nearly all of our possessions had been sold or given away, and the key to our rented house in Wisconsin was back in the hands of its owner. The address shown on our documents no longer pertained to us. Someone else was living there now, or would be soon.

We'd boarded the bus on the American side of the border, but it didn't go far before screeching to a halt. After traveling only a block or two, it crossed the international bridge, then stopped in front of the Mexican immigration/customs office (*Migración y Aduana Ciudad Juárez*).

Past contacts with police and other officials in Mexico and elsewhere had revealed two common approaches to bureaucratic procedure:

1. The inspector might be friendly, even jovial; but underneath his benign behavior and words is a foundation of utter seriousness.

2. He makes no attempt at friendliness, taking the fully down-to-business route through the interrogation and inspection.

Our inspector came from the second category: a young fellow who looked utterly serious throughout the encounter, backed by thinly veiled suspicion.

He said nearly nothing. Few questions. Strictly business. Polite enough, but keeping his distance. Thankfully, there was no sense of danger or imminent disaster. Our worry about possible demand for a bribe (*mordida*), or of outright theft of our funds, appeared to be a non-issue. But he insisted on seeing our all-cash travel fund. Thus, right in the middle of the open room, both of us had to reach into our underwear and manage to extract those fabric parcels containing three thousand U.S. dollars.

After counting them out carefully and patiently, he exercised one of his prerogatives as an immigration official who had found nothing questionable or suspicious. He disagreed with our arithmetic. As our penalty, he stamped our tourist cards in a manner that gave us only 90 days instead of the customary 180, insisting that we lacked sufficient funds to survive for more than 90 days in Mexico. Three months, instead of the six for which we'd planned. Pleas for reconsideration were ignored, leaving us just one option: halfway through our stay, we would have to go to the immigration office in Mexico City and apply for an extension.

Worse, after counting our money and declining half of our hoped-for (and expected) time frame, we had to get back on the bus, insecure in the knowledge that a whole troop of immigration/customs employees knew about the contents of our underwear. Were they all as honest as our inspector appeared to be?

Entry Point

Was he going to contact a criminal partner as soon as we walked out the door? We were sure we'd be robbed at the second inspection point 12 miles south of the border, which we knew about from rumors as well as guidebooks.

Amazingly, at the 12-mile point, nothing happened. As was the custom, an inspector walked through the bus, eyeing each passenger for a moment. But no action was taken, against us or anyone else on the bus. We were not questioned, stared at, or pointed out. Just the ordinary, quick check of passengers, not so different from procedures in other countries.

We were utterly amazed to survive and proceed southward, with no further inspections anticipated.

Of course, we still didn't know if bandits had been alerted and would assault the bus farther down the highway. Perhaps one or two of them were seated near us on the bus. For that matter, an immigration inspector in plainclothes might be seated behind us, waiting for an opportunity to spring into action.

This was Mexico, after all: land of *bandidos*, corrupt officials, underpaid government workers, *mordidas* (bribes). So everyone said, though our personal experiences south of the border have produced few such tangible dangers.

Invariably, whenever entering Mexico over the years, we wound up with a 90-day tourist permit, not the 180-day permission that guidebooks promised and other visitors seemed to receive every time. On one occasion, only a 30-day stay was granted – though a simple request for more resulted in a change to 90.

To someone who'd been a stay-at-home for much of his life, a lengthy residency below the border qualified as true adventure. But we could have done without that appraisal at the border.

We did stay for close to six months, being granted an extension after dealing with Mexican bureaucracy in Mexico City, as well as staying in a town that turned out to be less than joyful. That's where we had to wait for the new permit to arrive, allowing us to remain longer. Still, it was worth the effort and inconvenience to gain a couple of extra months.

In fact, we were so enamored by daily life in Mexico that I took the first step to possibly turning into an expatriate. A close relative had done so, settling in Europe. Rather than Mexico, whose residence requirements were a bit ambiguous, I tried for Canada, starting with the Canadian embassy in Mexico City – where I failed to qualify on the preliminary questionnaire. So much for taking on another life.

When we finally exited the country, we had quite a few pesos/dollars left. The inspector had been way wrong in his estimate of the cost of living, no doubt assuming a lavish gringo lifestyle. Or, maybe he merely wanted to exercise his authority and give one entering couple a hard time.

Yes, it was an anticlimax. Nothing dreadful happened. Yet, the incident in Juarez helped cement my uneasy discomfort when crossing any border, anticipating the prospect of facing inherently suspicious inspectors and interrogators.

7

Queasy Crossing

If there's one thing my wife and I both adore, it's boats. Big ships, little cruisers, sailboats. Even rowboats, especially if someone else is manning the oars. Just about anything that travels on the water: large, small, or in-between.

The excitement of boarding and exploring a ship – even a modest-size ferry – is cause for celebration. For ship lovers, if it floats and holds passengers, it's an opportunity to be savored and remembered.

Oddly, though, in our earlier lives, neither of us had that much experience with boats. Ships of any size, going any significant distance, were in short supply in the Midwest, where both of us grew up. Except for taking a ferry across one of the Great Lakes once, we'd spent our younger years on solid ground.

One of our most prized memories is the trip we took from England to Holland in the mid-1970s, soon after our marriage. Because the train ride from London to the coast at Dover was so uneventful, even ordinary, we were lulled into thinking that the rest of the trip would be similarly spiritless.

That's why, when we turned a corner during our walk from train to ship, well after dark, we nearly fell over when we saw the actual craft on which we would be traveling. Not only was it huge, at least to our eyes; it looked just like the oceangoing ships we'd seen in movies. They called it the Hoek van Holland ferry, but this was nothing remotely like the dinky ferries we'd taken when crossing rivers or modest-size lakes. This one sat on ocean waters.

Naturally, there were plenty of dining possibilities aboard ship, as well as slot machines and other casino machinery. No doubt, cabins were available for more affluent riders, but we were more than satisfied to take advantage of the neon-lit comforts and attractions available to all.

While crossing the English Channel, the ship headed northward as well as to the east, toward the Hoek van Holland. That destination was considerably farther away than the port of Calais, in France, for which ferry services also were available. We suspected, though, that the Calais ferry wouldn't be nearly as magnificent as our veritable cruise ship.

Not only was the night crossing fun, it was smooth and easy. No storms, no rough stretches, no obstacles or delays to be dealt with. By morning's light, we were headed straight to the dock in Holland, and would soon be on our way to Amsterdam via train.

A decade later, back in England for another family visit, we set aside enough time for another sea crossing. This time, we'd be traveling west. Destination: Ireland.

We assumed that any future relatively long-distance voyage would be unbridled pleasure. We were wrong.

Heading west from London by train, we approached the coast of Wales, along the Irish Sea. Although this ferry wasn't nearly as large or lavish as the one we'd taken to Holland, it was great in its own way: comfortable and roomy, just right for a joyful, relaxing daytime experience. The Sea was absolutely lovely, both visually and in its near-glassy smoothness.

Our arrival port was Dun Laoghaire, just north of Dublin, where we checked into a rather large, yet economical, hotel. Following a theater outing in the city, a train took us south to Cork, with a stop along the way at Wexford for a lunch of lovely mussels – a seafood that was entirely new to me. Our B&B in Cork was quaint and comfortable: a small house presided over by the most darling Irishwoman.

"Corkman, are ye?" I was asked by the operator of a newsstand in Dublin when I bought a Cork newspaper just prior to our journey. Once in the latter city, I almost felt like a resident.

While in Ireland, we'd hardly given a thought to the return trip. No reason for concern. Surely, it would be simply another joyful Irish Sea experience.

Instead, that initially easygoing eastbound journey soon turned into a horror show of illness and discomfort. Not much time passed before the smooth waters of the Dun Laoghaire port degenerated into ferocious, assaulting, battering waves that seemed to unleash a flotilla of agonies from within the earth. Practically within minutes, some passengers were looking sick. So sick, judging by their appearance, they might have been wishing for a quick demise.

Ah, but not the two of us. Not this time. Marianne's purse had brought forth a couple of motion-sickness pills that were supposed to combat seasickness. Despite my distaste for nonessential medication, I agreed to pop one.

They worked like magic. While other passengers moaned and groaned, writhed and suffered, as we learned later that long night, we dozed off quietly in our deck chairs, oblivious to the hellish scene around us.

Only upon awakening, and especially when going to the restroom, did we realize that anything unpleasant had happened, much less such a massive debacle. To be blunt, the walls of at least one restroom were strewn with residue from passengers' innards, suggesting voluminous episodes of agonizing vomiting. Hardly anyone, it appeared, had escaped the episode of abrupt, unexpected, unwarranted illness.

Curiously, the outgoing voyage had been so pleasant, it didn't seem all that memorable, truth be told. In stark contrast, the eastbound return pops back into mind in an instant, whenever thoughts of a prospective sea voyage – or any kind of voyage – come along. Does everyone best remember the bad times, pushing back the good ones into deeper memory?

Did this horrific experience sway our attitude toward ships? Not at all. Many years later, accompanied by my brother, I boarded what amounted to a cargo ship in Barcelona, Spain, for an overnight journey to the island of Mallorca.

Although the ship carried dozens of passengers, most of them appeared to be truck drivers who'd driven their rigs into the cargo hold. Staterooms were available for a reasonable price, but we'd opted for the basic fare, which included a reasonably comfortable chair in the public sleeping room. Not that I slept much, because the ship boasted a cafeteria, which was still open for business when we boarded. We'd missed dinner, but food remained available.

There's nothing I like better than dining aboard a ship, unless it's riding in a train's dining car. Something about that seemingly ordinary experience tickles a weird nerve of delight. To me, at least.

For some time after the cafeteria shut down for the night, I sat up front, watching the sea through a window. When the window view no longer sufficed, I walked out on deck to observe the night sea without obstruction.

Few, if any, tourists appeared to be among the passengers. To devotees of luxury cruise ships or oceangoing liners, this overnight trip on a commercial, workaday truck ferry might not sound like much. Oozing authenticity, shorn of ostentation, it was one of the best nights of my life.

Vying for visitor attention with the ferry from Barcelona is the vintage narrow-gauge railway that runs between Palma (Mallorca's capital) to Sóller, on the other side of the island. Six trains a day make the hour-long trip. Service began way back in 1912. Mere minutes of taking in the relaxed atmosphere of the town made this visitor hunger for an opportunity to move there immediately.

8

Hostility in the Hostel

Hotel people and hostelers don't always mix well. As a lifelong hotel fan, I prefer privacy: a soothing taste of solitude after each day's events. I arrive with luggage, not a rucksack. The camaraderie touted as a delight of the youth hostel experience held little appeal even when I was a youth. Far less so in middle age and beyond.

Still, I'd always wondered about them. Several friends and relatives – not exactly youngsters themselves – brought back intriguing reports from hosteling treks. One even offered to accompany me on a first foray into hostel territory.

In principle, I've always liked the idea of hostels. What better way for a solitary wanderer to feel the pulse of fellow travelers – though not necessarily any of the local folks. By hosteling, a cash-short visitor could focus on things to see and do in the area, without succumbing to luxury accommodations.

So, in the middle of a somewhat lengthy stay in Britain, I decided to answer that nagging question: Could a middle-aged private person spend a comfortable – indeed, enjoyable – night among a horde of youthful backpackers in a hostel.

I admit to having begun with a few preconceptions. Prejudices, even. After studying the American Youth Hostel (AYH) Handbook, along with skimming an article or two about hosteling, I couldn't help thinking of prison. Silly? Not when each hostel's on-site director is referred to as the "warden."

In most hostels, the sexes were segregated. Residents seemed to be subject to a lot of rules. Sensible rules, to be sure. Yet everything sounded so uniform, so standardized, so – sterile. Descriptions of the bunks, the dining hall, common room. All produced visions of movie gangsters behind bars, probably planning a riot.

Young backpackers can be a trifle forbidding as well. Okay, more than a trifle. A certain smugness seems evident on the faces of some 'packers when they confront a suitcase person. "I'm the *real* traveler," they appear to declare: tough, rugged, outdoorsy. Whereas any luggage carrier is obviously a pampered, dainty tourist.

Several incidents on British trains reinforced such negative perceptions. One time, a rucksack that had been stuffed precariously into the overhead rack came tumbling down onto a passenger's head. Was there a quick apology? There was not. The pack's owner acted far more irritated than contrite.

On other occasions, train aisles were strewn with rucksacks, knapsacks and so forth, tossed down without a thought of passengers who might wish to pass through. Some heavily laden hikers, boots and mats and paraphernalia swinging wildly from the basic pack, strode defiantly down narrow aisles, nearly daring anyone not to stand aside. More than one young rail traveler, in fact, complained of discourtesy and boisterous behavior among fellow hostelers.

To get a feel for the coming trip, we paid a quick daytime visit to a London hostel. A faded newspaper clipping on the bulletin board was not reassuring. Under a blaring headline, "Hell Hole Hostels," was a photo flaunting what were said to be typical hostel scenes. None of them were tempting.

One essential fact has to be kept in mind about hostels: You're expected to be sociable, if not gregarious. I am neither. Far from it.

Interaction isn't a requirement. Nobody will kick you out if you prefer solitude. But mixing with the other residents – whether they're rustic backpackers or well-off urbanites – is seen as part of the hosteling experience.

Not that I'm trying to feel superior about it. I just don't care that much about hanging out with people. Any sort of people. When I'm roped into doing so, I usually feel more comfortable with those who are least like me. Younger, of different race or ethnicity, with different attitudes.

I'd rather steer clear of Americans, in particular – especially those in my own demographic and social category.

Better yet, stay alone. Except for sharing with my wife, who hardly annoys me at all.

Late-night "bull sessions," or whatever they call them nowadays, make me cringe. Maybe it's because I can't stand arguments. Any "discussion" seems to end with loud voices and nasty tones: angry words spouting from distorted mouths that barely seem connected to what's supposed to be a brain sitting within that same head.

Rather than arrive alone at the hostel, I was one in a party of four: my wife, plus her brother and his wife. This hostel was established within an old mansion, oozing with character and history, far from the nearest town, set within the beautiful English countryside.

That was the good part, bringing to mind some literary locale, like Sherwood Forest. Oh, sorry, that was Robin Hood's territory. More like the forested glens of central England that lady authors wrote about in the 19th century. Sheep lazily grazing on the broad, lush lawn. A slow-water fountain rolling down a slim, gracefully-curved brook off to the side. Quiet – near silent – in daytime, apart from the light "baahing" of the wooly creatures as they researched the lightly-mottled terrain for the best grassy sustenance.

From the moment we stepped into the huge dorm-style room, available only to male guests, I could see that our first night was likely to be the kind I detest. The room was nearly empty when Larry and I commandeered one of the dozen or so bunk beds. Thankfully, he agreed to occupy the top bunk. I didn't relish falling out of that thing in the middle of the night, and would have spent the whole time imagining that happening.

We had an hour or two of quiet in the huge dormitory, permitting a bit of early dozing. Right around midnight, though, the rowdy young revelers stomped inside, voices unleashed at full volume, brains evidently further disconnected from their surroundings. (Well, that's how I felt about noisy people in those days.)

They all seemed to be yelling at once, creating a cacophony that made it impossible to make out any of the slurred, impassioned words that polluted the air. Provided one wanted to hear and understand them, that is. Which I did not.

Even covering my face with the thin pillow, forcing it against each ear with my hands, barely made a dent in the unwanted din. Dorm life can quickly turn into a party, we learned at our advanced age, curtailing the night's rest for those who will never be mistaken for partygoers.

As morning dawned after the first night, we made our own breakfast in the communal kitchen. That is, Larry did. Along with Katrina and Elizabeth, I simply sat and watched as he prepared the day's delicacy. Something I'd never tasted before, but had heard plenty about. Mostly, from people who'd sampled it once, but quickly vowed never to make that mistake again.

Haggis, they call it. They say it's a huge delicacy in Scotland, but something to avoid elsewhere in the British Isles and beyond. Tell you the truth, I thought it was pretty good. Not something I'd go out of my way to dine on again, but certainly not as hideous in taste as I'd been led to believe. Almost like the time, years later, when lunching with a friend in Paris, I ordered *foie gras* for the first time.

Yes, yes, I felt suitably guilty for making that choice, and had to struggle not to think about the pain inflicted upon little creatures to make *foie gras* possible, but there it was on the café menu. I just had to try it once. And was glad I did.

Now, if the subject of consuming food made from mistreated creatures ever comes up, I can say I've been there, took it in, and have no desire to partake of it again. Case closed.

In comparison, the second night at the hostel was bliss: as quiet and restful as anyone could wish for. A four-bed room (men only) with two spaces vacant, just like our wives had the night before. Larry again allowed me to claim the lower bunk, even though I knew he wasn't quite at ease in the upper spot. What does that make me? Contented. Quietly contented.

Looking back, I wish I could boast that my experience in the English version changed my mind about the communal experience, turning me into an avid hosteler. But that would not be true. I'm embarrassed to admit that I never did it again.

Some of us can appreciate the merits of the hostel experience, without necessarily wishing to go through them again. Asocial folks need not apply, unless private or near-private rooms are available. Bunk beds in a big room are definitely not for everyone. Most important, watch out for youthful imbibers in one of those vast dorm-style rooms, unless you're planning to party hard yourself.

Since that stay in the British hostel, I've probably overnighted in a hundred hotels, in half a dozen countries. And stayed for as long as a month in several more. Underneath it all, I'm *strictly* a hotel guy. A loner? Absolutely. Recluse? Not quite, but almost. Antisocial? More like non-social.

Mainly, when assessing a potential accommodation, my eye zips right past guidebook listings of hostels as if they don't exist. B&Bs? Perhaps. Airbnb, for sure. Maybe a hostel that also offers a couple of private rooms for the solitary among us. But mostly, I'm a hotel guy, pleased to bed down with myself in serene surroundings, obligated to communicate with no one.

9

Discomfort Zones

I love hotels. All sorts of hotels. Big, small, everything in-between. Also motels, furnished rooms, tourist homes – anyplace rented by the day, or perhaps the week.

Practically every time I pass one, I want to head for the front desk and check in.

Except for multiple-star, ultra-luxury examples. Traveling on business for a quarter-century or so, I occupied posh rooms in far too many high-end hostelries, few of which were memorable an hour after checking out.

My wife also is a hotel person. Our first date included an overnight event at a chain motel. Separate rooms, of course. Best to be discreet, whether you're in a no-star dump or four-star magnificence. At one point during our marriage, in the early 1980s, we lived for two years in a tiny room in a residential hotel in downtown Las Vegas.

Appreciation of hotel life wasn't a family trait. Except for annual visits to relatives in the Upper Peninsula of Michigan, my parents seldom went anywhere farther than 100 miles or so from their Chicago home. I recall staying in a couple of tourist homes during those trips northward. My first stay in an actual motel was in Escanaba, Michigan. Those tourist homes, each with a distinct character, provide more memories than that conventional motel.

As a young adult living alone, I never had a home, in the sense of a place that one owns. Most of those years didn't even include a rented apartment: nothing but furnished rooms rented by homeowners to earn some extra dollars each month, along with a few modest hotels.

Finding and selecting a suitable accommodation at the lower end of the price scale can be tricky. Some of our hotel/motel choices have brought to mind the query muttered by Ellen Burstyn in the 1974 movie *Alice Doesn't Live Here Anymore*. Why don't some of these places have a sign, "CHEAP MOTEL," she asks. Make it a lot easier to find appropriate, affordable accommodations.

Plenty of low-budget hostelries from our hotel history still produce fond memories. A few do not. At least a couple tend to deliver shivers of unease, forty-plus years after our one-night stay.

Winner of the worst-ever prize has to go to the Mallory. Since Marianne and I adore old hotels with some sort of intriguing history, the Mallory looked from a distance like a good bet.

Located on a busy yet leisurely downtown corner in a modest-size town in central Wisconsin, the old hotel – visually similar to a dozen, a hundred others we'd driven past – might indeed have had a notable history. It might even have earned some character in its heritage. Even so, there was nothing enticing about the place when we stayed there overnight, long after what might have been its heyday. No, long after its *decline* and imminent demise would be most accurate.

At least, when viewed from afar. Up close, the rough edges took precedence in our decision-making. Another factor: it was late in the day, and the chain hotels on the outskirts of town turned out be fully occupied. We'd already encountered a few "NO VACANCY" signs on smaller motels along our incoming route. So, the choices were limited.

"Can't be that bad," I said. "Anyway, it's just for one night. How bad could it be?"

"Horrible" is the response I wish I'd heard from someone in the vicinity. Instead, we tiptoed up the outside steps and eased into the lobby, trying to exude a confident demeanor. We'd stayed in countless hotels and motels during our married life and before. We were old hands. Or so we thought.

Although the desk clerk looked at us oddly, there was no problem checking in. Two rooms, four adults. Later in the evening, while sitting in the lobby, a family group came in and the clerk told them "this isn't your kind of hotel." Like us, they'd encountered fully-occupied motels on the way here. Unlike us, they chose to follow the clerk's advice.

Perhaps reminiscing about old black-and-white *film noir* movies, I felt an odd desire to sit on the window ledge, staring down at the street below and ranting loudly, or maybe muttering, about one irritant or another. Doing so was indeed strangely intriguing.

Dark, grungy and odorous, the down-the-hall bathroom proved to be virtually unusable, except for dire need. Taking a bath would be out of the question, unless you were one of the old fellows who lived here semi-permanently, and had no choice.

The foremost shock of our stay at the Mallory took place prior to our retiring for the night. However, we were lying on the bed when it happened. Suddenly, there was a huge, loud crash. Just as swiftly, we were on the floor. The bed had chosen that moment to collapse, dropping the mattress and its companion heavy metal spring to zero level. Thankfully, no one had his or her fingers hanging low, where they'd have been candidates for crushing.

Before checking out in the morning (early), we learned that the hotel was mainly residential, owned by a doctor. Which lowered my opinion of physicians' business practices.

A selection mistake of another sort also occurred elsewhere in Wisconsin, in the southeast corner of the state. At the time, I was test-driving a brand-new Chevrolet Corvette for a week. That was a major part of my job at the time: driving and evaluating the latest new automobiles.

For some reason, I was overly concerned about cost that week.

Pretty ironic, considering that I was tooling around in a high-priced sports car. From a distance, the motel looked ordinary and utterly unmemorable, but acceptable: like a dozen others along that stretch of U.S. Highway 41. My wife didn't like the look at all, but my uninformed opinion prevailed.

What we discovered after checking in was dirt. And dust. And an overall sense that the cleaning person hadn't shown up for quite some time. Trashy, in short; likely to be patronized for short time frames by quickie couples who weren't at all concerned about cleanliness in anything other than the sheets.

On my way alone from Chicago to California in the mid-1960s, I spent half my on-the-road nights napping in the front seat of my Plymouth sedan. One exception turned out to be among the cheapest places I've ever occupied. Located in western Missouri, the tiny cabin cost a whopping $3 a night, if memory serves.

The problem here was heat. No switch-activated heater in this place. Instead, an old-time heater sat against one wall, waiting to be filled with firewood (or something else that would burn) and fired up. Anyone who's tried to stay warm with such a device knows that often as not, little of the created heat reaches more than a couple of feet away from the stove. Inexpensive, yes; but also a cold and lonely night, prompting an early departure in the morning.

Considerably farther down the road to California, another low-rent room was waiting for me. But this time, the experience would be satisfying indeed. After driving for innumerable hours across the southwestern desert, I was exhausted, sweaty, hungry, and eager for a bed. Following a detour to the Grand Canyon, I headed straight for Las Vegas. Rather than go all the way onto the Strip, with its massive, flamboyant hotel-casinos, I opted for a motel on the outskirts. For a mere ten bucks, I got an elegant, sizable room that ranked as downright luxurious – like nothing I'd ever seen in my life. No discomfort at all, believe me.

Stopping for a night in downtown Denver, en route to Mexico

City via bus, we stepped into the past in a hotel across the street from the bus station. Tall ceilings, outmoded fixtures, and decidedly non-modern decor conveyed an irresistible sense of America's western past. One could almost imagine a cowpoke or two stomping down the corridor, well-worn boots hitting the floor to announce their arrival in town.

Highlight of that southbound journey was Santa Fe, a glorious location in New Mexico with an alluring feel of "old" Mexico – especially around the central square (which would be called a *zócalo* or *jardín* if south of the border). Thankfully, our hotel intensified that feeling of "almost" being in Mexico itself, and was only half a block from the square.

A couple of years later, following a transcontinental trek across Canada by train, we found ourselves in Detroit, ready to begin a three-week stint doing research for a possible book. Finding proper lodging took a bit of effort. At one spot, near the university area, the room we were shown looked suspiciously like one that was ordinarily rented by the hour. Bright red furnishings, mirrors, gaudy overall. Our suspicion was confirmed when the desk clerk asked Marianne if she would be accompanied by the same man for the entire three-week period.

Even when we weren't traveling anywhere, hotels were part of our life. Every now and then, we'd check into a local establishment for a day or two, if not longer. Sometimes, the hotel stay was practical in nature, offering a place to work on a difficult writing or research project without distraction. Other times, it would be strictly a getaway, taking advantage of the simple fact that we both enjoyed hotel life.

In the mid-1970s, our three-day stay in New York City, serving as a jumping-off point for flying to London to see relatives, did not start off well. Our plan to see three Broadway shows in as many days looked promising. Minutes after checking into our chosen budget-priced hotel, not far removed from Times Square, our attitudes took a bad turn when we pulled back the bedclothes and observed a cadre of bedbugs making its way across the sheet. Immediate checkout was followed by a move down the street, to a comparable hotel that turned out just fine. Surprising, because at a glance, the first room looked quite nice. Good thing we peeked beneath the blanket on that bed.

I was alone when I checked into the Broadway Hotel years later, largely because its $100 room rate was among the cheapest to be found in midtown Manhattan. Good thing, too, because the "room" was barely large enough to be occupied by one person. Dimensions were closer to those Japanese-style shelf-like accommodations that sprung up here and there in the 21st century. Only if I was lying down on the bed, on my side, was it possible to see the TV set. On the other hand, a perfectly usable private bath and welcoming lobby partly made up for the miniature room.

One hotel I'm sorry to have missed during its heyday was the Chelsea on 23rd Street, because of its long history of providing long-term accommodations to so many top writers, artists, musicians, intellectuals and other extraordinary tenants, from Bob Dylan, Leonard Cohen and Janis Joplin to Allen Ginsberg, Andy Warhol, and Tennessee Williams. Major renovation a few years back extracted most of the Chelsea's character, but most of the idiosyncratic guests had long since moved out by then.

Though far less renowned than the Chelsea, the Da Vinci Hotel had its own brand of charm, serving as a reasonably-priced midtown alternative to Manhattan's numerous luxury lodgings. A short hop away from Central Park, the Da Vinci exuded a European flavor, though the rooms themselves were on the ordinary side. Staying here while attending media events at the Javits Center left a few dollars in our pocketbooks to be spent on edibles – perhaps an overflowing corned beef sandwich at the Carnegie Deli, which sadly closed its doors in 2016.

One rule of cheap-hotel selection that I established early involved stairs. Exceptions certainly could be found; but in general, if you had to climb a set of stairs to reach the check-in desk, it might be best to look elsewhere. At the east end of our transcontinental train journey across Canada in 1983, in Halifax, Nova Scotia, I violated that rule. Nothing horrible transpired, by any means. It was simply a joyless night endured in a place that made us feel uneasy – even a bit unclean.

Early next morning, we moved to a more costly but highly recommended and far more relaxing accommodation of the sort that's featured in travel guidebooks. A fine choice, we agreed later. Sometimes, it's prudent to move to a classier accommodation to erase the memory of the dreadful room you'd occupied the night before.

More than one strange curiosity marked our week-long stay in midtown Toronto, including both the people and the place. Silly as it sounds, I was most troubled by an odd, unidentifiable object sitting in the middle of the public bathtub, which precluded any thought of bathing. I didn't want to go anywhere near the unidentified sitting object, much less make use of the tub. Marianne had a better impression than I did of this urban establishment, more rooming house than hotel or hostel or bed-and-breakfast, including its residents.

On a couple of other occasions, with room rent paid by a company, I stayed in the magnificent old Royal York Hotel downtown, or at one of the Four Seasons locations. But that curious place is the one I remember best.

Our hotel in downtown Winnipeg, in the province of Manitoba, was most notable for the bar downstairs, which catered to journalists from the city's newspapers. We stayed there more than once, for several days at a time, as a convenient point to visit friends. As a journalist of sorts myself, I felt drawn to that part of the building and intrigued by the photos of customers on the wall, even though I was not a consumer of alcoholic beverages.

Our room in Churchill, way up in central Manitoba on Hudson Bay and known mainly for its polar bears, was ordinary but satisfying. Some of the people in Churchill, not so much. We'd met some especially friendly local residents on the train heading north. But when we entered a café in town for lunch, we waited and waited for someone to serve us. No one in the rather crowded place made a move in our direction. Eventually, we gave up and went elsewhere for sustenance. Lack of any service has happened a couple of other times in our travels, including two occasions in Mexico. I'm still trying to figure out what the staff and/or patrons had against us, to compel us to leave without seeing any food.

Vancouver, far to the west in British Columbia, provided a couple of weeks' residence, at a pleasant and reasonable weekly-rate establishment. Its near-central location proved to be a fine starting point for walks around this vibrant, diverse metropolis, serving as the starting point of our coast-to-coast journey on Via Rail. Never did have a chance to partake of what some doubtless considered the main attraction: a bar featuring nude exotic dancers, entered via a set of stairs leading into the near-basement. In those days (1983), and for many years afterward, just about every city or town in Canada seemed to boast at least one nudie bar.

Not unlike the curious establishment in Toronto, our residence in Glasgow, Scotland, came across as vaguely odd, though perfectly clean and pleasant. Then again, Marianne and I probably qualified as odd, too, to at least some of the residents. Our favorite guests were the two middle-eastern gentlemen who couldn't resist stepping outside in their nightshirts, to see and feel snow for the first time.

When we arrived in Inverness, on the northern coast of Scotland, our selected bed-and-breakfast wouldn't be available until a day later. So, we had to quickly find a one-day alternative. That turned out to be a bedroom in a suburban home, somewhere in the outskirts of the city, fortunately reachable via city bus. Sudden changes in plan often lead to pleasant encounters. This time, we enjoyed an especially satisfying chat with two young women from Adelaide, Australia. That's when we learned that for many Australians, a trip to the European continent – or presumably, anywhere else – typically amounted to, say, six months away from home. Evidently, those Australians really liked to embed themselves wholeheartedly in the traveling experience.

Waiting a while was needed for the room we'd reserved on the Isle of Skye, too. This was another suburban ranch-style house, renting out space to passing travelers. When we arrived, though, after stepping off the ferry, no one was around. We learned that the owners were away for a few hours, so we had to wait for them to return before checking in. No problem. Skye is a lovely spot in which to spend a few hours with nothing to do.

Although London is filled with hotels, like most major metropolises, that's not the case in the south portion of the city. Visiting relatives who had no space available for guests, we had to find some sort of longer-term accommodation. After several inquiries made by our relatives, we were able to move into a room in a large house in the Streatham area.

While meeting the elderly woman who owned the home, a workingman who resided there permanently invited us to his local pub. I say workingman because he had hands and arms like thick tree branches, and looked capable of tearing down a tree, upon request, with his bare hands. Now, that was a fellow who worked hard all day and deserved an evening in the pub with his mates.

Basic was the word for the Hotel Santillana in Veracruz, Mexico. Located only a couple of blocks from the lively *zócalo* and the *malecón* walkway that overlooks the harbor, it served Marianne and me well for three weeks in the winter of 1980-81. Our room's private bath might have lacked a toilet seat, but a helpful fan rotated slowly in the ceiling. It's a Veracruz necessity not only in spring and summer, but welcome in December-January.

Clanging vertical-sliding metal doors assaulted our ears everyday at 6 a.m., when the businesses incorporated into the fish market across the street opened. Marimba music invariably followed soon. The fish market is long gone now. So is the train that brought us from Mexico City to Veracruz. But the hotel is still there, with about the same equivalent price as in 1981 ($13 per day), surprisingly.

We still have fond recollections of our weeks at the Santillana, though perhaps more about the tropical city than this particular lodging. Even that no-seat toilet helps make the Santillana one of our most memorable lodging places.

Much more recently, my brother and I stayed at the downtown Holiday Inn, a typical moderately-priced member of that familiar hotel chain. Our rooms were comfortable and clean, if a bit short on character. There's not much to recommend, except that I knew its history. A 1991 movie titled *Danzon* (named for a popular style of dancing) told of a woman who leaves her job as a telephone operator in Mexico City to seek a better life in Veracruz. She stays at the Rex Hotel in what appears to be a by-the-week room. Some years later, the Rex would be transformed into a Holiday Inn, perhaps after an additional iteration or two in between.

Traveling from the U.S.-Mexico border to Mexico City, we had to change buses in Chihuahua and stayed one night at a small hotel across the street from the bus station. Devoid of windows, it was a totally basic room, not memorable at all. With one exception: the adjacent café and its patrons. Namely, a group of unusually tall men, evidently basketball players from the U.S., flirting with their waitress while awaiting their meals.

Several years earlier, on our first-ever night in Mexico City (aka *Distrito Federal*), we stayed in a pleasant but unexceptional midrange hotel in the Zona Rosa tourist area. Except for a flower on the bed, reminding us that we'd been married back in Chicago not long before, there wasn't much to remember. What I do recall vividly is the brief walk I took to the nearby Insurgentes Metro station, where I stepped up to the counter at one of the food stalls and ordered *chicharron*. I'd never heard of it before, and was surprised to discover later that it was actually deep-fried pork cracklings, made from the skin of the animal. More importantly, ordering that delicacy taught a preliminary lesson on the importance of street food in Mexican life.

Though it had no discernible relationship to the French city, the Hotel Paris served as our favored home on several visits to Mexico City. No outside windows meant a total lack of urban views of anything, but most rooms opened onto a walkway around a large central indoor patio. That design mode turned out to be far from uncommon in the architecture of lower-end Mexican hotels. Inexpensive and dependable, the Paris had been recommended by friends who'd regularly made it their temporary home when in Mexico's capital city. Take a step outside and you were in the midst of a frenzy of activity all along the narrow sidewalks of the neighborhood.

Sadly, the Paris disappeared during a period of reconstruction in the city's *centro historico* (historic center). Fortunately, another old-reliable place was waiting for my patronage, only a block or so down Avenida Uruguay. A long-time favorite of backpackers and counterculture-type travelers, the Hotel Isabel quickly became my Number One choice. That was partly because of the excellent ground-floor restaurant, which served a *comida* (a several-course lunch) for an enticing price.

Rooms at the Isabel were larger than customary for budget-priced lodging, with a TV and phone (wi-fi, too), within a traditional-type atmosphere. That meant walkways on every floor, surrounding a sizable indoor central patio. Atmospheric and hostel-like, the lobby was a fine spot for a quick rest, if a bit on the dark side. Many customers looked as if they'd experienced plenty of hostel nights during their travels.

Most rooms, however, had windows facing the street: good news for urbanites unfazed by noise, but troubling for those who have difficulty sleeping in anything other than silence. The only problem I ever had at the Isabel was a busily buzzing mosquito, likely a result of the lack of window screens. To please the tightest budgets, smaller rooms, lacking a private bath, were available on the hotel's roof. One day when a fire broke out across the street, one of the maids – not so much younger than myself – was especially solicitous when assisting me to evacuate the building.

When in need of a splurge in Mexico City, no choice was better than the Majestic Hotel, facing right onto the renowned, massive *Zocalo* – featured in dozens of movies over the decades. No view of that urban square could be more delightful than the one from the Majestic's rooftop restaurant. Anyone whose room faced east could enjoy an almost comparable view of the activities below, including the early-morning raising of the country's flag.

Discomfort was the rule during the first days of our stay in Guadalajara. Our room's window faced a street that was frantically busy and in need of repair. One particularly harsh pothole sat right below our window. Not only in daytime but all night long, the entire hotel seemed to shake violently as one truck after another crashed and clanked over that obstacle. The aural assault reached its peak when we were suffering from agonizingly itchy insect bites, acquired during a side trip to the coastal town of San Blas. Later, we were able to move to an inside room, which was blissfully near-silent and devoid of commercial-truck commotion. Lesson learned: always feel free to ask to see another room, if there's any doubt about likely comfort.

Since we also liked to be in the midst of human activity, we were pleased to see that our hotel was right across the street from Guadalajara's huge, always-busy bus station. (As in most other

Mexican cities, the bus stations now are found somewhere in outlying areas rather than the *centro* (downtown).

A few doors down the street, Marianne and I had our most awkward dining experience ever. We loved tostadas, but feeling bold, I ordered one version that I'd never heard of. Bad choice. Sitting right in the middle of a totally flat tortilla was a pig's trotter, which I prefer to think of as a hoof. All we could do was stare at it. No idea which parts of it (if any) were edible, but the possibilities did not look promising. All we could do was sheepishly pay the bill and quickly ease out of the restaurant, leaving that particular portion of some hapless pig sitting untouched.

At the Hotel Central in Guanajuato, in the mid-1970s, we were given a welcoming front room that included a balcony, facing the old market. Decades later, I still like to look at a snapshot of myself, wearing my Mexican hat (not quite a full-fledged *sombrero*), taken while I gazed in the direction of that market.

Unfortunately, though, our strongest memory of that single-night residency in that central Mexican city stems from the horrific food poisoning that both of us acquired. Far nastier than the usual intestinal discomfort many visitors used to experience, this extreme version assaulted us shortly after arriving back at our relatives' residence in San Miguel de Allende, and kept us in bed, in agony, for days.

Speaking of San Miguel de Allende, our usual residence when not visiting relatives has been the Quinta Loreto. Still in business, the 1950s-style motel offers ordinary rooms, but a lovely garden atmosphere, ideal for bench-sitting. So is the *jardin* (main square), a couple of blocks away in this colonial city that's been attracting American and Canadian tourists and backpackers, along with scads of artists and writers, for many years.

Second only to Mexico City as a personal favorite, San Cristobal de las Casas is a good-size city in the southern state of Chiapas. Not far from the Guatemala border, that's the region that was taken over for a time, decades ago, by Zapatistas, backed by subcomandante Marcos. Unfortunately, the budget-priced bed-and-breakfast at which I stayed twice, for a month each time, went out of business not long ago. Including breakfast, I was able to stay in a snug annex room for about $13 a day, raised to about $20 for a bigger space in the main building.

Every morning, a different group of travelers showed up at breakfast. Even for an introvert such as myself, conversations were easy and pleasurable, whether in English or Spanish. One morning I sat with a young lady from Argentina who spoke no English; another morning, it was two young women from South Africa along with a young German fellow. He ran into a bit of good luck that morning, as the three of them decided to travel together for a while. Most tenants were full-bore travelers, staying for only a day or two before moving on to their next destination. Quite a few had been in Guatemala immediately prior to arriving in San Cristobal.

Most people probably couldn't imagine living for months, or years, in a room as tiny as mine at the Lakeland Hotel, on Chicago's Near North Side. My mini-lodging was on the second floor, way in the back, shared bathroom in the hall, with a window facing busy State Street. Washstand, but no TV or radio. Narrow room and narrow bed. Whether as a guest or during my short-term stretch as a night clerk, I had no complaints about the Lakeland.

Unlike most areas of the city, the neighborhood drew intellectuals and noted authors in the 1920s and 1930s, beat-generation writers and artists in the 1950s, hippies and gays in the 1960s, and countercultural adherents until that phenomenon faded away. New Yorkers may disagree, but it was a bit like a "second version" of Greenwich Village.

At the same time, a collection of working-class folks who liked the vibrant atmosphere of the neighborhood found a welcoming home here. Tastes change, though, and the Lakeland faded away quite a few years back, replaced by more modern residences, doubtless at far higher prices.

A mile or so north, facing the greenery and trees of Lincoln Park, with Lake Michigan just a bit farther off, the Hotel Lincoln was another residential hotel at the northern end of the bohemian, vibrant neighborhood. Positioned above the convenient and reasonable restaurant at the corner of the building, my spacious, bright and cheerful room had windows facing in two directions. No TV was included, but I rented one for most of my two-year stay. This time, I had a private bath.

When my wife and I checked into the Beverly Palms, a residential hotel in downtown Las Vegas, we had just returned from a four-month period of travel in Mexico, moving to another city every few weeks. Marianne had never been to Las Vegas, and fell for it during our first breakfast there, in a hotel restaurant right across from the bus station where we'd arrived. Hours later, we were moving our few possessions into Room 5, on the ground floor of the Beverly Palms. We quickly heard about the robbery and killing of a hotel clerk nearby, the night before, but chose not to take it as a negative omen or a portent of troubles to come.

Fremont Street, with its string of big hotel-casinos as well as smaller gambling establishments, was a block away. So was the El Cortez Hotel, built in 1941 and connected to the mobsters who would turn the modest desert city into a flamboyant entertainment center in the years after World War II.

Years later, I had the good fortune to stay at the El Cortez for nearly a week, while in Las Vegas for a convention. Rather than one of the "modern" (ordinary) rooms in the annex, I was upgraded to a sizable room upstairs in the main building, with no elevator but plenty of atmosphere. More than once, when close to dozing, I could almost see those New York gangsters seated on the couch, back in the Forties, planning their next move. Some of those hazy visions substituted Frank, Dean, and Sammy as the tenants, suggesting a bit later period on the time spectrum.

During our long-term Las Vegas residence, back in the Eighties, the El Cortez was our favorite. We could often be found enjoying the bargain-priced breakfast in its café. Because Marianne got a second-shift job at the phone company, a block from our hotel, we dined late nearly every night at one of the downtown hotel-casinos, taking advantage of their after-midnight promotional specials: the $3.99 steak dinners and 99-cent shrimp cocktails.

Down the street at the Palms, for the first time ever, we even had cable TV, feeding into a black-and-white set attached to the wall. Room 5 wasn't much bigger than our double bed. No room phone, but a public one down the hall, which we rarely used. With a window facing the street, the room was clean and comfortable, with a fine private bath and an intriguing array of residents. A "swamp cooler," which I'd never heard of before, substituted for an air conditioner. Some sort of cooling was definitely needed, with temperatures reaching as high as 114 degrees in summertime and a window that faced east to present the rising morning sun.

All told, the Beverly was a satisfying example of weekly-rate furnished residences. We stayed for two years; and as Marianne pointed out, it was a bit like living in the circus. For us, just right.

For some 25 years, my work as an automotive journalist took me to car-related events all over North America, and occasionally elsewhere in the world. Just about every one included a sizable room in one of the best hotels in the area, paid for by the car company that invited me. Four-star ratings were the norm; three-star, a comedown. Five-star, on occasion. Only once was I "forced" to stay at an ordinary chain hotel – something like a Comfort Inn. Ironically, that event was hosted by the Porsche folks.

For the most part, those luxury accommodations were lifeless and unmemorable. What bothered me the most was the fawning displayed by staff people toward the customers. How could they not see how phony it was?

Listening to the critical comments and overblown complaints of my colleagues at these media events, I often thought I must be the only journalist in the world with a preference for low-end, inexpensive lodging. At one dinner, I happened to sit with a young woman who had traveled extensively with her boyfriend in Central America. She regaled us with tales of lodgings a step or two – or more – down the quality scale from those I'd experienced and (mostly) savored.

They seemed to have had a great time "roughing it" in terms of lodging in a variety of countries. All of a sudden, I felt almost like one of those pampered top-end tourists whom I sometimes mocked for their insistence on endless luxury.

Those coddled guests might shriek when they confront an imperfection in their luxury suite, lunging for the phone to complain. An open-minded visitor – one who's fond of hotel life at any level – might be uneasy at first about a troublesome flaw, but wind up staying for a week, if not a month.

Now in our elder years, with no more business events to attend, we don't travel anymore. Do I miss it? Yes. Quite a lot. Especially the lodgings, not the flights or the test-driving. Even the flawed hotels added some unexpected but welcome flavor to our journeys. Except for the Mallory.

10

Highland Freeze

Ordinarily, the prospect for surprise is a bonus of traveling on the cheap. If you're not amazed or startled by something you see or hear during your travels, what's the point? If a dull life is your goal, plenty of big-buck tours or cruises are available – guaranteed to allow nothing very far from the ordinary to cross your path. Or, you could just stay home. That's the cheapest of all.

Once in a while, though, instead of producing a wistful memory, a surprise yields recollections of stress and disappointment.

Some folks who've never set foot below the U.S.-Mexico border are surprised to learn that Mexico isn't all beautiful beaches, blazing sun, gringas in skimpy bikinis. The central highlands north of Mexico City, for instance, can get cold in winter. Mighty cold. That's how it was when we found ourselves in those highlands, ready for a three-week stay in the sizable city of San Luis Potosí.

We'd been there once before, a few years earlier, on an enjoyable day trip from San Miguel de Allende, where we resided for five months. This time, instead of a generator of pleasant Mexican memories, those three weeks felt more like a prison sentence, fortunately with a welcome release date at its end.

It was winter in central Mexico as we pulled into the train station. January. This was the high desert country, far removed from the tropical warmth of Veracruz, along the sun-blazed Gulf Coast, where we'd spent the *previous* three weeks.

Our long-delayed arrival was due to an explosion in a train tunnel to the south, followed by a wide detour to another region of the country. What should have been a 9-hour train trip turned into a 37-hour experience. If anything, that unexpected additional-length journey heightened our expectations, and our hopes, about the city.

No one on the train, including the conductor, seemed to know what had happened and why we were so tardy. At one point, I could see that we were approaching a good-sized city. "Es San Luis Potosí?" I asked one of the fellows standing in the aisle. "No," he replied. "Es Aguascalientes."

Aguascalientes? From my study of maps of the region, I knew without question that Aguascalientes was in an entirely different part of the region, nowhere near our destination. Sure enough, the train rolled right through the city and out the other side.

Hours later, another city appeared in the distance. Could this be it? Before I had a chance to inquire, dozens – maybe hundreds – of human figures burst into view, running full-blast toward our train. A welcoming committee, out to greet us passengers? If so, they must have reached central Mexico by way of purgatory. Visions of that Biblical region, recalled from old museum paintings, assaulted our confused minds.

As they got close, we could see that it was a horde of young fellows rushing toward the train, while we were still a mile or so from the station. Why did they look so anguished? Why were they running so rapidly?

Finally, it dawned on us. Whole families had been waiting for hours and hours for this train to arrive, not only to greet incoming passengers but to board it themselves. Because it was so late, the train's coaches would be packed with humanity. So, as best we could determine, each family had sent one of its boys – presumably, the one who could run the fastest – toward the still-moving train, so he could claim seats in one of the cars for his family.

That presumption appeared to be affirmed when all of the boys, ignoring the doors at each car, began climbing through the open windows to get inside. Before long, the aisle was so packed with human figures that no one could even think about moving to another spot – or of getting to the exit.

How Marianne and I managed to make our way down the aisle, inch by inch, and depart from the train along with our luggage, I cannot tell you. Basically, we managed the impossible.

In those days (this was 1981), Mexican railroads still carried passengers, and the train stations were usually near the city center. Our chosen low-budget hotel was barely a block away from the station. Like a thousand others in this country, it was small and ordinary, yet suitably promising for our three-week stay.

Before signing the registration card, I asked to see the room. A reasonable request, I thought; one I'd made many times, in Mexico and elsewhere. The clerk looked at me blankly, uncomprehending. Odd, since he seemed to be an intelligent young fellow, well-dressed and alert, like a student. And my gringo-based Spanish, while far from perfect, had nearly always been understandable to hotel clerks and other service workers, at least for basic requests.

For instance, the waitress at our hotel in Colima, later on, described my speech as *clarito* (clear). I was quite pleased by her modest praise.

Of course, I knew my Spanish pronunciation couldn't ever cause anyone to think I was Mexican. But because I spoke slowly and emphatically, if quietly, so as not to make a fuss, most people understood well enough. Depending on the subject and speed of speaking, I could – and did – carry on occasional conversations. Brief, but real. They wore me out, but I could ordinarily be understood. And vice versa. Yet, his face registered no comprehension at all. Not this time.

"*Puedo mirar el cuarto?*" I asked again. Still no response. I knew there was more than one word for "room," but figured he would get the idea even if a different one was considered the norm in this particular city. I tried a few gestures to suggest a desire to see the room, but I've never been good at talking with my hands, so I wasn't surprised by my lack of success this time. Still, even if he couldn't quite grasp the words or hand signals, you'd think he would grasp the concept. This was a hotel after all, with a constant flow of incoming guests. Surely, plenty of them must have asked to see a room in the past. How many other questions are there, in an encounter between guest and clerk? Could he somehow be fixated on *not* understanding me?

Because there were at least two distinct ways to say "look at," I'd used the one I thought was best. After repeated fruitless efforts, I tried the other word, without much hope. Suddenly, it dawned on him, as if the proverbial light bulb popped on above the clerk's well-groomed head. "*Ay, verlos,*" he exclaimed, *el cuarto,* as he reached for the appropriate room key. Evidently, I'd been victim to that complicating fact: that in Spanish, two or more distinct words often mean roughly the same thing. And there's no guarantee that the "wrong" one will be understood. *Ver. Mirar.* To see, to look at. *Cuarto,* too, was one of several words that defined a room, whether in a hotel or apartment building.

"*Exactamente,*" I replied with a sense of great fought-for satisfaction.

I took the key with a smile, which was returned in kind, and we headed up the stairs. The room was small, as expected, but fine for us. Basic, but that was our preference. Private bath. Clean. Odorless. Everything we needed.

Except, as we learned a little later, for hot water. The water was icy cold, warming for only a few hours each day. Because we normally hand-washed most clothing, that was not good news. Especially since it was midwinter, fairly high up in the mountains.

Not only was it cold outside, with patches of snow on the sidewalks, but the room was cold. Frigid cold. Seeing-your-breath cold. All the time, day or night. Few low-level Mexican hotel rooms offered heat of any kind, and this one was definitely not an exception to that rule.

That was the rule in cheap Mexican hotels, including those where wintry winds blow hard and the sky occasionally erupts in a flurry of white flakes – just as it did back home in Chicago. Heat and air conditioning were for the luxury crowd, even in regions that got very hot or very cold.

What it did have was a private bath, which was the one luxury that we invariably preferred not to do without, if at all possible, during our months of wandering through Mexico.

With our accommodation details settled, calmed down from our chaotic arrival at the railway station, we set out to explore the neighborhood. Right next door was a fairly large restaurant, which we valued more for its convenience than its food. It also had something we'd never witnessed before: the presence of Mennonites, struggling to sell their homegrown food products. Especially, their cheeses.

Groups of Mennonites, we learned, had migrated to Mexico many years earlier, hoping to maintain their simple religious lifestyle without interference from the government or neighbors. Not a word was uttered by those we observed in the restaurant, who would just hold their product out for inspection by diners at each table, one after the other. They did not look overjoyed to be spending their days hawking the community's wares, but that was clearly part of their value system. These were silent salesmen; but since they were "in business" at this location daily, we had to assume that their sales totals were sufficient to bring them back each day.

A large restaurant downtown demanded a fairly long walk, but had one feature that easily overcame all other amenities: electric heaters positioned along the baseboards. It was one of the few places in the city where we could sit for an extended period and warm ourselves in toasty comfort before heading into the cold again.

Two forms of freeze became evident during our stay: wintry weather and unwelcoming people. For some unknown reason, people here weren't very friendly. Some came across as nasty, or insulting. Some seemed to feel superior. With few exceptions, they were not at all like those we'd encountered elsewhere in the country – for instance, in Mexico City, Veracruz, Guadalajara.

It wasn't because San Luis Potosí was packed with tourists, either. Unpleasant reactions came from locals. In fact, we rarely saw anyone who looked foreign, or American; or who acted or spoke like anything other than a Mexican. At least, not in our part of town.

The most upsetting incident took place when Marianne took a few clothes to the local laundry. Her attempts to say a few words in Spanish were mocked in the most disdainful manner. *Servicio Cortés* (Courteous Service) was obviously not this store's motto.

We'd always tried to avoid being labeled as "ugly Americans." More than once, when asked, we had declared ourselves to be Canadian. That is, safe and subdued; not American loudmouth and barbaric, as many expect elsewhere in the world. I didn't like falsehoods; but in 1981, in much of Mexico, asserting your American derivation did not automatically yield a warm, courteous welcome.

Glad to get away as soon as possible, we stayed the full three weeks only because we'd applied for extensions on our tourist cards, and the new cards were coming in the mail, addressed to *Lista de Correos* (General Delivery) in San Luis Potosí.

Nearly everywhere in Mexico, you never know what to expect at the next corner. Today, of course, that scene could be a dangerous zone. Yet, those of us who long for that country below the border manage to overlook the risk, relying on elementary caution to keep ourselves safe while delighting in the experiences that lie ahead. Thankfully, the local folks had been, and continued to be, considerably more congenial in other parts of this exotic and alien – yet ever so enticing – nation.

11

Ready? Go!

Ruth Ann was nuts. Not raving mad or anything. But someplace off the beam, out in left field, as they used to say. No question about it. Just about anybody who dealt with her in those days had to agree.

Personally, I knew it only too well, having spent plenty of time among truly crazy people back in those days. Sick, troubled people. Most of them, I'd met or observed during a stint in a mental institution, a few years earlier. As a patient, not an employee or visitor, I have to admit with all due honesty. Voluntary, but a patient nonetheless.

We met in the mid-1960s, a couple of years before the counterculture became the big thing in much of the country. Ruth Ann was well ahead of them in terms of living life as an outsider. *Way* outside. What might be called an *outlier* in today's fancier times.

Why had I taken up with her? Mainly, because she was there. She was no great beauty. Too skinny to attract a lot of notice, but cute in kind of an oblique way. Bright red hair. The lush kind you hardly ever see. Sometimes, I could hardly take my eyes off it. Never seen a woman quite that redheaded, before or since. Yeah, red "down there," too, I learned before too long. I knew you'd be wondering about that.

Ruth Ann never worked anywhere for long. She got jobs easily, but none of them paid well, or were even semi-permanent. Just a way to amass a small nest egg for the next stretch of non-employment, whether sticking close to home or on the run.

She ate little beyond French fries, washed down with Pepsi-

Cola, but always insisted on having enough money to pay her insurance. Health insurance, in particular, though she seemed to be in amazingly good health considering her limited diet. Since I considered insurance companies to be the pariahs of the universe, I couldn't quite grasp her fealty to them.

Ruth Ann didn't care much for sex, but gave in now and then. Bed sessions were nothing to get excited about. They didn't necessarily take place in a bedroom, either, except during periods when she was living at home and her parents were out for the day. Or, during the time when I had my own apartment rather than occupying a bed at my mother's place.

Some grappling took place in whatever car she happened to own at the time. You probably won't be surprised to hear that. It was the Sixties, after all. Trouble was, except for the time when we first got together, she nearly always drove small cars, and often brought her dog along. The limitations were obvious. This was not the kind of threesome that might prove entertaining. All in all, I could take or leave dogs, but leaned toward the latter, especially on the road.

Still, I'd had so little experience with women, and even less *good* experience, that occasional time spent in her company – with few clothes present – was good enough for me.

When we had sex, which wasn't often, she would insist that coupling not be quite complete. That way, she could tell herself that she hadn't really had sex at all. Hadn't quite gone "all the way," as they used to call it. Just the preliminaries. "Not all the way in," she sometimes pleaded.

I went along. Going part of the way (close enough, truth be told) was sufficient.

She could have been called "frigid," I suppose. Worried about her reputation. Which was strange, because she claimed to have been forced out of the small town she was living in, not long before we met. Supposedly, that expulsion stemmed from an altercation over somebody's boyfriend. She practically bragged about having been tagged as unwanted, shunned, and ultimately ousted from that community. "They ran me out of town," she explained one evening.

If her story of ejection was true, I don't know how that concern about reputation came about. Didn't make sense. Of course, with Ruth Ann, not much did.

Like I say, odd, especially since she seemed prone to putting herself, at least occasionally, into position for serious misbehavior. Who were "they," anyway? No telling.

Weird as she was, Ruth Ann changed my life. It's true. Over a couple of years, in our sporadic, tense – even combative, ostensibly boy/girl relationship – I went from someone who rarely left my neighborhood to an intense if short-lived existence as a veritable vagabond. By the time we split up for good, I'd turned into someone who was always ready to head out to parts unknown, at a moment's notice.

That's because Ruth Ann was a traveler. A rambler. An adventurer.

Her inclination to wander popped into the picture in what seemed like minutes after we first met. "How about Iowa," she suddenly declared. "Want to head that way?"

I didn't know what to say. We were in Chicago at that moment. It was almost dark; maybe 9 o'clock at night. Iowa was on the other side of the Mississippi River, straight west, probably close to 200 miles away.

"When?" I asked.

"Now. Right now. Want to go?"

Surprising myself, I blurted out a "Yes. Sure." So, our first "date" consisted of a long, purposeless nighttime drive. No movies, no restaurant dinner, no formalities. Just a stretched-out session behind the wheel of her massive Plymouth Fury convertible, its top down to take in and enjoy the dark sky above and the lightly-traveled road ahead.

Even after our lightly romantic relationship faltered, we continued to take occasional trips together. Why? Because no one else I knew had such a nomadic nature, or anything close. For all of the time we were together, and a couple of years after that, she was nearly always willing to jump into the car and take off for somewhere. Or to nowhere in particular. Unscheduled, unplanned, spur of the moment without any itinerary.

Why did we go? To Iowa? Georgia? North Carolina? "Because it was there," as was said about climbers taking on the biggest mountain, was the only solid reason I ever came up with.

Typically, we might be sitting on her front porch, chatting with others in the three-flat building, when one of us brought up some destination. "Let's go," the other might say. And off we went. Right then. Not tomorrow, not next week. Now. Gone for a couple of hours, or a couple of days. Despite our separation, we both retained that unquenchable urge to take off without notice, and felt free to travel lightly. Luggage? A bag of French fries and a couple of Pepsi cans, and we were ready to travel, whether 10 miles or a thousand.

She was ahead of her time with cars, too. A growing number of young women had their own cars by the Sixties, but most were on the modest side. Ordinary, practical sedans. When I first saw Ruth Ann, she was 22 years old, driving that huge 1957 Plymouth Fury convertible, with golden paint and a big, powerful V-8 engine. Tall tailfins – among the highest available in that period of automotive excess. It was one of the flashier cars of its day. She looked tiny sitting at the wheel, but drove with a high level of ease and expertise.

After that, most of her cars were compact size or smaller. We drove a compact Ford Falcon between California and Chicago. Long before Toyotas became popular, she owned a 1967 Toyota Corona, followed by a 1971 Corolla. One of our trips was taken in a 1965 Opel Kadett, whose steering system was so twitchy it was tough to keep it centered in its lane on the highway.

Ready? Go!

Our impromptu journey to North Carolina came to a halt at Cherokee, in the western section of the state, so we never got to see the mountains and scenic greenery farther on, but it didn't matter. When we felt like stopping and turning around, we did. No regrets.

In Georgia, the site of her family's ancestry, I got to experience the Deep South for the first time, apart from a visit to a relative in Florida at age 15. We even drove through the town where the Scottsboro Boys were famously lynched, back in the Thirties.

Heading toward New Orleans in 1969, after our hesitant affair had ended but our trips continued periodically, we hoped to enjoy Mardi Gras. Except for a short nap in a rest stop, we almost drove straight-through, only to discover that the carnival was almost over. Even so, we saw enough to accumulate a modest stock of those colorful beads tossed to the audience by costumed folks on the parade floats. Ruth Ann hung them carefully on our rearview mirror, which seemed to be the customary practice.

Before moving on from Louisiana, we tried to sleep in the car in a city park, but were promptly ordered to depart by a cop. Driving into Mississippi, we got a look at the devastation remaining from the hurricane that had hit that area not long before. While spending the night in a motel in Gulfport, I was startled by Ruth Ann's request for a massage, while topless, despite our no longer being a couple. I complied.

During our return trip, a guy at a rest stop in Illinois boasted of making that trip in half the time it took us, meaning 100-mph speeds most of the time. We were never concerned with elapsed times, or any kind of time. Just go, keep going, and turn around when and where we wanted. That was always the rule.

Early in our relationship, I flew to southern California for a holiday: my first flight ever. Ruth Ann drove out there alone, a bit earlier. To me, it looked like paradise, and I began to entertain thoughts about moving to the state permanently. Meanwhile, we drove back to Chicago together in her Ford Falcon.

Our close relationship was long past when we drove to Colorado Springs, so I could attend the Studebaker Drivers Club's annual gathering. As happened now and then, we got there too late. Nearly all the participants had left, except for a handful of stragglers. Such results seemed to be inevitable, some of the time, when indulging in an unplanned trip.

As a rule, Ruth Ann shunned hotels, which she seemed to consider excessively risque, if not shameful; but motels, for some unfathomable reason, were okay. Even for sex, very occasionally. Seldom did I try to decipher her motivations or her barriers.

Because Ruth Ann fancied herself a big-time real estate speculator, many of our trips included a visit to a vendor of empty lots. Sometimes, she wound up buying one of those lots, unable to grasp that the guy selling them was the one destined to make all the money. He was the "con man." She was the "mark," convinced that those various small properties, located all around the country, would eventually make her rich. Who knows, maybe they did.

She bought lots of lots, around the country. Finally, she bought a house in Florida, several years after I'd last seen her. At least, that purchase had some practical value.

While out west, we spent a bit of time in Arizona, where she could look at properties, including a deserted cabin out in the desert and a subdivision lot closer in to civilization.

Another encounter with a real estate agent took place in southeast Michigan. This vicious-looking, pseudo-patriot right-wing gentleman informed me that he was trying to run a leftist schoolteacher out of town. In his mild-mannered opinion, anyone who did not get a lump in his throat when the National Anthem played had to be severely punished. And if that lump-in-the-throat failed to appear in the dastardly Commie culprit, he would be happy to put it there.

One Sunday morning while en route to North Carolina, we pulled into some small town in Kentucky, in need of breakfast.

Ready? Go!

Practically every patron in the restaurant looked up instantly, heads swiveling toward us, when we entered. It was 1969, and I was sporting a dark black beard. Over the previous year, since the disastrous protest and police response at the 1968 Democratic National Convention in Chicago, any evidence of hippie attire or facial adornment was *verboten* across much, if not most, of the country. Especially when outside of urban areas.

Now and then, Ruth Ann did plan ahead, for a longer journey. She even planned the intended itinerary, with the help of those old AAA Triptych maps that featured routes boldly marked with a Sharpie-type pen. GPS wouldn't come along until decades later. For some reason, she disdained those drivers who relied upon their own personal familiarity with maps and routes.

Only once did we disagree emphatically on a destination. I'd heard about the music festival set to take place at Woodstock, New York, and wanted to go. Ruth Ann put her foot down on that one. She detested the counterculture and everything connected with it. She, herself, could be considered a similar sort of eccentric outsider, but she was also an ardent capitalist. A nearly-impoverished one, but an ardent admirer of business, traditional values, and respectability. Hard to explain and understand the irony there. How we managed to get along, considering my leftist political views and leaning toward the counterculture, remains a mystery.

Our relationship didn't last all that long, but the vagabond nature remained as part of my psyche for the rest of my days, even though most of those days would be spent right at home, or close by.

I failed to realize, until much later, how much she influenced my life – then and now, more than half a century later. The reasons may have been different, but with a few odd deviations, she led the kind of off-the-map, unbridled life I'd always fantasized about, and read about in books like Kerouac's *On the Road*. I got at least a welcome taste while we were together.

Untied Knots

Without my time on the road with Ruth Ann, I would never have been able to take a cross-country driving trip on my own, after we'd separated. For years, even if I wasn't traveling anywhere, I'd sit and dream about it, knowing that I'd done so much of it in the past. Plenty of times. And when the time came, much later, for me to metamorphose into a seasoned traveler, flying 20 or 30 times a year on business, I was ready to take that plunge. Thanks, Ruth Ann.

So, was she really nuts, after all? Or just eccentric, like myself.

12

Roadworthy

My tailpipe fell off in New Mexico. The car didn't get much louder, I had to admit. Besides, a missing tailpipe wasn't a disaster. A relatively minor issue, especially on a decrepit old clunker.

Still, it was the second mechanical problem on this trip. Back in St. Louis, the fuel pump on the old Plymouth stopped working. Turned out to be a simple "fix," and I'd been lucky enough to be able to pull into a gas station where someone analyzed the problem right away, So, I really couldn't complain.

It was the middle of 1965 and I was on my way to California. Like countless migrants before me, from covered-wagon days to Depression-decade "Okies," I was hoping for a new beginning out there. Not unlike the wandering hoboes of the past, as well as the more recent beat-generation hipsters, inspired by Kerouac to take to the westbound road.

Most of the trip would take me onto the Interstate highway system, which served as a modern alternative to the old Route 66, vestiges of which ran parallel. Whenever feasible, I turned off the multilane Interstate and spent a while on the two-lane 66, imagining some of the dispossessed families that had traveled that path during the Depression, en route to the allegedly golden paradise of southern California.

This would be a different kind of cross-country trip, far removed from the typical holiday outings that had to fit within a one- or two-week vacation period, as allotted by your employer. I had no schedule to maintain, no real mileage or time goal. Nobody was expecting me. Hardly anyone knew I was on my way to anywhere.

I've always liked cars, but not so much driving them. Especially over long distances. For me, 300 miles was a long, long day. So, my 2,000-mile westward journey was likely to take a good six days. At least.

Though decrepit, my car at the time wasn't all that old. Even so, it wound up burning something like 24 quarts of oil between Chicago and Orange County, California. Hard to keep track, but I had to be sure to check it with every gasoline fill-up. And to have a couple of cans of oil at the ready, at all times.

I'd given up my job as a public aid caseworker in Chicago, mainly because my mental state kept getting worse. Psychoneurosis, it was, officially called "anxiety and panic reaction." For most of the previous eight years, it had served as a disability, ruling my entire life. As if that wasn't bad enough, I was drinking way too much. Taking plenty of prescription tranquilizers, too.

I just couldn't cope anymore; my mind was destroying me, rapidly. My condition had kept me out of the military draft, which would have been a disaster; but I desperately needed a fresh beginning.

I'd also realized that caseworkers were more like policemen than social workers – evaluating clients, but not helping them all that much. Unlike many caseworkers, who took that job as a stopgap until something better came along, it was one that I'd sought out and really wanted. Getting hired had been difficult, because of my time spent in a mental hospital, three years earlier.

I'd left my last job because of the mental stuff. Even though my work as a public aid caseworker let me spend two days in the week out of the office, visiting clients at their homes, it was more than I could handle. Days in the office were worst of all. Sitting there in a state of fright, trying to keep from shaking and fading away mentally. If that happened, I'd have no choice but to run out of the building, without a word to anyone, and somehow get home as quickly as possible.

All these years – decades – later, I still feel guilty about leaving that way. But at the time, there was no choice. When the worst burst onto the scene, I had to get away, as rapidly as humanly possible, seeking the hoped-for safety of home.

A year before, on my first-ever airborne holiday, I saw southern California for the first time and was captivated by what seemed to be a modern paradise. Why search for anyplace else? An unexpected offer from a relative who'd moved out there, stating that I'd be welcome to stay with them for a while, proved too hard to resist. I thought getting away from Chicago influences and memories would turn the tide.

Anxiety and fear were the foundation of my daily life in those days. Big time. Unfazed by the tranquilizers I gobbled down several times a day, my distress eased a bit by the alcohol I was consuming every evening. I'd taken my first drink something like eight years earlier, and almost immediately transformed into an alcoholic.

Agoraphobia was a major part of my affliction, though I didn't realize that until later. Literally, that means a fear of open spaces. Or, more commonly, of being away from the security of home. Even if home wasn't all that secure. Whatever and wherever home happened to be, that's where you felt safe. Safe enough, anyway.

Some guys could buy a car in one city, hop in, and drive a thousand miles, hardly stopping along the way. Not me. Never did enjoy driving that much. Not really. Not since my teens, anyway.

My 1958 Plymouth was the cheapest model, a Plaza, "stick" (manual) gearshift on the steering column. A beat-up rattletrap already, even though it was only seven years old. It looked and felt more like seventeen.

I'd bought it used, of course. Much used. That was a certainty.

I'd never had a new car, or even a late model, in those days. Nothing but old wrecks. Buy them cheap, drive them until something breaks down, get rid of it and buy another. My hands were each vehicle's last stop before the junkyard. Or the crusher. May as well let it be squeezed into scrap, and start over.

Was I nervous, starting out? You bet. What I experienced was a confused mix of foreboding and eagerness. To cope with my intense anxiety and fear, I was forced to hold my head with one hand and drive with the other, nearly all the time, for the whole trip.

I don't mind telling you, I was nervous about the journey. Fearful, to tell the truth. Even under ordinary circumstances, I was a bundle of anxiety, burdened by a scattering of debilitating symptoms. All mental, but formidable obstacles nonetheless.

I'd stopped to visit a college friend, staying with him the first night. Then onward, southwest bound, first on the Interstate but looking forward to traveling on segments of old Route 66. Much of it was still there, in the mid-Sixties. Still a functioning, official national highway. A few years later, Route 66 would be remembered mainly in books and songs, doomed by expansion of the multi-lane expressways. Before long, it would essentially disappear, though a few stretches of pavement still remain today.

I pulled off the Interstate periodically, to take either 66 or some old two-lane road for a while. That way, I passed through a tiny corner of Arkansas, one of many states I'd never entered before.

Oklahoma City was a shocking sight, with its oil wells pumping away, fully active, right on the state Capitol grounds. In the state's front yard, you might say.

Half the nights were spent sleeping in the car. Usually, in the parking lot of a big truck stop. That seemed about as anonymous, and safe, as I was likely to find. Seldom did I manage more than a couple of hours' sleep, if that.

One night in southwest Missouri, noting the falling temperatures, I paid a whopping $3 for a little cottage. During the night and especially toward morning, I had to fuel the fire, which – as best I remember – meant reloading the stove with firewood.

Because my alcoholism was an ongoing issue, I had to stop periodically for a couple of beers. Somewhere in New Mexico, for instance, I sat at the bar with a few Indians. That's what they were most often called in those days, though nobody seemed to have asked them their preference on that score. "Native Americans" and "indigenous people" came later.

When I reached Flagstaff, Arizona, I turned northbound, toward Nevada. Always wanted to see Las Vegas, and this was my chance.

After my late-afternoon arrival, following miles and miles of Arizona desert, I checked into what seemed a veritable luxury hotel for $10 a night. Actually, it was a commonplace motel at the south end of the Las Vegas Strip. After a nap, I headed for one of the Strip's hotel-casinos. It was well after midnight, and I stayed until (or near) dawn, enthralled by all that I saw on the casino floor.

One of the most startling sights in my life was the vista of smog-ridden Los Angeles that appeared upon cresting one last hill in the westbound lane of Interstate 15. I'd heard and read about the sickly-looking cloud of pollution in that part of the country, but seeing that ugly, yellowish fog in person, hovering all along the horizon, put the issue of pollution into a new plane. After that sighting, whenever a conversation turned to vehicle emissions and similar topics, I couldn't help but instantly re-imagine that first sighting I'd experienced.

The trip took eight days total, with a couple of detours along the way.

Several months earlier during a visit to Chicago, one of my cousins who lived in Orange County, California, invited me to stay at his house if I decided to head west. He didn't realize what he was asking for. I overstayed my welcome by far, moving into his home not once, but twice.

In between, I rented an apartment in a typical southern California residential building with an outdoor pool; but I grew so anxious, so quickly, that I couldn't stay there more than a day or two, despite having paid a month's rent in advance. Being awakened abruptly by loud sounds from an adjacent apartment, heard through the thin wall, helped trigger an all-out panic that I couldn't overcome even a little.

A bit later, I managed to move into a small apartment in the same city as my cousin, remaining there for the balance of my stay.

So, was that exciting new life out west ever found? It was not. Shortly before my arrival in southern California, the job market seemed to have shrunk sharply. The same thing would happen years later when I (and my wife) decided to settle in Las Vegas. After expanding for years, with low unemployment, "Sin City" suffered its first serious recession.

I managed to fill the gap with a pair of short-term jobs: taking the local census, followed by three weeks as a box boy at the Broadway department store. Then, I somehow managed to obtain a full-time position with a Boeing supplier, writing parts lists.

That office functioned with a very loose setup that should have worked perfectly for me. Although we were required to be in the building for our entire shift (no surprise there), nobody cared what we did when there was no work to be done. Tasks tended to arrive in spurts, which had to be completed as quickly (and accurately) as possible. Beyond that, in the interim periods, we were free to read, chat, or just about anything else. Sounds ideal for someone in my condition, but I was too far gone by then. Too mired in ceaseless anxiety, dread, and panic.

While in California, I had sought psychiatric help, but was informed that if I required hospitalization. they would ship me back to Chicago rather than treat me out there at a public institution. Unless I could pay full price for treatment, of course.

Interviewed for a caseworker job in Santa Ana, I was dead certain that I'd flunked the interview, conducted by a panel of managerial employees. I barely gave the devastating experience a thought after dashing out of the building afterward, except for the fear and guilt that plagued me for months afterward. During the interview, I felt as if I was shaking apart the whole time, sure the interviewers couldn't wait to get rid of me and turn to a calmer candidate for the job.

I didn't have all that many dollars tucked away when leaving Chicago, and my cash supply was dwindling fast. After five months, with mental problems getting worse once again, I gave up and hopped a plane back to the Midwest.

Much to my surprise (shock, actually), I was hired by that social service agency in Santa Ana, but not until I was back in Chicago and received a postcard saying come to work on so-and-so date. Too late. By then, the desire for a fresh start had evaporated, and I felt even less able to consider another trip than I had before.

Obviously, none of us ever know what lies ahead if we take a turn in life, whatever its direction might be. If all goes well at first, will it stay that way? If it's bad from the start, was the transition a total failure?

Looking backward, had I not returned, the freelance life I managed to establish back in Chicago might never have come to pass, with results that would be impossible to speculate upon. Naturally, I would never have met my wife either, not written any books, and never had my long life as a low-level journalist covering the car business. Even though I wasn't delving into matters of importance, I was officially a member of the media, at a time when it still enjoyed some respect, unlike today. Maybe my failed adventure wasn't such a loss at all.

13

Get It While It's Hot

Heading home after lunch one afternoon, my wife and I noticed a small group of women clustered around the entrance to our residence. It wasn't a house, or an apartment building. No, our abode – the place we lived in for two years – was a residential hotel. The kind of hotel that was already disappearing from most cities, or already gone, but served as home for a substantial portion of the casual population of Las Vegas. That is, for people who intended to stay for a week, maybe a month; but might instead wind up at the hotel for a year if not more, paying by the week.

Room 5 was our home in downtown Vegas, on the ground floor of the Buena Vista Hotel, just steps away from the 24-hour-a-day action and dazzling neon of Fremont Street. Sixty bucks a week, including a private bath. While we were there, they even installed cable TV, hooked to the black-and-white set that came with the room. Double bed, small dresser, tiny desk. No phone in the room; only a buzzer, to let you know that a call was waiting for you at the public phone at the far end of the corridor.

No cooking facilities were provided, but we didn't need anything more high-tech than a heating coil to warm up soups and such. We'd be eating nearly all of our meals at a restaurant or buffet within one of the downtown or Strip hotels.

Not much of a view from our room, either. Only the slightly more costly hotel across the street, which was visible because we had a front room. Overall, the room wasn't much bigger than the double bed.

Unlike the Strip, which started a couple of miles to the south, Fremont Street was the heart of *old* Las Vegas, with a checkered history as a tiny desert metropolis dating back to 1906. Not until well after World War II, when the Strip – Las Vegas Boulevard, the main entertainment street – was developed did the city's population even begin its explosive growth, which persisted over the next half-century and beyond.

We'd arrived in Las Vegas in 1981, after four months of travel through Mexico. Already, some of the old luxury hotels along the Strip were beginning to disappear, replaced by ever-larger and more luxurious establishments. Old Las Vegas was still part of the picture, but a decade or so later, not much would be left of the city's earlier hotels, restaurants, and entertainment facilities.

One of those downtown hotels, the El Cortez – our favorite, it turned out – had been constructed in 1941, well before the arrival of "Bugsy" Siegel and the gangland boys from back east. More than any other individual, Siegel was credited with turning the dusty desert town into a metropolis of dazzle and glitter, catering to high rollers from across the globe.

There were no high rollers living alongside us in our residential hotel, a block away from the El Cortez. Lots of *low* rollers – some of them pretty far down on their luck. Others eked out a sometimes precarious, sometimes steady living from jobs at the bigger hotels and casinos with their integral bars and restaurants. From the beginning, Las Vegas has been a city of service workers, though the forms of service have changed over the years.

Yes, that includes sex workers, which brings us back to the ladies hovering in front of the Buena Vista that afternoon. Despite being illegal in Clark County, plenty of women squeezed out a living of some sort by offering their bodies for rent, short-term. Elsewhere in the state, randy gentlemen could find full-fledged, fully legal brothels. Las Vegas has always marched to the beat of its own, carefully selected drummer.

As we approached the hotel's entry door, it became evident that the women hanging about weren't exactly what you'd call ladies, in the usual sense. More like ladies of the evening; or in this case, of mid-afternoon. None were dressed especially scantily, but their choices of fabric and color were the type that sent signals to any likely prospects who were paying attention.

One of them stepped forward, just a bit closer, seemingly prepared to ask a question that was a regular occurrence in her profession. But before she got the words out, another woman – one I recognized from chance encounters in the hotel corridor or the laundry room – stopped her abruptly. "They're okay," she said, indicating that neither I nor my wife were potential clients for sexual services. "They live here."

The first woman, more flamboyantly dressed than the others as well as more aggressive, wasn't about to be dissuaded quite that easily. "Got to get it while it's hot," she proclaimed, tossing a final come-hither glance in my direction before slowly turning back to her colleagues and competitors.

As a rule, the women who plied their trade on the street were as polite and restrained as anyone else in the hotel. Cell phones hadn't even been invented yet, so the daily activities of the ladies in question had to be arranged in a more direct manner.

Accosting a gentleman on the street – downtown or along the Strip – was a popular pastime. Nothing threatening, though some recipients of the ladies' attentions looked pretty uncomfortable. Just a couple of words indicating their interest in establishing a brief relationship, for which a fee would have to be paid. Negotiations, as in any business, often followed the opening bid.

Unpleasant encounters with disastrous ends did happen, but rarely.

Walking alongside one's wife or girlfriend was an unreliable barrier to the attentions of passing night women, regardless of time of day. Just another objection to be overcome, like any salesperson.

Even though I never accepted the offers of afternoon or evening entertainment or companionship, it wasn't because of my wife. Marianne was unusually tolerant and non-judgmental.

A few years earlier, while strolling through the Red Light district in Amsterdam, she'd asked if I wished to strike up a short dalliance with one of the ladies displaying her wares behind a plate-glass window. I declined, of course; but the knowledge that the choice was entirely mine enhanced my appreciation for Marianne's maturity and character.

Invariably while traveling, and she spotted a scantily-clad or, less frequently, topless lady lolling about, Marianne would point out that person like a tourist guide who didn't want you to miss any crucial sights.

She was actually the one who had suggested settling in Las Vegas for a while. When we stepped off the bus from Phoenix, following our lengthy stay in Mexico, she'd never been in Las Vegas. I had. By the time we finished our promotional-priced breakfast at a restaurant across the street from the bus station, she was ready to start looking for a place to live.

Daily life in Las Vegas, she often said, was like living in the circus. A *hot* circus, for sure. During our two-year residence, the thermometer reached a peak high of 114 degrees – decidedly uncomfortable to a pair of born-and-raised midwesterners.

Air conditioning? No such luck. Sure, the huge hotels blasted frigid air right out the always-open front doors, but our little hotel room contained no such comfort. Nothing other than what they called a "swamp cooler." Better than nothing, but hardly capable of overpowering three-digit summer temperatures.

We soon learned to look for shade whenever the sun was out – which seemed to be always, except for midwinter. *Any* kind of shade. Even the slight protection from harsh solar rays provided by a light pole at the curb, while waiting for a bus or the Walk light, could provide a touch of most welcome relief.

Beyond downtown and the Strip, of course, Las Vegas differed little from other desert cities. Those neighborhoods sounded dull and dreary to us. We fit right into our life at the heart of what came to be dubbed Sin City.

Speaking of buses, those were our sole means of in-city transportation. Only once or twice did we rent a car, to get out into the desert, and it wasn't easy. Because we did not *own* a car anymore, we had no car insurance. As a result, auto-rental agents were flummoxed about how to handle our paperwork.

No matter. We got by nicely making use of the city's bus service, which ran on a surprisingly reliable schedule and could take us almost to the edge of that unique metropolis, where the real desert began.

Most likely, even some long-term residents were unaware that bus service existed, beyond the popular Strip buses that rolled along Las Vegas Boulevard. They'd have found it hard to believe that bus ridership could be relied upon as a low-cost alternative to owning an automobile.

Jobs were hard to find in Las Vegas in 1981, even at the hotels. The city's first recession had occurred not long before our arrival.

When Marianne finally got a job, after applying at a dozen or more possible employers, she had to pretend to own a car. The job was secured through Nevada's public employment service, and when I looked over the list of available positions, every single one carried the notation "Must Have Own Transportation." In the end, she was hired by the phone company and started work on the second shift – at a location less than a block from our hotel.

Because she got off work at midnight, we had a schedule that fit right into Las Vegas life, but would confuse some of our middle-class friends and acquaintances back home. Dinner was nearly always at one of the big downtown hotels, taking advantage of the after-midnight specials. Four-dollar steaks and dollar shrimp cocktails were still the rule; or perhaps, a bargain-priced lobster tail.

Breakfast typically consisted of a minimal meal prepared with our heating coil, or obtained from a nearby takeaway. Several times a week, we could be found at lunchtime feasting at one of the budget-priced hotel buffets, where the food was a lot better than TV comedians suggested in their mocking routines about the city.

Doubtless a few criminals were among the hotel guests. One young fellow a couple of doors down from Room 5 kept his door partly ajar, all day long, when he was inside the room. As it happened, the city jail was barely a block away. Most likely, he didn't want to feel closed-in, trapped, now that he was supposedly free, out in the world rather than restrained within a barred cell.

Not everybody knows this, but despite the blazing sun in summertime, Las Vegas can get cold in winter. One day in January, we were surprised to see snow on the sidewalk. It had fallen only in one tiny area, for a short time, but it was actual, authentic snow.

Another thing lots of people don't realize: not everybody gambles. Or if they do, it's probably just an occasional activity. A coin in a slot machine when passing. Or a ten-buck investment at a Blackjack table, once every couple of weeks.

Mostly, I liked to be around gambling, but I wasn't that keen on getting into it myself. I knew how most of the games worked, and had a basic sense of odds and probabilities; but few of the casino games tempted me to learn more, in order to play seriously. And if you're not going to devote some serious attention to Poker, or Craps, or whatever, why bother at all? Marianne and I were more attracted to the extravaganza shows on the Strip, or to the serene desert beauty of the region, than to the casino tables or machines.

My father had been a gambler, at a time when Nevada was the only state with legal gambling. He never went more than a couple of hundred miles outside of Chicago. But when out of his regular neighborhood, he had a kind of sixth sense that let him know just where to find a nearby bookie, or a bartender who took bets, or a purveyor of sports-betting cards. Lifelong gamblers are like that. It's as if they can smell a gambling joint, or sense a game taking place within a two-block radius.

I often wondered what he'd make of the many venues for legal betting these days. He passed on long before any state other than Nevada, along with Atlantic City, New Jersey legalized gambling. I suspect he wouldn't be as drawn to wagering. Too sanitized. Part of the appeal, I think, stemmed from the illicit nature of the activity.

Anyway, I've long been attracted not to the betting, but to the milieu, the surroundings of establishments where gambling is happening. Which usually means casinos. Which, if you're looking for the finest ones in the country, still means Las Vegas in the south of Nevada (and Reno up north).

Just about every morning, the warming sun streamed through the window curtains of Room 5, unwelcomed by those who, like ourselves, had gone to sleep only a few hours before – if at all. Unless it was winter, that sunlight would be heating our tiny living space in a hurry, barely impeded by the dubious action of the swamp cooler on the wall.

There was no work of any kind for me, and no writing assignments available from former clients. After standing for a long while in one unbelievably long employment line at the newly reinvigorated El Rancho Hotel, I finally realized that seeking a job at the hotels and casinos was futile. Even long-term hospitality and gaming employees couldn't find work. Not with so many of the unemployed gathering at every spot that seemed to promise a possibility for employment.

Fortunately, Marianne remained employed through the entire balance of our residence in Nevada. We managed to get by on her income alone, because we lived so simply. Yes, it could be done, even near the middle of a loud, flamboyant, incandescent 24-hour-a-day carnival.

Not unlike those Las Vegans who owned homes or rented apartments toward the city's outskirts, far from downtown or the

Strip, we enjoyed a quiet, easy, low-stress – indeed, restful – life. In fact, it was akin to what legendary expatriate author Henry Miller had described in his autobiographical novel *Quiet Days in Clichy*. Just what we needed at the time.

Coincidentally, much later in life, I spent a month in Clichy, just north of Paris, and it was indeed a quiet and peaceful place. A far cry from Las Vegas, though immediately adjacent to lively Paris.

Even the circus sheds its outsider appeal after a time. So, after our two-year stretch, we moved on to Canada, looking forward to getting as much travel as possible out of a pair of 30-day rail passes, valid in each of the provinces. After that, who could say? We were still looking for adventure and foregoing – perhaps shunning – certainty and familiarity.

Even though we've since returned to Las Vegas only as tourists or on business, I've often wondered what happened to our hotel home. Last time I visited, it was still operating. Everything looked about the same as it had a couple of decades earlier, but there was no sign of the ladies who had promised a hot time on the premises.

14

Smitten

"Nice Move!" I almost said it out loud. "Smooth." That was my instantaneous, silent reaction as I watched her make a swift, wholly assured position change, blending her motorcycle precisely into the outer lane. Evidently undertaken as preparation for a right turn ahead, that simple lane-change maneuver brought to mind the impeccably flowing motions of an easygoing river, meandering yet forceful.

Except for a momentary glance at her face when she issued a nimble downward twist of the head to check traffic in that adjacent lane, I saw her only from the rear. Young, for sure, riding a slickly modern yet semi-traditional motorcycle on an ordinary state highway through the Chicago suburbs. And doing it really well.

One of my few regrets in life is that I've never owned a motorcycle. Ridden one occasionally, but never drove one home to stay. I even took riding classes at one time, but never took the next step. And never stopped thinking about it, after all these years.

Plenty of women, young and not-so-young, ride motorcycles nowadays. In my younger years, not so many.

Obviously a civilized, urbane rider, she wasn't attired in black leather and rough denim like some raucous refugee from *The Wild One*, seeking the attention of a sullen Marlon Brando wannabe. Instead, she wore an intoxicating, snug-fitting, rich purple T-shirt. No tacky brand name or slogan on the back. Short-sleeved, above pure white slacks. Or were they darker? Hard to remember for sure, after being so transfixed by that simple, breathtaking purple T-shirt.

White shoes. Yes. Unusual looking. Her hair was tucked neatly into a subtly colorful helmet, but no other safety gear could be seen. No gloves, no heavy boots.

Surely, she was on her way to some grand adventure: one on which I would desperately desire to accompany her. Whether behind her on that motorcycle seat built for one, or on a separate machine, gazing at those graceful two-wheeled maneuvers.

Realistically, I had to admit, she might merely be on her way to work or school, like every other day. Sad, but likely true. Another fantasy dashed by reality.

Though intense, my rapid-fire thoughts couldn't be called lustful in nature. Okay, maybe just a hair in that direction. But she was too perfect, too unmarred, too young for me to entertain even the mildest lascivious thought. No, it was more a matter of simply wondering how sweet it would be to hit the open road behind her, headed for ... well, who knows what destination. Or better yet, no destination, no hard-and-fast goal at all.

One thing for sure: my imaginings, any fantasies, didn't involve the current, elderly "me" accompanying her on that quest to somewhere. No, they were of the long-ago "me," the young version, more comparable to her own age. And in those long-ago days, I'd been so uneasy with girls that I would never have been so bold as to risk even speaking to someone like her.

Today, I'm the equivalent of her grandpa. Maybe even her *great-*grandpa, for pity's sake.

Momentarily, I was sorry I didn't have a camera right at hand; but on second thought, glad I kept her presence, her existence fresh only in my mind, not as a photographic image. Far better not to have intruded upon her privacy except this tiny bit, from afar. That was enough. And it was good.

She turned right at the next stoplight, heading in the direction that I, too, intended to take in a few moments. Could that be a favorable sign? Of something? But to my distress, she was two cars ahead of me, with a van blocking my view as she waited for the green arrow to illuminate.

By the time I had a chance to see past intervening traffic directly ahead, she'd disappeared. She was gone in a wisp, much like she'd arrived on that suburban road, never to return.

Or would she? Might I be plying that same route daily, at the same time, just in case she returns, astride that heavenly two-wheeler? Could I be that foolish, at my hugely advanced age, rapidly running out of time left on earth?

It's possible. Otherwise, she's tucked into a secret corner of my feeble, fast-graying brain. I like it. A lot.

How do any of us ever know how, or if, our presence might have struck an attentive chord in a passing stranger – appearing in a moment, gone in another, but leaving an indelible, non-erasable image behind.

Back at Home

Tales of troubled folks – stuck on the home front – seeking a way out, whether they realize it or not. Some are wholly fictional, but most stem largely from real life.

15

Desk Duty

Out in the dusty lobby, the old lady wasn't bothering anybody. Just sitting, staring. Sure, she didn't really belong there. I knew that. She wasn't a guest at the hotel. That's the rule. The requirement, which lets a stranger occupy a seat in the lobby.

Still, why should I have to insist that she leave? And call the police if she refused?

Because I was in charge, that's why. While taking home something like minimum wage, from 5:00 to 11:00, six days a week, my word was law at the Delaney Hotel (Weekly Rates, Private Bath, TV available).

Outside the hotel, my word was shit, counting for nothing. But for six hours a day I was virtual lord, master, king. Whatever you wanted to call it. Maybe all of those together.

The hotel's owner left by 5:00 nearly every day – provided he'd showed up at all. "It's all yours, Sharkey," he'd said to me as I arrived behind the front desk and he was halfway out the front door. The hotel wasn't mine, obviously. It was his. He'd inherited the place from an old uncle or something, and had no interest in it. Not the rooms, not the guests, nothing. Whenever he made an appearance, he just gathered up the rents they'd all paid, looked around a little, and went his merry way.

This same scenario had happened so many times, I'd lost count long ago. Maybe the same old lady, maybe a different one. Didn't matter. Getting her out with the least commotion was my job. And I'm embarrassed to say so, but I was good at it. Isn't that great? I was skilled at booting little old ladies out into the street; or calling the cops if they resisted.

Who was she, anyway? Was this really one of the old women who'd been here before, sitting quietly, unruffled, in the lobby? I just couldn't tell. They kind of looked alike, all of them. Coat too heavy for this weather, but worn tightly closed at the neck. Worn-out old-lady shoes, scuffed and tired. No lipstick or anything. No jewelry. But a hat. They all had hats. Hats that had probably been stylish at some time in the distant past. But not anymore. Nobody wore hats anymore, except little old ladies in the lobby of the Delaney. Waiting for me to act.

Did she live around here? Except for the Delaney, this was kind of an expensive neighborhood. I couldn't afford to live here, that was for sure.

Anyway, what was I, some kind of policeman? When I took this job, I thought all I had to do was rent rooms occasionally (not many people came to inquire) and take rents from the residents. They all paid by the week, or even by the month. So there wasn't much rent collection duty, either.

Little old ladies weren't the worst, though. At least they didn't often resist, or try to fight. No, the worst were the couples. Married couples, or whatever they were. Gay couples, too. Like the man and woman in 216. Every Saturday evening the two of them would stroll out of the elevator like lovebirds, cooing and preening. Not a worry in the world, all dressed up for a night out. They were probably 40 or 45, and acted like they'd been together a long time.

By midnight, they'd be back. Screaming, clawing, frantic. Often as not, she'd already be marked up from a fight somewhere along the way. Scrapes, cuts, maybe a bit of blood oozing down her cheek, making its way onto her party dress.

Usually, when they came back, he'd be quiet. Not always, but usually. She was the one yelling, trying to drag her longish fingernails down his face, or flail at him with her arms like some mechanical boxing toy. Even knee him in the groin, if she could get close enough.

He was a muscular-looking guy, but if he'd been doing any talking at some point, he was finished now. He was obviously drunk, but the kind of drunk who shuts up eventually. She was the hysterical drunk, the angry boozer, ready to fight some more, letting the world know what a rat he was and how he had ruined her life.

Maybe he had. How would I know? All I knew was that I couldn't do a thing to control her outbursts, her attacks. Except call the cops. Which I did, almost every single Saturday night around midnight. Might as well have made that call automatically, before they actually walked in the door.

A district police station was only a couple of blocks away, so a pair of cops usually showed up pretty quickly. But they didn't seem to be in any hurry. Why should they? There were no surprises at the Delaney.

"You two again?" one cop would cry out as they ambled in the front door, hands on their billy clubs. "Don't you ever give it a rest?"

His name was Bill. Johnson, I think. Black guy. Nice enough, for a cop. But he and his partner had been here so many times, seen this exact same scenario so often, that you could tell they were just exasperated.

They didn't really want to haul the couple in, though that happened now and then when they got too frisky and things looked a little dangerous. Especially when he came out of his quiet stupor and started grabbing at her, or trying to slug her with his sizable fist. Then, Bill would make quick use of his club, and practically in an instant, cuffs would be holding the man's hands behind his back.

Funny. I can't remember their names. The couple. Just "the fighters" is how I thought of them.

Both of them were pleasant enough when they stopped at the desk in the daytime, sober, evidently with no recollection of the turmoil they'd created just a few feet away, a few hours earlier. Markovich was the name on the registration card, I think. Something like that. But first names? Maybe those just never came up, when talking about rent due or a light burned out in the shared bathroom on their floor.

Anyway, their plight didn't help with my quandary of the moment: how to get rid of the latest old lady.

As I glanced over to the couch where she sat, she looked as if she'd not moved a muscle since my last observation. Sitting upright, hands folded. Prim. Proper, really, despite her worn-looking coat and exhausted shoes.

In an earlier time, she might have fit right in. Years ago, the Delaney was supposed to have been a fairly classy place. Lots of well-heeled folks had lived here, paying by the month. Or maybe by the year. Dowagers in decade-old attire probably sat on that very same couch, whiling away each day.

Lots different from today, when you have to chase after tenants to get their weekly rent. Or, now and then, have to gather up all their stuff, store it away, and change the lock on their door until they pay up. Or disappeared, leaving their stuff behind. It happens.

So, anyway, I couldn't wait any longer. Step One, as always: ask her what she's doing there. Most often, they'd give no response at all, just look up with an innocent demeanor at the interloper who appeared to be questioning them about something. Whether they were actually confused or just play-acting didn't matter. Frankly, I didn't care. My job was to chuck them out unless they were paying guests; and like I said, I was good at that part.

This lady was no different. "Can I help you?" I asked as I approached her slowly. She barely raised her eyes, giving no sign that words were being formed in reaction. Again I asked, "Is there something I can do for you?" She looked frightened, yet somehow firm in her resolve to remain sitting there, mute.

"Are you staying in the hotel, ma'am?" Her eyes practically

looked right through me. She seemed even tinier than before, as if she were starting to disappear into the folds of the leatherette upholstery. "Unless you have a reason for being here, ma'am, you'll have to leave. Otherwise, I'll have to call the police."

If she understood what I was saying, she didn't show it at all. Silence.

"Hey, Ma!" A loud voice echoed through the dusty lobby, coming from the entry door. "What you doin' here?"

He was a big man, muscular, almost tough-looking. His sport coat looked a size too small, the sleeves not quite reaching his wrists. The collar of his flashy, nearly incandescent sport shirt sat wide open over the coat's upper lapels.

"She's your mother?" I asked, rhetorically.

"That's right. Been looking all over the block for her."

"Well, she's just been sitting here," I said. "I was trying to find out who she was, what she wanted here."

"Yeah, well, she's done this before. We were down at Anthony's, the Italian place on the corner? All of a sudden, I come back from the head and she's gone. My wife didn't even see her leave."

The man reached down, took her arm. Achingly, slowly, she got up from the couch, clinging to his elbow. "Sonny," she said in a whisper. Nothing more. Just "Sonny."

"That's right, Ma. Sonny. We need to get back now. The family's waiting. Food's probably all cold by now."

"She's okay then?" I asked, backing away toward the front desk.

"Yeah, sure. She give you any trouble?"

"No, no, nothing like that," I replied honestly as they strode slowly, carefully out the front door.

No matter. Another old lady would be on that couch tomorrow, sitting upright, prim and refined. If not tomorrow, the next day. And the next.

No matter how much I disliked doing it, I'd have to throw out one of them. After all, I was on front-desk duty. I was in charge.

16

Bad Sports

Stan was not a fan. Sports fan, that is. Things would have been easier, a lot easier, if he was. But growing up, he was one of those kids who was invariably chosen last when picking sides for softball, basketball, whatever.

For good reason, too. Stan stunk. Throw a ball – any kind of ball – in his direction, and you may as well have tossed it right at the ground. Because that's where it would be, in a moment.

Not that Stan was the only misfit in the neighborhood, when it came to sports. One difference, though: he just didn't care. The others were hurt by all the taunts from the athletic crowd. "Butterfingers." "Loser." Plus a few cruder terms as the boys grew older. More than once, Stan had seen his best friend Greggie run home, almost in tears, after a game – stabbed by those pre-teen and teenage verbal assaults.

But Stan? He just didn't give a shit, if you'll pardon the expression. Sports? Not for him, that's all, whether as a participant or a watcher. He always had better things to do than sit in front of a TV with his eyes glued to some game or other.

Otherwise, his high-school life had been fine. He got good grades without struggling hard. Hardly at all, in fact. A couple of good-looking girls seemed to like him well enough, even without any athletic exploits to brag about. He danced reasonably well – even the fast ones – and had his own car. Who needed a little round object or a slab of wood to make their life more complete?

As might be expected, the sports fans got even more intense as they hit their late teens and edged into the 20s, finished school, got jobs, started families. Most of them stopped playing themselves, but directed that excess energy into their role of all-out, our-team-first fans.

They knew all the players on the city's teams, as well as the university competitors. They had all the statistics memorized. Some of them had season tickets for one team or another – at a price that almost caused Stan to lose his breath. Or his lunch.

"Can you believe it?" he said one morning to his deskmate, Randy – another non-fan. "Harold came up with over two thousand bucks for a season ticket. I mean, you could buy a pretty good used car for that."

Stan had been surprised to see how many non-fans there were in the office at Argos Publishing. Half a dozen, at least. Other places he'd worked, he had been the only one. Far as he knew, anyway.

The idea came to him at an opportune moment, just as he'd tossed a wadded-up sheet of scrap paper toward the wastebasket across the aisle. As it glanced off the rim and dropped inside, Randy let out a snarly cheer. "Go, Stan!" he called out. "Do it, Stan!"

Stan stood up and took a mock bow, raising his hand to quiet the crowd of one. "All in the wrist," he declared with a modest nod of his head, loosely waggling his hand at the wrist – the wrong hand, actually – to demonstrate his prowess.

Actually, he had to admit, he was surprisingly good at tossing paper balls into the wastebasket. Why that was, he couldn't imagine; but for whatever reason, he hardly ever missed.

In a matter of seconds, the whole scenario came to him, like a jolt to the brain when witnessing an accident. Teams. Tournaments. Maybe gambling. Prizes, too. Except, only the non-sports would participate. Jocks and fans? Out of luck.

He loved it.

Maybe the fans would just scoff and sneer, derisively snorting:

"Yeah, look, a game for losers only." Then again, maybe not. Maybe they couldn't resist being part of a new sporting event, even if it didn't meet the usual criteria. Or, *especially* if they didn't.

All the more so if they had gambling. Stan knew for a fact that a couple of the fan types were heavily into wagering. Some of them bet on everything, it seemed, from football to horses to cards. Or whether Harold, a self-described ladies' man, would be successful in asking that new girl in accounting for a date.

Still, was Stan the only one who was good at tossing the crumpled paper ball? If the other non-sports couldn't get it near the basket, the whole idea would collapse.

They'd need a contest, for non-fans only. Surreptitious at first. Let out only a few hints that something was happening, so they could retreat if need be. If some of the non-sports needed guidance, maybe he could try and advise them on how to shoot more accurately.

Stan almost laughed out loud at that one, causing several heads to turn his way. Imagine, him, Stan the non-fan, coaching a group of players. His overbearing – even cruel – high school gym coach, who'd given Stan a hard time every single day, would faint away if he could ever see such a turn of events.

He didn't think there were any books on the subject. No experts. Anyway, he'd look into the possibilities later on, if and when they got rolling.

To Stan's surprise, the initial steps didn't take much effort at all. Nearly every time he brought up the subject to anyone, he got an immediate "Yes. When do we start?" Of course, he was careful whom he talked to about the contest. Any hint of sporting interest and the conversation was over. Or more likely, never got started at all. This would be a closed competition, and he was going to keep it that way.

He would like to have done it at the office, after hours, but feared that management would not look kindly if they heard about it. Both the game itself and the wagering that would take place.

A preliminary game was scheduled for Friday evening, an hour and a half after their official workday ended, in the back room of a nondescript bar Stan patronized now and then. He'd paid the bartender a few bucks in advance for maintaining the privacy of the group. A rough-looking gentleman, he was heavily muscled with a perpetually displeased expression, so no interlopers were likely to get past him. Drinks were ordered right away, but they didn't dawdle or sit around chatting. Everybody seemed eager to get started.

Stan had commandeered a few wastebaskets from the office, along with a stack of waste paper. Printer paper, which would be good for crumpling.

Nobody seemed too concerned about who would go first. Being first (or last) didn't seem to provide any particular advantage. They weren't forming teams, either. Not for this first trial, at least. Everybody agreed that Stan should keep track of the "baskets" and misses. He'd come up with the whole thing, after all.

By the time the first contender was ready, crumpled "ball" in hand, an even dozen guys – plus two ladies – had shown up.

"No real rules this time," Stan explained. "We just want to see how you do. So, crumple a few sheets of that paper, and just start tossing at one of the wastebaskets. Keep track of how many hits and misses you have, and I'll keep score for all of us."

Not everyone proved equally adept (or inept), of course. As always in such contests, a couple of participants shined, while a few others were lucky to the paper wad anywhere near the region of the wastebasket.

Several of the participants were surprised to find they had a bit of talent for this new sport. "Never been good at anything in the athletic department," said George from marketing as his paper ball dropped into the wastebasket for the third time in a row. "Uh course, I've never really tried at anything, either. I hate to say it, but this is kind of fun."

All of the contenders had avoided play of any kind in high school. Grammar school, too. Nearly everyone had a tale of shunning and avoiding all sports, and the humiliation suffered. They seemed glad to talk about those bad memories. "In college, I didn't even know where the football stadium was," said Bruce the copywriter. "Or, the team colors. Never admitted that to anybody, but it didn't mean a thing to me." Something like half of the group nodded in agreement at that one.

More than half grumbled about the sports aficionados who chattered and argued incessantly about their favorite games and preferred players. You know how they are. They know every teeny little detail about the sport that captures the greatest share of their attention. And if nothing more can be said about that one, they're ready to jump right into a discussion of any other athletic endeavor that somebody brings up. In other words, boring, boring, boring.

They decided early on that no fans would be permitted to join. It would be strictly for losers. Proud losers, naturally, who manage to steer clear of most of the sport talk around the office, or wherever else they go.

Stan was surprised how quickly the sign-up sheet filled up. Everyone who'd been at the preliminary event signed in, plus a few who heard about it later. As long as they weren't hotshot sports enthusiasts, Stan let them in, until the sheet was full. A couple practically begged to be included. Or at least, put on standby. He'd never seen such enthusiasm about *anything* at work.

A couple of total strangers also pleaded to join. They might as well have been strangers, because they worked in the lower depths of the building, seldom seen by anyone.

No women would be included on the teams. They were uninvited, uninformed. These players were men. Pale, white-collar white men, for the most part, but male nonetheless.

Within what seemed like hours, if not minutes, a rumor about the competition was circulating in the office, among the female employees. Exclusion from the new activity did not go down well, even with women who could never be described as feminists. Stan barely managed to hold his ground on that one, and felt certain that some of the female workers managed to get a bet down, anyway.

By afternoon on Monday, back at work, at least some of the office "sports" seemed to know about the contest. Several expressed interest in participating. Stan had to tell a few falsehoods to deflect their queries away from the competition.

Prior to Official Game One, hints and rumors circulated around the office, including the prospects for betting. Even some of the non-sporting folks seemed to take an interest in the possibility of investing a few dollars. Scheduled participants started betting amongst themselves, and were glad to take wagers from fellow workers who knew about the competition.

Betting started small and easy. No more than $5 could be wagered by each player. Even money: if you bet $5 and win, you pocket $10. Stan was unanimously chosen as the "house," handling wagers and winnings.

Soon, waste-can basketball was drawing almost as much attention in the office as major league baseball and the upcoming football and basketball seasons.

It didn't take long for gambling to get heavy. Well past that initial five-dollar limit, even before the first game. With amazing haste, unpaid debts were accumulating, some of them reaching frightful levels for middle-class office workers. Work quality and quantity even began to suffer a bit, as both the participants and the observers turned their attention to the upcoming game and away from their assigned tasks.

Potential participants practiced in slack time at the office, which was becoming nearly as lengthy as work time. So it seemed, anyway.

At one point, a worker Stan didn't know came by his desk, watched for a moment, crumpled his own scrap paper into a ball and made a fancy shot. A third said "bet you can't do that again," echoing the setup developed by Paul Newman, portraying ace pool hustler Eddie Felsen, in that great old movie, *The Hustler*. Naturally, Newman did make that shot one more time, then slipped out the door after pocketing his winnings.

Just one day before the game, the participants broke up into small teams. Stan arranged them so each would include at least one star and one loser – as evenly organized as possible. To keep things at something approaching evenness, he decided to make up odds, so bets on the most promising players would pay off less if they won. "Just like racehorses," he admitted to Harold just before Game One began.

This was getting too serious. Some players began talking about coaches. Stan wondered if cheating of some sort might be next. All the overblown stuff that made up pro sports. For some of the players, the competition began to seem like the main reason for the company's existence.

The bosses didn't like it, but couldn't bring themselves to step in. Actual work appeared to be getting done faster than ever, so the players would have sufficient free time for the game. Besides, some low-level managers were involved in the game themselves, as eager bettors.

Amazing, Stan thought, how quickly everything can change in a situation that was supposed to be a bit of fun. Usually, for the worst.

After all the hype and gambling talk, the game itself was almost anticlimactic. Mainly, an opportunity for gambling. But to the fellow whose trash-tossing skill was his one and only "athletic" ability, who stood apart from the pack, it was a rare opportunity to prove himself. And some of them did, surprising even themselves.

Stan knew it was all over when a few sports fans demanded to join the competition. The non-sports wound up ahead by a fair amount, but that was their one and only victory. After another session or two, the sports guys got better, the non-sports faded, and everyone seemed to lose interest. Except for the gamblers, of course.

No matter who won, the non-sports were still back where they started in terms of respect. Still outsiders, who were only good at this one thing.

Back at the office, wadding up a crumpled sheet of paper snapped away from a stack of blank contracts, Stan stared at the wastebasket. He thought. He pondered. He raised back his arm and shot the paper wad in the desired direction, flying through the office air with only the hint of a wobble.

He missed.

Even so, for once in his life, his puny sporting life, he'd won.

17

Hotel Del Rey

Even though the name of the place translates to "hotel of the king," there was nothing regal about the Del Rey. More accurately, it was hardly fit for a peasant. Even so, I'd been there two months already, with no plans for leaving anytime soon.

Actually, I had plenty of plans. But I wasn't dumb enough to think any of them would come to pass in the foreseeable future. They never had before. Why I kept coming up with them, I just don't know. I mean, stuff keeps popping into my head: ideas, schemes, propositions. Considering that I'd never once done anything about a single one of them, in all these years, I'd have to be an idiot for continuing to pay any attention.

What can you do, though. Each new idea sounds so logical, almost foolproof, when I first think of it. Most of them, anyway. Besides, I don't have the knowledge about financial matters to know whether they make any real sense or not.

I think it has something to do with living in the hotel. Or *any* hotel, and I've been in plenty of them. Weekly Rates. Share Bath, to keep it cheap. No phone, no view to speak of other than an airshaft. Just a narrow single bed and, if you're lucky, a little dresser and a couple of hangers for your stuff. Faded list of rules on the back wall in the lobby, which hardly anybody takes note of – and fewer yet abide by.

Something about living in a single, small room with only a small TV for company – and not always that – kind of narrows life down to basics. When you're at that level, without distractions, ideas that slip into the brain face few barriers. They ease right into your consciousness, and make sense from the start.

That one time when I had an apartment – an actual flat, with three rooms and furniture that didn't look like dogs and cats had been living in it, all torn up and tatty – I hardly had any ideas at all. Probably none, now that I think of it.

In the Del Rey, though, I spent most of my day – every day – thinking. What else? I had no job to go to, nobody to see, nowhere to be.

So much time had passed since I lost my last job, I could hardly remember when it was. Or what the *job* was, for that matter. When you're a minimum-wage guy, invariably taking the first job anybody offers you after long days of looking and asking, the details don't matter much. All of them pretty much run together, anyway.

Tending bar, loading trucks, busing tables. Shuffling papers in some office. It's all the same. You get up, you go to work, you do something for a bunch of hours, you go home. Whatever home might be at that particular time of your life.

Best you can hope for is a boss who leaves you alone most of the time, who doesn't stand over you glaring. Or yelling. Threatening, even. Too many of that kind around.

Fortunately, I'd managed to save a few bucks at that last job, which lasted longer than usual. Something like four months, in fact. Maybe five. Close to a record, for me. One time, I lasted only an hour and a half before this hardass supervisor got so far into my nerves that I had to walk away. Or, if I remember right, I yelled out that I was going to kill him.

I wasn't, really. I'm actually a peaceable guy. No violence. I try to avoid trouble, not make it. I just get fed up in a hurry. That's happened a lot. It's the way I am.

Good thing I don't like guns. If I carried some kind of weapon in my pocket, I might have ended up using it once or twice. Showing it, anyway.

Untied Knots

Listen, I'm going to tell you something I've never told anyone before. Hardly ever. Once in a while, years back, when I lived in a tiny room on an upper floor in this building near downtown, I'd look out the window and see all the citizens just strolling by. Not a care in the world, it looked like. Regular folks, breezing through their lives.

Yeah, I know now that wasn't true. Most of them probably had hard times, like me. But when I got pissed enough, I'd sometimes pretend I was holding a rifle or something and point it at one of them. Then make like I was pulling the trigger. "Pow, pow." You know?

Nowadays, I know, I'd be in jail if somebody heard me admitting something like that. Or the nuthouse, more likely. They'd say it was an indicator of likely dangerous behavior ahead. Put me away, just in case. But back then, couple of decades ago, it didn't seem so bad. Just pretending. Ease the tension, like.

That's not what happened, though. Instead of any kind of satisfaction, all I got was guilt. Big guilt. Like I say, I'm not a violent guy. Stay away from guns. Hate the damn things, actually. No way.

I mean, I never wanted to hurt anybody. Inflict any kind of harm. It was more like those video games that came along later. Just a distraction, blowing off steam. Right? Erasing tensions without harm to anyone.

That's how I see it, anyway.

When the incident began – the *big* one – I just happened to be sitting in the lobby. Didn't do that very often, so it was just chance that I was there, sitting in one of those overstuffed old easy chairs, reading the paper.

It started out small. Mid-afternoon. Two guys came out of the stairwell door, yelling obscenities, making threatening gestures. I couldn't make out what they were saying, and didn't much care. Just kept my eyes focused on the paper, raising it just a bit to half-shield my face from view.

Hotel Del Rey

Judging by the tone of their words, I would have bet that a woman was involved. Sure enough, this startling blonde comes dashing out of the doorway behind them, causing everybody's eyes to turn her way. Male eyes, at any rate; but probably all of the lobby's guests. Nearly every seat in the room was full, which was usually the case through most of the afternoon.

She wasn't exactly crying, but I could spot tears in her eyes. A tissue was in her hand, which she brought up to her face, evidently trying to wipe it dry. "Stop it!" she screamed, almost as loudly as the two men. "Stop it right now!"

In an instant, the whole scene changed. What had seemed like a brief scene in a movie – probably a "B" movie – suddenly took a beastly turn. To us bystanders, seated comfortably around the lobby, it felt like slow motion. Couldn't have taken much more than a second, in all. One of the men spun around, raised his arm, and slammed his fist into the lady's face. He must have hit her really hard, because I could hear something that sounded like a bone cracking.

Suddenly, I knew I had to intervene. Not that I wanted to. Never did anything like that before. Not in my whole life. But something about the incident – its distressing, violent nature – unleashed a flood of best-forgotten memories, making it impossible for me to ignore.

Next thing I knew, the guy's fist was heading my way. Amazingly, despite my utter lack of experience with fighting of any sort, I managed to twist my head sideways, so his fist glanced off my chin. I think I managed to hit him a couple of times over the next few seconds, but can't say for sure. I can say that he connected again with my chin, as well as my belly and my shoulder. By the time I fully realized what was happening, I was headed for the floor, dizzily flooded with pain, applied enthusiastically by this aggressive resident.

Adding insult to injury, when I was taken to the hospital to have my injuries checked out, I was quickly reminded that I had no health insurance. Even before any medical person took a close look at my condition, a financial adviser turned up with papers to be signed. Including an agreement to pay the full cost myself.

An hour earlier, I had only a couple of hundred dollars in the bank, but at least I had no debts. Now, I owed the hospital some unknown amount. I'd read how they tack on all sorts of extra charges in cases like this. No telling what the grand total will be. Most I can hope for is that they let me pay it off on time, making monthly payments. I hate monthly payments. Credit. I lead a simple, unfettered life. Just the way I want it. But no choice this time, when the money-changers rush through the door.

On the plus side, I have to admit that I was feeling at least a little bit proud of myself. On the whole, it was well worth a few bruises, or a broken bone, or whatever they find and fix. I'd defended a lady's honor. Even if she wasn't totally honorable.

18

Wakeup Time

When I awoke, it was with a jolt. A fiery spark made its way down from the front of my head, threatening to take my barely-open eyes along with it.

My throat felt like someone had applied sandpaper to it, back and forth, all night long. Rough-grit sandpaper, the kind meant to assault reluctant knots in a chunk of wood. It hurt too much to cough, even though my nose was running and the need to clear it seemed urgent.

Lots of things used to seem urgent. Not anymore. Now, every day was pretty much the same. All bad.

Opening my eyes took more effort than I thought I could muster. Oh, the burning: two piercing needles of light came calling, sent by the bright early-morning sun that forced its way through the mud-splattered windshield.

I was in a car. Again. Front seat this time, scrunched and twisted into what felt like a contortionist exercise. Except that my agility was long gone. So, all the awakening brought with it was pain, galloping along each extremity, threatening every joint and muscle.

And nerve. Especially, the nerves.

Was this my own car? Did I even own one? I couldn't remember.

I used to have a car, I was sure. Pretty sure. Yet, the feel of the fuzzy seat upholstery, the smell of the floor, didn't seem familiar. Odd.

Still, it must be my own car. Otherwise, how did I get in?

Unlocked? Not too likely; but it happens. I guess. How could I *not* know whether the car was mine. That was crazy.

But that wasn't even the first question to be raised. *Where* was I? *That* was the big one. And how do I get home from here? Will I be welcome there? Or am I one of those loners they talk about on the news. Friendless. Unattached. Even dangerous.

More importantly, where *was* home? I'd had so many, though none qualified as a home in the normal-people sense.

I needed to stay calm, to think, even if doing so made my head and eyes hurt. Every other second, I was injected with a fiery wave of pain, but I forced myself to open one eye ever so slightly. Agonizing sunlight streaming through the smeared windshield told me it must be at least 7:00 A.M. Not much traffic, so it couldn't be much later than that.

Exhausting as it turned out to be, I struggled into a seated position behind the steering wheel. Keys. See if you have keys. Groping into my pants pocket, I found some. Two sets. Car? House? What?

One must be for a car. Yes. This one. I peered closer at it. Says "Dodge" on that little tag. Is this a Dodge? Maybe. Despite my inebriated haze, it was starting to seem just a bit familiar. Only a little.

Sure enough, one of the keys slipped into the ignition. Turned, too. To my surprise, the engine fired up quickly, almost instantly.

Could have fooled me, but evidently this car was mine. But then, I'd owned so many junk cars over the years, how could I be expected to know? One's about the same as the next. As soon as it gives out, to the junkyard it goes, soon to be replaced by another cheapie. Maybe one bought right at the junkyard itself, rather than from one of those "We Finance Everyone" used car dealers.

Of course, I shouldn't be driving at all, with all the booze I put away every night. Every day, too. I knew that.

Guilt about my behavior crept regularly into my mind, though it never kept me from grasping for that next drink. And eventually, way too often, I'd wind up driving home, or heading somewhere else. Most likely, another bar. Maybe, if I was flush, a strip club. Not a bad way to pass a few mindless hours, staring at naked girls. Feels good, whether you're drunk or sober. So, why not? I sure didn't have any other opportunities to gaze at women without clothes on.

Don't know why that kind of stuff popped into my head on this gray-hurt morning. I didn't think I'd been to a strip club that night. But that didn't matter. The question was, where could I go now. Which way was I supposed to start off? To where?

Peering past the windshield, nothing looked right. Still, it seemed like I'd managed to park properly. Or, someone had. Maybe I hadn't been alone. No, probably not. I was nearly always alone while drinking. Start out by myself, finish by myself. However long it took.

At least, the car wasn't sticking out into the intersection, or anything like that. Wouldn't be the first time, if it were. That much I remembered.

Though it hurt like blazes to twist my head around, I tried looking into the back seat. Wrappers. Sandwich wrappers and greasy paper bags. Success! Looked like they could have held 'burgers and beef sandwiches. Italian beef. My main sustenance, nearly every day.

Yep, this was my car, all right. Had to be. In certain circles – at certain taverns, I mean – I remembered that my cars were well known as repositories for the waste from fast-food meals. Don't know why I always tossed the trash back there, and then failed to clean things out until the back seat started to smell. But then, I don't know why I do much of anything anymore. Anything at all.

Without expecting any success, I started to rummage around for a bottle. Most likely, if there had been one in the car earlier in the night, I'd finished it. Sure enough, I could see or feel nothing like a bottle, whether full or empty.

Wait! Under the seat, way back. Yes, it was a bottle, all right. I didn't even have to pull it all the way out to realize that it wasn't empty. Some kind of special sense that drunks have, I guess.

Okay, no point waiting any longer. I squinted my eyes ahead and studied the rearview mirror. Clear. I think. I put it into gear and started off, easing out of the parking spot. Slowly, carefully. Didn't want to draw anyone's attention so early in the morning.

After moving only a few feet, I stopped abruptly. Come to think of it, I wondered if I had a license. A valid one. Seemed like I'd had some issues on that score.

Was it Sunday? Is that why traffic was so light? Was I somewhere on Saturday night that led me to drink into oblivion again? How did I misbehave this time?

Then it came to me, like a stray bullet to the brain, losing speed as it entered. A wedding. Holding a drink. Just a shot glass, filled to the brim with whiskey. Undeniably overfilled, as if asking for trouble. Or with something else liquid and lovely. Toasting the bride, then abruptly seeing the amber fluid leap out of the glass onto the bodice of her bridal gown, oozing across the angelic white fabric.

At least I wasn't the best man, I was pretty certain of that. More like the *worst* man, I was sure. Even "man" seemed to be stretching the point. Drunken lout was more like it. I'd heard those exact words before. Somewhere. Maybe last night, at the wedding.

Is that what it was? Really? Now, whose wedding could it have been? I hardly knew anyone. How could I be acquainted with a woman who was getting married?

Maybe it was the bridegroom whom I knew. But who in his right mind would have invited a drunken slob to his betrothal? Only an idiot, that's who. A total fool.

Maybe one of them was a relative. Did I have relatives? *Live* ones? Couldn't seem to remember.

Forcing my mind into reluctant service, I seemed to remember a brother. Older, I think. Couple of cousins. Couldn't quite picture any of them. Not right away, at least.

All of a sudden, somebody started banging on the car window. Driver's side. Scrutinizing him through hazy, watery eyes, I could tell who it was. George. My God, he's my best friend! No, my only friend. My brother, too.

He looked angry. No, furious. I pushed down on the window-opening button, but let up after a second. No! I couldn't talk to him. Couldn't face him. Not without knowing what I'd done. I had to get out of there, this instant.

Before I could say a word, I snapped the gearshift into Drive and hit the gas pedal. Not hard. Not stomping it. But the car roared ahead. Enough to force George to leap backward, away from the moving car.

A second, two seconds later, a sharp, crisp clunk rose up from the car's underside. I couldn't have gone more than a hundred, two hundred, feet. Sounded almost like I'd hit something. An animal? Tree branch?

Or, someone? A person? Good Lord, I hope not. What had I done? Jesus, I'm going to jail. What do I do now?

Will they all hate me? Thoughts from my endless list of drunken misdeeds flashed through my mind at drag-racing speed.

I reached down for the bottle. Naturally. How could I not? It's a natural motion. When in trouble, the hand immediately reaches for that bottle. Whether it turns out to be full, or only a few drops of that delectable liquid remain at the bottom.

Anyway, what difference did it make now?

19

Winding Down

Harry hated his penis. Always had. He'd hated it when he was a kid, in gym class, when the bigger boys would giggle and guffaw while pointing toward his scrawny physique and, especially, his puny unit. Glimpses of his skinny anatomy in a mirror didn't help, either.

Years later, he realized that apart from a couple of teenage near-adults – hairy guys who probably had to shave twice a day – who flaunted and even shook their sizable dangles as if they were gifts to the gods, most of them were around the same dimensions.

Some shrunk away when in public view; others maintained their regular size. But the differences weren't nearly as great as those big boys had made it seem.

Besides, who cared how big the thing was when it was idle. Harry once heard a character in a movie say, "I'm a grow-er, not a show-er," acknowledging its minimal importance until called upon for sexual purposes.

Of course, in those high-school shower rooms, the promise of sexual encounters with an actual person was far off. A moot point. At least, he figured it was, for himself. Couldn't say for sure about those older hairy apes, though. Possibly, some of the exploits they bragged about with girls might have been true. Who could say.

He hated it even more when girls entered the picture more prominently. As a teenager, he'd been scared – petrified, actually – of the opposite sex. Other fellows went out on dates regularly, often boasting afterwards about how far they'd gone with the girl.

"Third base!" his best friend Eddie might say the next morning at school. "Feeling everything. Right under her clothes. Bra off."

Winding Down

Harry did none of that. He could never muster the courage to ask any of the local teen females. Hardly ever, anyway. For the most part, the closest he came to girls was in ballroom-dancing class, which his mother had forced him to attend. As soon as his hands touched the dancing girl of the moment, he'd start to breathe hard, and sometimes even twitch. Worse yet, he could feel the steady growth of the troublesome appendage, struggling to keep it from becoming noticeable.

No telling what the girls thought. No one ever said anything, but he left each class mortified, vowing never to return.

On the other hand, he adored the feelings he experienced when dancing with one of those girls. He'd never admit it to anyone, of course. But as soon as he thought of what it felt like to touch a girl's body, even through a heavy sweater, his reluctance to return to dancing class vanished as if it were a whiff of passing cloud.

Just the thought of caressing the small of her back with his fingertips would excite him unbearably, both physically and within his anguished head. Actually doing it almost drove him crazy with ecstasy. Even today, so many years later, recollections of those tiny touches brought long-forgotten sensations to life, both in his groin and in his heart.

Sometimes, later in life, Harry wondered how many of those over-endowed 15-year-old boys now had to take ED medications to "perform" at home. Probably plenty of them. Harry secretly hoped it was plenty.

Batch of useless skin that cannot help but lead to trouble. *Big* trouble, all too often. Best to hide it away, keep it concealed, act as if it's not there at all.

Now that he'd reached the dreaded "senior citizen" time of life, Harry noticed that his own appendage still seemed to function. Without pharmaceutical assistance, too.

Not that he had many occasions to find out for sure. Even in his 20s and 30s, Harry had never been much of a ladies' man. Not at all, to tell the truth.

Every few years, he'd managed to initiate a relationship, tentatively but hopefully. They'd last a week, a month; two, maybe even three. Then, the couple would just drift apart, typically without saying a word. She'd just be gone one day, and he never made the effort to follow up and see what happened.

Nothing much had ever really occurred between the pair, and sex was only a sporadic diversion. Both parties were simply unable to find much reason to stay together. Not much reason to move apart either, except that it was easier.

Even his marriage had been tentative and brief. Two largely pointless years. No children, thankfully. Nancy hadn't wanted any, and Harry had never even acknowledged the possibility – except when he worried about accidental pregnancy, which was most of the time.

That wasn't quite the same as making a choice about children. Harry, to be honest, never gave children of *any* sort much thought. He didn't dislike them, exactly. They just played no part in his life, and he had no desire to spend much time with young people. He had a couple of nieces, but hardly ever saw them. Friends' children had come along, grown up, and gone, without attracting much notice from Harry.

Clearly, lots of men love their male organs – and have no hesitation about using them, making them available to a succession of women from teen years all the way through old age. Harry wouldn't know where to begin, though he still thought about it quite a bit.

Sexual urges had not diminished like he thought they would, as he grew older. Not for him, at any rate. He spent way too much time trying to keep himself from ogling shapely women on the street, and scanning the Internet for pictures of attractive ladies with few clothes. Turns out, there seemed to be millions of them out there, posing either for exhibitionism or money. Maybe both. Or because they had to. He felt a twinge of guilty nausea at that thought.

Even after he'd grown a little more at ease with girls – or women – in his 20s, the die of reticence had been fully cast. The very idea of asking someone out, much less suggesting – or implying – the prospect of a physical tryst made his palms sweat and his head spin directly into a piercing headache.

How could it be so easy for others? Though Harry was no handsome lothario, he wasn't exactly hideous, either. Women didn't turn and run as he approached. They didn't look his way either, but he wasn't some Frankenstein monster.

Odd, though. Looking back, he recalled more than one occasion when a woman he knew slightly had given signs of what may have been romantic interest in him. But in his fear and ignorance, Harry had failed to recognize her interest or possible availability. So, nothing ever came of those lost encounters, except that they contributed to more than a few fantasy trysts in his later years, probably providing more stimulation than a real-life liaison might have.

Besides, if he had followed up on one of those possibilities, the chance that even the tiniest bit of sex might emerge that evening was remote at best. By the time Harry was in his 20s, he could count on one hand the number of times he'd gotten anything much beyond a peck on the cheek. Or, a firm handshake at the end of an awkward evening, making it clear that another meeting was not in the cards.

Harry had never paid for sex. Never would. He couldn't understand how such a thing was pleasurable. Even so, he wanted one more tryst of some kind before expiring. Before it was all over, for good.

But with whom? And how? He couldn't interest persons of the opposite sex when he was young. How could he possibly do it now.

Younger women, he knew, would just mock his shrunken,

reticent unit. Plus his flabby, sagging physique. Most certainly, he needed to find a *mature* partner. He'd read that older women outnumber men, which made sense statistically. Men simply tend to die sooner, he recalled. Was this true? Or did he imagine it.

He knew no women, except for those at work – and those only slightly. Strictly business. In addition, he knew no one in a position to introduce him to a lady. So, any meetup had to be almost accidental, but not too much of a coincidence.

All of his reticence and fear changed the moment he took up with Nina.

Harry had decided to start going to film club meetings. In no time, to his surprise and pleasure, he met this fetching older woman, probably not too much younger than himself. Before he knew it, the two acquaintances became friends, then a couple, meeting several times a week for dinner, drinks – even dancing, one evening when they both were feeling lively.

When they eventually got together in a romantic way, after a few kisses and a bit of groping his seemingly decrepit organ actually responded to the occasion. "Like a young fellow," he told himself – but he certainly couldn't bring up such a notion to Nina. Nor to anyone, needless to say.

Yet, when the time came to couple more intimately, he stopped short. Like a balloon losing its air, he began to deflate. Suddenly, images of each of his stillborn romantic endeavors of the past – a total that didn't even approach double digits – flew into his brain. In retaliation, he pulled back from Nina's waiting body, almost leaping into an upright position.

"What's the trouble, hon?" she asked, sounding more curious than critical.

Seconds passed by slowly, without a word spoken. "Been a long time," he finally replied. "Can hardly remember the last ..."

Nina responded with what could best be described as a sly grin. Not the kind men get, imagining the delights that might be coming their way in a matter of minutes. She spoke gently, softly. "Been a while for me, too."

"Yeah," Harry answered, with a wistful tone. "But not so many times, actually. I wasn't one of those kids, those young guys, running after girls. Or being run after, either."

After a few hesitant moments, they settled into each other. Softly. Silently. Harry realized right away. as they came together for a deep, deeply-felt kiss, that he didn't detest that bodily part quite as much as usual. No, not so much at all.

20

Scandal in the Dayroom

Her name was Mary Ellen, and she was a beauty. I mean, the kind who won beauty contests. Slim but curvy. A smile that could flirt gently yet boldly, revealing the quietly intense seriousness of the busy, admittedly agitated mind inside.

Laid-back, greenish eyes twinkled hints of secrets that might never be disclosed; or perhaps might be, any moment now. Short hair, just a touch disheveled, but carefully maintained. A mellifluous voice, complemented by a bare touch of huskiness, as if it had consumed and savored a few too many filter-tip cigarettes.

Though quiet most of the time, she unquestionably knew a lot more than she let on. In fact, as I learned later, she was a seriously smart young woman. Maybe even near-genius, who knows. Or at least, a head above any of the females she hung around with. A head, a mind, that was as beautiful inside as out.

She was a musician, too. Not professional, not playing for money. Not yet. But in my strictly amateur estimation, not far from that caliber. With a bit of luck, she might have transformed herself into a mildly-iridescent star at some second-tier record label. Or, at least, performing late-night sets on smoky stages at small, darkened venues – content with scattered applause while struggling to cope with lewd catcalls.

That's what I thought, anyway. How I fantasized her life before we met, formally. Then again, what do I know about music. And musicians. Or anything, for that matter.

Not just one instrument, either. She could play the piano, whether by ear with gusto, or reading music carefully when a quieter sound was needed. Accordion, too; and in her hands, that antique instrument – so often ridiculed as an unsophisticated joke – acquired a new breath of life.

Mary Ellen was learning the clarinet, too. Or was it the flute. One of those two.

Her shapely fingers also could strum a few tremulous chords out of the old guitar that usually sat within its case, stuffed into the back of the closet in her room.

Someone said she'd been an actual, for-real beauty pageant contestant. Someplace out west. Not just some hick town, either. Almost won, too, they insisted. Second or third place, something like that. Take a quick look in her direction, and you wouldn't doubt that claim for a second. You'd just wonder why she hadn't taken the top prize.

On this particular evening, her good looks, her liveliness, her gracefully feminine nature, got her into trouble. For one reason, and one alone: Mary Ellen was a drunk. You'd never suspect it. The kind of drunk who looks perfectly normal, until alcohol takes over.

She was also crazy. Not *psycho* crazy. Just troubled, tormented. Fighting off some sort of demons, trying to drown them if nothing else. Pretty much like the rest of us in the Psychiatric Institute, to tell the truth.

Mentally ill, to be genteel about it, at least in the opinion of the court system. After some sort of rambunctious misbehavior, no doubt involving alcohol – plenty of it – a judge had sent Mary Ellen to the psychiatric hospital, which was where we met. In the dayroom, where the patients spent the better part of their time when not asleep or lying awake during the long nights.

No one knew she was a drunk. Not at first. She was one of those alcoholics who do nothing bizarre, who don't scream and shout, or speak in garbled, unintelligible phrases. Crazy talk.

Not until that evening in late spring. I'd been there for a month or so. Checked in voluntarily, no longer able to cope with everyday life, with the workaday world. Anxiety and Panic Reaction, the admitting shrink called it.

I couldn't argue with that assessment. In fact, those few words described me accurately and precisely. I'd been afraid, panicky afraid, day and night for months. More like years, really.

Unable to function anymore, I was unbelievably relieved – elated, to tell the truth – to learn that I could be admitted to the psychiatric institute. Without a moment's hesitation, I'd gladly signed myself in for a minimum of 30 days. When that time was close to running out, I was overjoyed to be advised to remain longer.

Mary Ellen, on the other hand, was not in the hospital voluntarily. Like about half of the patients on our floor, she'd been committed by the court. Hardly any of the involuntary patients were happy to be there. Many of them talked constantly about how they didn't belong in such a place; how they hoped to get out as quickly as possible; the steps they intended to take to secure a release. The sooner, the better.

Why, you could go crazy living in a place like this, they'd insist. Amazing how many times I heard that one.

Who knows, maybe it was true. Being realistic, though, a lot of them were pretty far gone from their first moments on the ninth floor, before they saw or talked with anyone in authority.

Not all of them acted crazy, necessarily. But after being there a while, you could start to see it in their eyes, in their speech, in their overreactions to simple events. No doubt about it, most of them were exactly where they should have been, despite their protestations.

On this particular day, the staff made a big mistake. They were always looking for new ways to keep the inmates – sorry, patients – busy and entertained. So, one of the nurses came up with the idea of a contest. A beauty contest. For a bunch of mentally ill people, many of them way short on self-confidence and big on feelings of inferiority, a contest of *any* sort could be troublesome. But a beauty contest? With winners and losers? That one was insane. Stupid, too. So naturally, the staff set it up.

Rather than make it a daytime event, which was the usual way, they decided to start right after dinner. The announcement came at breakfast that morning. Immediately, a few of the female patients perked up. Big surprise: each of the eager participants was pretty good-looking. Unlikely to be the big loser, for sure.

Ordinary-looking women seemed more morose.

Men (and boys) didn't seem to know what to think. Most were heterosexual, at least in theory, so the prospect of being permitted to gaze at some hot-looking women wasn't exactly something to dread.

Randolph, one of the loudmouth, macho residents, started to whoop and holler, almost leaping into the air and practically licking his lips. Illicit relationships were hardly unheard-of on the ward, but most patients were surely celibate during their stay at the institute.

Mary Ellen didn't respond at first. When she did, it was with a quietly raised hand, responding to the call for contestants. Looking back now, something in her eyes suggested secrecy. Or maybe I was just imagining things, looking for reasons after the fact.

Dinnertime conversation was more animated than usual. One or two guys recalled strip shows they'd seen, trysts they'd experienced. Or claimed to, anyway. One attractive middle-aged woman admitted to having participated in a beauty contest, years earlier. Or maybe she was boasting. Hard to tell what was true, when you're conversing with mental patients.

As soon as dessert had been consumed, the group rose almost as one, to settle themselves on the couches and easy chairs in the main part of the dayroom. As the festivities began, Norman took over his regular role as DJ for the occasion.

Each of the contestants took a few minutes to prepare for the event, returning to their own rooms to change clothes or just do a bit of primping.

Elizabeth, the first participant, looked scared as she approached what amounted to center stage, her feet slowly pitter-pattering on the hard tile floor. She wore a pretty modest swimsuit, which revealed her elegant shape but nothing startling.

Rita was next. More rambunctious, though not a beauty. Joking, making faces, her interpretation of a come-hither smile.

Mary Ellen was third, and she wasn't back yet from her room. Seconds, then minutes ticked away. Melvin – looking like he was about to burst from holding a huge secret – finally opened up to the group of fellows with whom he was sitting.

"Mary Ellen. She's next. She's going to come out naked. I heard her tell one of the girls before they went to their rooms."

He'd spoken quietly, but all the guys looked stricken. Whether from delight or fright, lust or embarrassment, I couldn't say. Maybe all of the above.

Just about everybody in the male group started talking at once. Clearly, they seemed split in their opinions. Should they step in and stop the contest? That was the view from Edward, one of the older patients. Or should they just let it happen, consequences be damned? Kenneth, who came across as a tough, young street guy, leaned firmly in that direction. Judging by the slight nods from several of the boys, that was the majority view.

Samuel, who always seemed to be worrying and fretting about something, wanted to tell the staff right away, and let them take care of it. One quiet guy, whose name nobody seemed to know, wondered if Mary Ellen would get into trouble, even if nothing dramatic happened.

Paul, who occupied the role of quiet intellectual among the male patients, was adamant. "We can't do this," he insisted. "It's just not right."

If anything, I was more torn in both directions than anyone. Of course, those opposed were correct. Allowing a naked woman to prance into the room, to be judged by a bunch of mental patients, simply wasn't fitting no matter how far you stretched the rules of behavior.

What I guess is the devilish side of my brain took the opposing view. It was simple. Mary Ellen was the hottest-looking woman on the ward by far, and that included the staff members, a couple of whom were plenty cute. Watching Mary Ellen parade past without a stitch on sounded like a moment in paradise. Maybe we'd all get in trouble afterward; but meanwhile, what a sight that would be!

I'd seen beauty queens before, and I'd seen naked women. Not surprisingly, the thought of putting the two elements into a single person produced stirrings in the groin area. Sizable stirrings. And I knew I wasn't the only one experiencing such a response.

We never got a chance to present our opinions or take action. The naysayers won. Somebody – never knew for sure who it was – went to the overseers and tattled on Mary Ellen's plans. Nobody had noticed who had slipped away from the group, either the men or the women. Or if they did, they weren't telling.

Mary Ellen suddenly appeared at the corner of the dayroom, but her body was barely glimpsed by anyone before a couple of aides grabbed her. She screamed, she shouted. She began to cry. Even threatened to harm herself. Losing control, it must be said, is how it usually goes when one of the patients feels under attack, whether from the staff or from her mental-hospital mates.

One of the women jumped up, slipping her sweater off, in an attempt to cover up the culprit. By then, Mary Ellen was being restrained by three or four male staffers. Everyone else was quiet, though obviously agitated, holding themselves back. Judging by what they said later, when the incident was over, nearly all had felt ashamed, mortified, though only a few seemed to blame Mary Ellen.

Mary Ellen wound up in a locked ward overnight; and likely, a lot longer. Rumors of using electroshock began to circulate. Some wondered if previous shock treatments could have triggered the incident somehow. We never saw her again, so who knows?

Now and then, a patient would suddenly disappear. Who could say why? Maybe they misbehaved, maybe some previously unknown fact about them came to light. Or, just being moved to another category of nuttiness, warranting a more rigorous treament mode.

Most of the men felt guilty, at least until the shock of the incident faded away. I think they did, anyway. Or hope they did.

Doubtless, some – maybe most – were more disappointed than regretful. None of us ever got more than a fleeting glance at her naked body, though its mere existence, if momentary, quickly bore its way into the lustful but distorted brains of at least a few male residents. Most likely, a female or two as well.

"She's just a drunk seeking to be disorderly," said the quiet, nameless guy. Maybe so. But for some of us, at least, Mary Ellen was never forgotten.

21

Slipping Into Stupid

Let's be clear here: I was a smart kid.

No point being coy about it. In grade school, I was the brightest boy in my class. *Any* of my classes, because the admiring teachers double-promoted me three times.

They don't do that much anymore, I'm told. But in those days, in Chicago's Public Schools, seriously smart kids often were offered a chance to skip a semester. Or two. In my case, three. So, I spent only half a year in first grade. Same thing in fifth, and again in seventh. In second grade or so, the teacher gave me arithmetic problems and reading tests that ordinarily went to kids who were four or five grades ahead of me.

Skipping a grade (or half a grade, to be precise) was fairly common. Skipping three was not. It meant that I graduated from elementary school at age 12, making me the youngest kid in my freshman high school class. Also the youngest when I graduated, four years later, at 16. And that was a big high school, with some 4,000 students.

Not by a lot, I have to admit. The girl who lived in the apartment upstairs also graduated from eighth grade when she was 12. In high school, one boy in my class was just a month older than me. Another was three months older. Nevertheless, I held the title: youngest kid out of 640 graduating seniors.

They used to call me a "brainiac" and such. That designation wasn't necessarily meant as a declaration of admiration, though. Far from it, as a rule. More often, it came with at least a twinge of resentment. No surprise there. Back then, in working-class Chicago, everyday conversation typically included expressions of the same sort of anti-elite, anti-intellectual attitudes that persist today among so much of the citizenry.

Grown men who worked with their minds in those days, rather than their hands, often drew more subtle scorn than any kind of acknowledgment of their well-earned success. Intellectualism was seen as unmanly or feminine. In many quarters, a male person would be presumed gay ("queer," in those days) if he read books.

Only once did my academic prowess reach past the schoolyard fence. The resulting incident became both a highlight and a lowlight of my life. After winning my school's spelling bee, I did likewise in the district contest. For a short while, I thought I must be the best speller in the world. Then, I participated in Chicago's all-city bee. To my shocked surprise, I was beaten. By two kids whom I'd bested previously. A lot went wrong later; but at least once in my life, even if it was at age 11, I experienced the feeling of being the best at something. Pretty darn good, at any rate.

Unlike grammar school, I didn't have the top grades in high school. And I have to admit that it still irks me, all these years later, to remember the absurdity of some of the classes where I didn't fare so well. Wood shop, for one. Electric shop. Though highly rated academically, it was a technical high school, for boys only. Every kid took four shop classes. Oddly, I did pretty well in sheetmetal shop. No idea why.

As a total non-athlete, too, with no interest in sports of any kind, gym and swimming classes were a disaster.

Anyway, I was used to being Number One (okay, a close second or third now and then) in elementary school. Then, as I eased through freshman and sophomore years in high school, I kept slipping. Not dramatically. Just enough to be irksome.

Not that finishing 26th out of that 640-student graduating class was bad. Not at all. Pretty darned good, actually; and I was pleased by that ranking. But if that score was a tad lower than expected, the real downhill slide started in college.

First off, I couldn't go from high school directly to college. No money. No knowledge of scholarships, either. No high-school counselor ever mentioned the subject. For some weird reason, I took (and passed) the entrance exam at a prestigious School of Journalism, but that was wasted effort.

After securing my first full-time job, I registered for night classes at a well-known university downtown, earning "A" grades without trying too hard. A couple more classes at a community college went well, too; but during that semester, the curse of mental illness struck fast and hard. Eventually diagnosed as Anxiety and Panic Reaction, it cast a bleak shadow upon my entire life for the next few decades. Fearful of everything. Afraid to leave home, but seldom comfortable there, either. Vestiges of it still have an impact.

As if that wasn't a sufficient obstacle, just before my 17th birthday I discovered the allure of alcohol. Most important, the first time I took a drink, I liked it. A lot. And wanted more. Before too long, still in my teens, I'd turned into an all-out alcoholic, racking up enough episodes of bad behavior to prove it. Including, I'm ashamed to admit, a lot of inebriated driving. Thank heaven I finally stopped, cold, soon after turning thirty. Never took a drink again.

This new combination of psychoneurosis and excessive alcohol consumption triggered a true, undeniable downhill slide, starting with my first full-time semester at the Chicago branch of the University of Illinois. First off, I flunked the school's English placement test, despite getting an "A" in that subject at another university. So, I had to take a remedial class.

Because I'd had such an easy time in high school, getting mostly excellent grades with a minimum of studying, I figured that method would work again. It didn't. Somehow, I managed to get through four years, at two U of I campuses, and be rewarded with a B.A. degree. Took me seven years, because I started and stopped three times; but I wound up with a diploma.

Of course, I'd spent much of that time intoxicated, as my grades demonstrated. At one point, I had to repeat a semester of German because I'd been drinking all night before the final exam, and didn't show up. I even rejected the professor's offer to retake the exam, certain that I would be no more able to pass it than I was before.

Foolishly or not, I took the Law School Admission Test, intending to spend my senior college year there rather than in the Sociology department. On the first day of class, I realized that my conception of law school – and of the legal profession – had been woefully incorrect.

Worse yet, I misbehaved badly during and after a party in my residence, barely escaped a DUI charge, and wound up having to explain myself to a disciplinary law-school panel.

Alcohol is at least a partial explanation for decline of intellectual prowess. Maybe the whole reason. Heavy drinking kept me from doing much of anything I'd hoped for with my early adulthood. What happened in my twenties sent me toward middle years having missed the preparatory period that permits most of us to make some initial progress in our chosen (or accidental) careers, as well as in life itself. Wasted, for the most part.

Mixing abundant alcohol with heavy doses of prescription tranquilizers, it's a miracle that I survived that period.

To my mind, life has been a long list of failures and rejections, rarely balanced by success of any sort, no matter how small. No awards won; successful at nothing; no noteworthy achievements; nothing that might be deemed worthy of recognition.

My few commendable accomplishments seemed so trivial in scope, inconsequential in importance, overwhelmed by a host of failures and rejections. A lifetime of humdrum, utterly unimportant work, demanding little intellectual ability and close-to-zero skill.

My obituary should read, simply: "He took up space. Now he doesn't." A colleague told me that once, though he was speaking about somebody else. Or was he?

Yes, I know. All of this sounds like whining. Feeling sorry for oneself. Guilty as charged, I'm sorry to report.

Because of lack of any tangible skills or talents, intellectual life had to be my forte. I should have somehow found a way to survive, if not quite thrive, by thinking, pondering, analyzing. Unfortunately, that's long been a veritable impossibility for a shy person lacking in self-promotion ability and unable to acquire an advanced degree or other valued credential.

Frankly, there's little or no place in modern life for non-academic thinkers to become known, prominent, listened-to, notable. Nowadays, after working as a long-time writer/journalist, mostly covering the automobile business, any efforts seem like yelling (or writing) into the wind, one's hopefully wise and worthy words scattered like depleted ashes from a campfire.

What we have today are "influencers," whatever that means, along with podcasters and Tik Tok-ers who manage to acquire thousands, millions, of followers – even if they have little to offer that's worth following. That's how I see it, anyway.

"Know-nothing" isn't merely the name of a long-defunct political party from the distant past. Not long ago, some famous economist – or was it a columnist – referred to today's version as "willful ignorance." Sounds like a concise description of a recent ex-president, doesn't it?

Tell you the truth, it hurt to finally realize that I wasn't nearly as smart as I once thought, or as I appeared to be. Or hoped to be. And still wish to be, all these decades later. I often think of a lady who walked up to me at a bus stop one day and asked if I was a professor. I was secretly pleased.

Stupid, I know. Still, they say a person with an IQ of 180 lives in a different universe than one with 160, who in turn occupies a wholly different intellectual space than one with 140, and so forth. When you have nothing to fall back on other than your mind, those differences matter.

Starting out high, then slipping down, eventually finishing life mentally unrewarded. That's my story.

Why could I not keep up that 12-year-old's momentum? Instead, that may have been the high point of my intellectual life. Not unlike professional (or amateur) athletes whose peak periods of skill or talent are gone by their 30s, if not 20s.

In the movies and TV, and doubtless in real life, we sometimes picture high school as a high point for jocks, and for others in the working class. But it can be so for young potential scholars, too: starting high, slipping downward, eventually finishing life mentally unrewarded. In a world dominated by ignorance, matters of the mind don't get much respect.

22

Inhuman Relations

I'd been here before. Not the exact same place. Not this precise room or building. But one just about exactly like it.

Dozens, actually. More than that. Might even be a hundred by now. They used to call them Personnel Departments. Then, they turned into Human Resources, or something like that. A fancier phrase for the same old job, evaluating job applicants and weeding out the riffraff, the rejects.

I was one of the riffraff. In those days, I had no trade, no profession, no skills. No experience at anything useful, either.

Still don't. Not really.

Anyway, back to my own job search on this particular day, quite a few years back. And how I got to that so-familiar personnel office, waiting to see the personnel manager or some assistant.

This time, I was applying at a big printing company for a timekeeper job. In the typesetting department, the newspaper ad said. Instead of doing actual work myself, it sounded like I'd be keeping track of the output from the authentic workers. The ones some people refer to as working-class heroes. Used to, anyway, in the old days when real men toiled at physical work and belonged to unions.

Sounded good to me, in any case; but with any job hunt it doesn't pay to think positive, to get your hopes up.

Not that I could actually envision myself at work in this place. Or anyplace, to be honest. When you tote up as many rejections and turndowns as I've had, you don't think about actually being hired when you're going through the hiring *process*. If it happens, fine. But being shown the door, sometimes after only a few minutes, is way more likely.

One simple fact is hardly ever mentioned: if you're rejected at Company 1, it's likely to happen again at #2, 3, 4, and beyond, all the way to the end of your worklife.

Besides, it wasn't going to be exactly a thrill-a-minute position, or one that leads to anything. No job that I'd be considered for met either of those qualifications. When you're on the bottom rung, you stay at that spot. Moving from one company to another, or to another job in the same place, changes nothing. Sure, exceptions are out there. I could probably count all of them on a couple of hands.

Even though the company seemed up-to-date in a lot of ways at the time, their hiring *process* was the traditional kind. Fill out an application, talk to the interviewer (in-person, not via Zoom or whatever). Explain why you're so eager to have this particular job, at this particular company. Then, make up some kind of story in case you're asked where you expect to be in the company in ten years, or some such nonsense. (Answering "out the door" or "far away" is not considered an acceptable response.)

Sorry, I keep digressing away from the scene at that printing place. Well, every attempt to get hired in those days was about the same. Day after day, you trudge to employment offices, barely aware of each company's name, much less what they do, or make. You fill out countless applications; pretend you really want *this* job, for *this* company. In reality, you have roughly zero knowledge (or interest) about either. Don't care a whit, either, which makes it hard to pretend fake enthusiasm.

Remember that scene in the movie *Saturday Night Fever*, in the hardware store? Tony Manero (played by John Travolta), after quitting in a huff, slinks back to ask for his job back. Does he really want it? Heck, no. He'd rather spend his days – actually, nights – at the disco, showing off his dance-floor skills. Who wouldn't?

"You've got a future here," says the store owner to young Tony. Yeah, sure. Like the opening scene in that movie, with Tony toting a pair of paint cans down the New York street, swinging them in unison with the soundtrack. That's what he's supposed to look forward to for the next ten, twenty years.

What choice does he have, though. Nobody is paying him for his dance-floor finesse. So, like all his buddies, like everyone in the neighborhood, he needs a conventional job, no matter what it is, to pay for daily life. If not the hardware store, other possibilities won't be any more appealing.

Well, that movie was in the 1970s. It's not much different today.

"Mister Quinn?" The well-dressed lady I'd glimpsed before had emerged from within the confines of the personnel office, to call out my name. "Here," I replied, starting to get up.

"The manager will see you now." I headed for the door behind her, which was halfway open.

"Have a seat," the manager said, pointing idly toward the no-frills chair facing him from across the desk.

We went through the usual routine, as if I'd never heard it all before, glancing at my application before each question, making it sound even duller than it was. Name. Address. Lived there how long? Your last job? Doing what there?

Then, the big one: "Why did you leave?"

That's a toughie. I was sort of fired. But not exactly. Hard to explain that I never got along with my supervisor, and things erupted one morning. Before I knew it, I was jobless, out the door, not exactly sure which of us had made that new status clear.

Ah, didn't matter anyway. It was a black mark. And this interviewer's job was to catch those black marks and use them against you. That's how it seemed to me, anyway.

Sometimes, those interviews were long, drawn-out affairs, inducing drowsiness. Worst of all were the ones where they made you take one of those moronic psych tests. The 50-question ones. Even for a petty low-pay job that may (or may not) eventually lead to climbing one or two steps up the long, tall ladder to occupational success. Or not.

At least, I never had to take that 500-question monster I'd read about – MMPI, I think it was – where they try to drill deep into your mind to see what kind of person you are, and whether you would fit in at this company, in this position. That's what they claimed to do, more or less. By wearing you down with that endless list of personal questions. Intrusive ones. Nothing to do with any job you might be applying for, in my view.

I remember reading about advice given by some expert on how to "pass" that big test. How to "beat it," I think is the way he put it. He wrote: answer its questions as if you were your most middle-of-the-road, ordinary acquaintance, standing out in no way. It probably worked. Of course, they always insisted there were no "right" or "wrong" answers, but we know that's a lot of bull.

One time, when I was still in my teens, I asked an interviewer about the company's pension plan. Why? Because no matter how hard I tried, I couldn't think of any other question. I was that uninterested. And probably, so exhausted from going through the same routine day after day.

Whenever job-hunting became necessary, we had to grow impervious to rejections. Likely, a long, seemingly endless series of them.

No matter what anybody says, the purpose of every application, résumé, and interview is always the same: weeding out and rejecting imperfect applicants, thereby narrowing the field. Rejecting is the important part; hiring comes second. Often, a distant second.

For low-level work, there's seldom any arguing about wages. Take it or leave it. Negotiation is for the better people, the ones making big bucks.

Thus, you wind up accepting what's available – if anything – and pretending to like it. Turn down a job offer? Not likely. If offered the job – *any* job – you take it. Never know how long it will be before another offer comes along. And certainly no assurance that it would be any better.

So, don't quit a job unless you have another one lined up. I learned that lesson from my father, but rarely followed that rule myself. Nearly always, I wound up quitting a job abruptly, with nothing else waiting. Is that the workaday version of the Golden Rule? More like equivalent to pyrite (fool's gold).

Some employment-seekers could pick and choose from several offers. They might even be sought out by companies, rather than have to apply. Rarely, if ever, would those of us near the bottom of the occupational scale face a choice between two worthwhile job offers. That was the stuff of dreams.

When the bosses talk about the subject, they make it sound like everybody has a job they actually want. Not those on the bottom, but most people. They don't seem to think much about all of us who take what we can get, accepting something on a markedly lower level than we'd hoped for. I mean, in all my years of job-hunting, I wouldn't even consider applying for *worthwhile* jobs. The kind that really do turn into careers that a person might want to have. I knew I'd never be hired for those. So, why bother?

For instance, as a high school graduate I wanted to be a journalist, and was accepted to a major journalism school. But because neither I nor my parents had money for education, and I knew nothing about scholarships and such, that wasn't going to happen. Without a degree in the field, I would never have applied at a newspaper or magazine. I knew I had no chance, unless there happened to be an opening for an office boy or data clerk.

They don't get the need for urgency, either. Sometimes, a person needs a job now. Right now. Not next week, not next month. Today.

Did you ever see that movie, *Kramer vs. Kramer*? When Dustin Hoffman loses his job, finances are tough and he's in the middle of a divorce. He needs another one immediately. So, he talks to a former colleague, ready to accept a loss in pay. What does his pleading get him? "Come see me after the first of the year," the guy tells him. Amazingly, when he replies that he's available this minute and no later, he gets an offer for a lower-level position, paying considerably less. But a job, starting right away. Doesn't often work out that way in the real-life corporate world.

Those in the supervisory class always seemed to assume you would be salivating to move up the ladder at the company, too – even if the ladder to success was broken, or missing. Plenty of us are satisfied staying where they are. Besides, I've never felt like I belonged to any organization. I mean, I never hired, fired, or supervised anyone. Nor wanted to. After-work, organized "company" activities? Too much like the dystopias of Orwell's *1984* and Huxley's *Brave New World*.

Enjoying one's workday was a mostly foreign concept to me. Toleration was as far as I could go, with only one or two exceptions. I was more in the mold of that song, "Take This Job and Shove it." That's probably why I still enjoy those old labor songs and stories about quitting one's job abruptly and taking off – to wherever.

So, was I a slacker in those days? Anti-work? Yes, I admit it. I've often been one of those clock-watchers the bosses used to complain about. Layabouts. Bums. Better than being a lifer, an organization man, waiting and vying for advancement. Lifelong careers? No thanks. Not for me.

Back in my early job-seeking days, most employees got paid vacations. Couple weeks, maybe. Not like Europe, where workers got a month or two off each year. But enough to take the edge off.

Paid holidays, too. Sick days. Even pensions, if you last that long.

Yeah, I know. Not everybody got those benefits. But more so than today. In the 21st century, the high-level workers get them all. The rest of us, not so much. Or, with all those gig workers around, none at all. We all know that, don't we?

Everything is different now. Hiring (or more accurately, rejecting) is done online. No need to trudge around to company offices, or be interviewed by anyone. At least, not right away. In fact, the applicant can easily appear via Skype or something. And be dismissed from consideration readily, practically anonymously.

Now, you don't have to wait for a human personnel person to utter an insincere "we'll keep your application on file" as he or she points you toward the door. No, a string of computer codes – an algorithm – handles the task of rejections.

More and more, those algorithms make the hiring decisions, either in full or tentatively. Well, those algorithms were set up by a person (though that's changing). No need for *any* humans there at all. Mainly, the algorithm is supposed to determine whether you would or wouldn't fit in. Not like a personal appraisal, but the same result. As if fitting in is the Number One attribute to have. Which it sure seems to be.

I swear, old Mister Jenkins (my first boss) or his descendants are back there somewhere, setting up their algorithms to convey the "no thanks" message that I would have received in person, in the old days.

Behavioral interviews are the latest. They watch your expressions, your hands, twitches, glances aside. Just about what Winston, the depleted "hero" in *1984*, faced every day, constantly watched via telescreen.

Nowadays, application forms have been disappearing. Except at entry-level or barely above, job seekers need to have résumés printed up. Or more likely, they apply online, with no paper needed at all. In the old days, I could have filled out an application in my sleep, I'd handled so many of them.

Even decades ago, when a company sought to appear modern, a test of some kind of was likely to be given. Even for the simplest jobs – the ones for which you barely needed a brain – they liked to test you. Especially that quickie 10- or 12-minute test with 50 questions, which was supposed to tell the interviewer whether you should be considered, and where you might fit best within the organization.

At least, I *guess* that's what they were trying to figure out. I took that thing so many times, I could get practically all my answers right in the allotted time. But I found out that too high a score wasn't a good idea. They might think you consider yourself too good – too brainy, "above" the others – for, say, a menial office job. Best to provide a few wrong answers, or leave some of the spaces blank. Unless you answer the questions like a typical employee, you're not going to become one of them.

Sometimes I wonder if these personnel guys know that half the applicants – probably more – don't give a crap about this job, this company, or much of anything else. They just need money, and acquiring a spot somewhere as an employee – selling your soul to the system, some would say – is the only way to get it. Short of turning criminal.

Just one time, way back in the past, I experienced a completely different hiring process. The state employment service sent me to a technical catalog publishing company that needed a copywriter. I'd never held a writing job of any kind, but seemed to have a bit of a knack for it. So, they gave me the kind of test that should have been universal. The editor handed me a few information sheets about a product, and told me to write a couple of paragraphs to promote it. I must have done okay, since I was hired with no further fuss.

As I soon learned, though, they hired – tentatively – just about everyone who didn't completely flunk that eminently practical test. One difference: we were given a two-week trial period. Do the job effectively, and it's yours. Fail, and it's the door for you. Turned out to be the longest connection I ever had with any employer.

Despite being run by a loud, boisterous, angry-sounding man, that company was ahead of its time in other ways as well. When I was having trouble working in the office, they introduced a way to let me do my job at home. This was long before computers and the internet entered the scene, half a century before Covid made working remotely a familiar concept.

Quite a difference from my very first full-time job, at age 16. Not only was a lengthy psychological evaluation administered, but the human-resource folks seemed to assume that I was seeking a lifelong connection with the organization.

For that timekeeper position, much later in my shaky, ill-defined "career," the company skipped the fitting-in tests, so the interview didn't last long. "We'll let you know." As usual. The words may change, but the outcome is always the same. "Thanks for coming in. Don't let the door hit you on the way out. But keep on going."

Sounded like a good idea to me.

23

Mail Call

All my life, I've been excited about mail. When I was young – a kid of eight, maybe ten – I waited anxiously each afternoon, after I got home from school, for the mailman to arrive. As soon as I spotted the postal carrier, either walking leisurely behind his cart or lugging a heavy-looking leather pouch on his shoulder, I made a dash for the front door. Rather than merely preparing to gather whatever happened to arrive in my family's mailbox, I nearly always secretly hoped for the kind of mail that never comes.

My near-compulsive interest in the daily mail delivery was unimpeded by the fact that during childhood few, if any, letters were addressed to me. As I would explain years later, I never stopped waiting for that singular letter that would change my life: that one great opportunity that each of us should be offered at some point.

I'm still waiting.

Now, I'm old enough to remember fondly the impact of radio in kid days – as well as its tie to the tangible delights that might arrive one day at the hand of the local mail carrier. As described by humorist Jean Shepherd, youngsters in those days would listen avidly to serial broadcasts on the radio. When the announcer informed the young listeners that they could order a premium item related to the story or its characters, and have it delivered by mail – well, who could resist? Recollections of one of those items still pop into my head now and then: a replica bullet on a ring, authorized by the Lone Ranger himself.

Sometime long ago, I read this Damon Runyon short story,

Mail Call

about a wife who laments the loss of Jim, their long-time mailman. Her husband reminds her that she only ever got one piece of mail. "Yes," she responds, "that's the one I mean." I could easily identify.

No doubt, plenty of people aren't, and never were, all that enthusiastic about mail. All too often, letters brought bad news and disappointing messages. For many of us, the disappointment stemmed from patiently (more likely, impatiently) awaiting – hoping for – *good* news that never came. Each day brought potential promise, which just might be sitting in the big leather bag astride the shoulder of the mail carrier as he approached.

Postal mail used to be important in so many ways, beyond personal communication, especially in the early days of the nation. Families bought most of their goods, other than food products, from the big mail-order businesses: Sears Roebuck, Montgomery Ward's, Butler Brothers. Today, our mailboxes are overloaded with solicitations and product promotions. Plus political pleas. In a word, junk that promises little or nothing of value.

What is it about postal mail that makes it irresistible and memorable. For one thing, it has a formalized format, including a salutation, a close, an offer of good wishes, and a signature (whether one's full name or a nickname). E-mail, our modern scourge, nearly always lacks all those features. Texts drop all the way down to basics, lacking even a semblance of finesse.

A letter has substance. It's communication that feels alive, handled by humans, not conveyed over a wire or through the air. E-mail is a wisp of nothing unless it's printed out, which hardly anyone seems to do anymore. Texts barely seem to exist, yet they're the method of choice when a message is considered urgent and important. They're the princes of brevity: far too direct and impersonal. Even more than the other two means of personal communication, most texts aren't exactly about crucial matters.

Not every communication is urgent, you know. A printed letter carries an aura of importance, even when it's imaginary. Well, I'm one of those traditionalists who doesn't necessarily read – or even open – a letter right away. Instead, I might set some of them aside, held back while waiting for the right time.

Same thing with writing letters, or answering them. Rather than rush into them, why not wait until the time is more suitable?

As a young adult, I was such an enthusiast about the Postal Service that I even became a postal employee – a mail carrier with my own route – for a couple of years. Trudging along the sidewalk, stopping at nearly every residence to tuck a few items into the mailbox, I seldom felt tired, even though half of those homes had stairs to climb. Even the frigid midwestern winter didn't bother me all that much. The time I got a touch of frostbite was my own fault, for wearing worn-out gloves that had little holes in a trio of fingers.

I didn't even bother to use the cart provided by the Post Office. I simply slung that heavy leather bag, packed tight with letters, magazines, sales circulars, and even small parcels, over my shoulder and carried on.

Even though I had the longest route in this Post Office branch, I managed to finish well ahead of schedule.

When e-mails first came along, I was almost torn between the human mail carrier and my new desktop computer. Sure, those paper letters had a look, a feel about them that could never be matched by an electronic equivalent. Still, the ability to receive an e-mail mere moments after it was sent – now, that was undeniably progress. Besides, an e-mail could always be printed out, thus taking the form of an actual, traditional letter.

The anticipation – and the daily disappointment – escalated, now on two fronts. But e-mail was a perfect example of using digital technology only to the point that it was personally beneficial, improving some aspects of one's life rather than complicating or reducing it. Postal mail seems personal, even when it's not. E-mails feel disconnected from their source, having been sent into the air rather than conveyed from hand to hand.

Mail Call

Naturally, all these years after first obtaining an e-mail address, I am bombarded by vastly more messages than I ever got via the postal service. Just like everybody else who's joined the digital world. But since 98 percent (at least) are junk and most of the rest don't amount to much, the disappointment I used to feel when the local mail carrier failed to deliver anything exciting has eased a bit. Now, it seems like a good day when one e-mail is welcomed and appreciated; or better yet, received from someone I like to hear from and respond to.

24

Whites Only '59

Wherever you happen to work, a lot of the rules of the job are unspoken. Never mentioned in ordinary conversation. Not written down anywhere, either.

No, they're informal. Casual. Understood, somehow. Everybody seems to know them and, for the most part, abides by them.

Except the newcomers, of course. The new hires. Break one of those unspoken taboos and you'll hear about it soon enough, you bet. Even if you had no idea that you were breaking any rule, or bending it mildly. Or even that such rules existed at all.

The hotel business was no exception. It was full of secretive rules. Requirements, even; stuff that you were expected to know, even if no one had ever told you about them. If anything, hotels – especially small, residential hotels – were overloaded with little rules, as well as a few big ones.

At the Lakeland Hotel on Chicago's Near North Side, there was just a single big one. A whopper. Break it, and you'd be out the door in a flash. Maybe worse, if old man Kenton got wind of your transgression.

Nobody would ever admit the existence of such an unwritten rule. If the subject ever came up, denial was a near-certainty.

Couldn't be simpler or more direct: Anyone working the front desk must never – ever – rent to a negro. That was it. Absolute, direct, no exceptions.

"Negro" was the most acceptable term used to depict African-American people back in '59. It wasn't the one that plenty of white people used, in everyday life. What eventually came to be called the

Whites Only '59

"n-word" could be heard – uttered in full – all over the city, but especially in working-class and low-income neighborhoods.

Far too many Chicagoans observed no linguistic niceties. The eventually-forbidden word was shamefully commonplace. You might hear it anywhere, even in seemingly polite conversation among "better" people. I'd grown up in working-class white Chicago, where the full n-word was an integral element of the local lexicon.

The hotel's owner let the clerks know the unofficial rule, without necessarily saying it outright. He might have simply assumed that every white person knew it automatically.

This was five years after the Brown decision by the Supreme Court, striking down "separate but equal" treatment in public schools and paving the way for the coming-soon Civil Rights Movement. But not yet. Not at the Lakeland Hotel. Nor at the three other properties owned by this family of "hospitality" entrepreneurs.

Chicago had a long history of racial enmity, highlighted (actually low-lighted) by the 1919 race riot. The city's South Side was perceived by Northsiders as practically a foreign country, visited only for special events at, say, the International Amphitheater. Lily-white enclaves dotted the South Side, but the white perception was that the whole vast area was mostly Black.

I was working the front desk in 1959, evening shift, 5 to 11 p.m., four nights a week. That amounted to a part-time job, but it wasn't unusual to be asked to take over another clerk's shift, whether days, nights, or evenings.

Because of the hotel's location in a popular, culturally diverse and historic part of the city, it hosted quite a variety of residents: some long-term, others for temporary stays. Most were quiet and polite, keeping to themselves. A few were wilder (and more interesting, I have to say), perhaps because Rush Street, Chicago's top entertainment center, was only a block away.

Ms. Vickers, for instance, was stunningly good-looking. No surprise, because she worked as a showgirl at a well-known gentlemen's club of that day. (Gentlemen's clubs were different in those days, featuring beautiful young ladies but no nudity or sexual activities.) One evening, late for work, she stopped at the desk to ask if I had a couple of rubber bands. As she explained, the garter holding up her stockings had broken, and she needed a temporary substitute.

I complied. Needless to say, it was difficult to look away from her shapely legs as she installed the replacement parts. For my minimal effort, she even rewarded me with a cup of takeaway coffee when she returned later in the night, refusing reimbursement.

Two sisters lived together on the second floor. Both were friendly, but I quickly developed kind of a schoolboy crush on one of them. When I heard about a party they were holding in their room, I secretly hoped to be included on their short invitation list. No such luck. Not that it mattered. I was never going to approach either of them beyond a quick wave or greeting in the lobby now and then. Besides, I was too uneasy in groups to take advantage of such an offer.

Years earlier, the area had been the center of "bohemian" culture, home to many of Chicago's famous – or notorious – writers, artists, street-corner philosophers, and the like. Bughouse Square, barely a block away, still featured impromptu public speakers, bringing their soapboxes to better address their audiences as they ranted, harangued, debated, and otherwise wrestled with the language to present their typically idiosyncratic political, social, and cultural ideas.

As a night clerk, I saw rules and workings of the hotel up close, including those that were never stated clearly. As a resident, I could observe the barrier between myself and the workings of the hotel.

Several instances of blatant racism still cling to my mind, all these decades later. Most painful was the reaction when a long-term resident, who'd always appeared sophisticated and gentlemanly, came running down the stairs to yell at me. "Get that girl out of that room!" he screamed. "Out of the hotel!"

Those might not have been his exact words, which got lost in the confusion of his ferocious verbal assault. He was livid beyond belief, to the point where he looked as if he might be inviting a heart attack or stroke. Why? Because a male college student on his floor had left the door of his room open and – horrors! – was sitting on the bed studying textbooks with ... a Black Girl!

I knew that because I'd followed up on his demand to deal with the situation immediately, and went up to see the offensive tableau for myself. I chose not to evict the young fellow instantly; but he must have realized that something was amiss, because he shut the door of his room. That didn't stop the accuser from continuing to rant loudly, but the evidence was no longer visible, so he left the hotel. Maybe to attend a Ku Klux Klan meeting.

Chicago was still heavily segregated. In fact, it was often called the most segregated city in the North. One major east-west thoroughfare was named Division Street for good reason. Black Chicagoans were almost entirely consigned to the South and West Side neighborhoods, while whites resided on the North Side.

For weeks, a fellow who lived in the hotel annex across the street stopped at the desk nearly every evening to ask if one of the rooms near his was available yet. He wanted to get a room nearby for his friend. Over and over, I had to tell him that no, they were all still occupied. All I could do was hope no one moved out, because I happened to know that this polite, sophisticated gentleman's friend was Black. A couple of times, he had come in to make the inquiry himself.

One day when I arrived at work, I learned that a room in the annex had been vacated, and then rented to someone else. I was the one who had to inform the hopeful applicant for residency.

Near the end of my tenure at the hotel, I committed the unthinkable. Yes, I actually rented a room to a dark-skinned guest. It was approaching midnight when this young Black woman appeared at the desk, asking about a room for several days. Well, I'd been pondering the racial situation at the hotel for quite some time. I wasn't in the mood to tell a falsehood and inform her that she was out of luck. Instead, I handed her the hotel register.

What was my reward for helping to ease the path toward integration? A couple of days later, she skipped out. I wound up packing her stuff, including "dainties" (intimate apparel), ro be placed in storage. In another context, this task might have been at least mildly stimulating, in addition to embarrassing. Not this time. How ironic that my first check-in of a person of color soon turned out to be a skip-out no-pay.

In 1950s Chicago, you didn't have to explain that Blacks weren't welcome. Just about anywhere on the North Side, except for one small enclave in the Uptown neighborhood (where household workers employed by wealthy patrons in the rich lakefront suburbs lived), Blacks were emphatically unwelcome.

Not totally absent, though. A single Black family could be found here and there, accepted by the area's whites because they'd been there a long time and were seldom seen. Not only did they make no trouble, they made no effort to bring in additional Blacks. So, they were barely noticed by anyone other than immediate neighbors.

My high school, for instance, was said to have one Black student out of a population of 4,000. I say "said to have," because I never laid eyes on him in four years.

Nowadays, even people with a racist history are likely to employ that euphemistic "n-word" when referring to a Black person. It's considered more genteel, less aggressive toward the Black race.

Back in the Fifties and into the Sixties, white folks often just said it outright. As weighted a six-letter word as you're ever likely to find. They just said it out loud, or softly. Angrily, or in ordinary speech. Unhesitatingly. Almost proudly, in some cases, but always with a basis in white superiority somewhere down in the heart.

Those of us who grew up hearing the word in full, especially in working-class urban America, yet managed to shun the use of it, could feel left out of things. Maybe we weren't really white. Or, not white enough.

As the Sixties emerged, the prospect for true integration finally was in the air, but only after numerous battles were fought, and only in part. Soon, Chicago residents would be assaulting Rev. Martin Luther King Jr. during his visit to Chicago, firing verbal hate of an unfettered magnitude, shocking to many non-racists. Physical violence, too, from working-class Chicagoans who felt threatened by a possible influx of dark faces in their neighborhoods.

Later came a growing influx of Latinos, bringing to mind the old song lyric by Big Bill Broonzy: "If you're white, it's all right – if you're brown, stick around. But if you're Black, get back ...."

Expressions of ingrained racist menace, seen by everyone on TV in the Sixties and approved by so many, seemed out of place at the Lakeland, which sat in such a "sophisticated" neighborhood. In this part of the city, not unlike the University of Chicago area on the South Side, interracial relationships weren't so fraught with fear. A live-and-let-live attitude was the norm.

Gays, for instance, were commonly seen and heard in this diverse Near North Side area, whereas their mere existence would have been taboo in most other city neighborhoods. Interracial relationships were not yet common, but not entirely hidden behind closed doors, either. Certainly not in this part of town, where the counterculture would be developing a few years later.

Most jobs I had in the Sixties, after my hotel stint, were open to persons of color, but that was clearly untrue of the majority of openings. A handful, like the catalog publishing company for which I worked as a copywriter, gave practically anyone who applied a tryout. If they showed they could do the job a week or two later, they were hired. If not, they were shown the door. That was a huge exception to the hiring norm.

The company janitor was a Black man, in accord with the

Chicago custom of the times. But one of the half-dozen copywriters was a Black woman. In the judgment of the publication company's owner and editor, getting the work done promptly and properly was all that mattered. Who manned the typewriter was irrelevant.

So, why did I rent to that young lady approaching the hotel desk? Was it because she was sexy? Exotic? Good-looking? Congenial? Maybe I just couldn't say "no" anymore. I'd like to think I was acting on principle, ignoring the risk involved.

Conversely, why didn't I rent a room to that friend of the annex resident? Because he was a man rather than a hot-looking woman? To protect him from the trouble that I knew would be coming soon if he moved in? Or because I hadn't yet developed sufficient confidence to "buck the system" and simply "do the right thing."

Like most residential hotels, the Lakeland is gone now. Destroyed a couple of decades ago, replaced by fancier residences for an affluent clientele that cannot imagine living semi-permanently in a cramped hotel room. For all of its flaws, led by endorsement of rigid racial attitudes, the hotel – and the offbeat neighborhood around it – possessed a version of character and quirkiness that's absent from today's flavor-free chain accommodations, which value luxury far more than uniqueness.

Many of us who've lived and/or worked in such establishments, even for a short while, have been sorry to see them disappear. Too bad some of their owners – like some tenants – were unable to see beyond their innate racism.

From the Archive

Stories by James M. Flammang, written in the 1980s or before but never published – until now.

25

The Last (Debt-)Free Man

He was running. Running a few steps in one direction, stopping abruptly, then taking off again the other way as they came at him from every corner. Hordes of stylishly dressed, pleasantly smiling young men, each one displaying a colorful, enticingly-shaped object, tried to attract his attention. The objects were all different, all bright and shiny and vaguely alluring; there were so many that he could barely identify any of them.

As he ran back and forth, around in a tighter and tighter circle, the objects became clearer. He could make out a huge 3-dimensional color television set, an endless row of leather-bound gold-embossed encyclopedias, a dishwasher-vacuum-quadraphonic sound entertainment system, an electric can opener with dozens of strange attachments clinging to it in the manner of a Dali surrealist painting.

And signs. Signs everywhere, printed in bold letters with fluorescent patterns that bored into his eyes:

"SUPER SUMMER SALE – TODAY ONLY"

"FOR THE MAN WHO NEEDS EVERYTHING"

"MAGNIFICENTLY CRAFTED TO REVEAL
THE REAL YOU"

"BARGAINS OF THE MILLENNIUM –
NO MONEY DOWN"

Hundreds, thousands of signs crushing him down to the ground, leaving him gasping for breath, crying and moaning for relief.

He jerked awake.

The signs were gone. The mass of salesmen had departed. He was alone again with Mister Jeppson.

"How are you feeling now, son?" Jeppson asked, a comforting, fatherly smile on his clean-shaven, well-groomed face. "You seem to have dozed off for a bit."

He was vaguely aware that he had not really dozed at all, that he had been drugged somehow. Or hypnotized. And the nightmare of signs and sales was not an accidental nocturnal happening, but a part of the total process to which he had been subjected for hours now. Or was it days? He couldn't tell, it seemed like years. But his clothing seemed to be clean and freshly pressed, so it couldn't have been very long.

"You were perspiring quite a bit, my boy, so we took the liberty of dressing you in a new suit of clothes. Very fashionable, I might add; takes years off your appearance."

Of course, he realized in despair. This wasn't the suit he had worn when he arrived at the office. The shirt was different, too: much newer and in keeping with current fashions. Probably his underwear was all new as well, perhaps in one of those hideous contemporary patterns with the price displayed in the stitching.

He groaned, falling back in his chair. What was the use; he couldn't fight them any longer.

But no, he thought. He would not make it that easy for them. They couldn't just install a new suit of clothes on him while he was unconscious and unable to resist. With a sudden burst of energy, he tore off the shiny, strangely-tailored light green coat and began to strip down.

"Give me back my old clothes" he yelled, his voice almost cracking from the strain. "They're mine."

"Oh, I'm afraid we can't do that," Jeppson said with a smile. "Why, they're on their way to the incinerator right now. That suit must be four years old, at the very least; should have been atomized long ago."

"Get them back!" Beads of perspiration were forming on the man's forehead. His hands were beginning to tremble. "I don't want these new clothes, I want my own clothes. You have no right."

Jeppson shook his head, reaching for the intercom button. "No, you're correct, of course. We had no right, not precisely. Though I fail to understand what you have against this beautiful new suit, which can be yours for a modest $189.95."

"I don't have $189.95, and I don't want your stupid suit. I want my own suit; it belongs to me. I paid for it years ago, and it's mine."

"Susan," Jeppson said into the intercom, "please get this man's clothing back. That tatty old suit we were going to send to the incinerator. And bring it in here when you find it, please."

Jeppson turned to the man, his smile returning. "You're absolutely sure you don't want this lovely suit? Naturally, you need no money right now. All that's necessary is your signature, and we take it from there. You would be right in the fashion limelight this season, I can assure you."

"Limelight. Fashion. What do I care? I've been telling you over and over that I'm perfectly satisfied with what I have now. You've no right to keep me here, to keep harassing me."

"Well, that's not exactly true, I'm afraid. We debt counselors have a good deal more leeway nowadays, ever since the universal debt collection laws were passed.

"Admittedly, most of my clients are considerably different from yourself; the other side of the coin, so to speak. They have taken on debts – or, as we prefer to call them, life investments – quite willingly, in order to provide themselves and their families with some of the finer things. Our country, our world, is constantly developing and producing more and better products to make our people's lives easier and more enjoyable. And everyone wants to take advantage of each of these technological advances."

The man laughed out loud. "Like that tape player gizmo you tried to get me to sign for? The 24-track gadget with 16 speakers? Including two that attach directly to your head? That's the great technological advance that everyone wants?"

"Scoff if you like, sir," Jeppson shrugged. "Thirty thousand of those players were sold in the first month they were available. And customers are on waiting lists everywhere for them; they've been back-ordered for weeks now. The factory cannot hope to catch up with the demand."

"At $1,500 a copy? I'm not that crazy, to stand in line to throw money away on junky gadgets."

"$1,499.95," Jeppson corrected. "No money down, of course. And we do have an economy model for persons such as yourself, who do not demand the absolute finest in listening pleasure."

"No!" the man screamed. "No, no, no. Don't you people understand that simple word? It's an old English word, everyone has heard of it. Or do you prefer *nein*, or *nada*, or *non*. *No lo quiero*, I don't want any." He sat back in his Loungeabout reclining chair, his energy ebbing away again. How long had he been here, anyway?

"Yes, you have made your attitude perfectly clear, strange as it is. But we are merely taking this opportunity to talk it over with you. To show you everything that our modern world has made available for your enjoyment, things which you may have been unaware of. I understand you have been somewhat out of communication with the business world for some time. My agents tell me you don t even have a simple television set in that, uh, home of yours. We can make some allowance for that fact, but we still must determine why you continually persist in your resistance to progress."

"You hypnotized me," the man accused, pointing a finger at Jeppson. "Or drugged me, or something. You're trying to force me to sign for one of your stupid pieces of garbage. With those subliminal pressure tactics. I've read all about it. I know what you're trying to pull, and I won't allow it."

"Oh really, now," Jeppson said soothingly. "You know that is quite unnecessary. Many years ago, it's true, our advertising industry made some small experiments with subliminal sales techniques. Showing an ice cream bar on a movie screen, for example, at a speed too fast for the audience to be consciously aware of what they were seeing. Those techniques did bring about a modest increase in ice cream sales in the lobby. But believe me, we eventually found those methods to be wholly unnecessary. The public wants – no, demands – what industry can produce; we don't have to trick them in any way. You don't really believe otherwise, do you?

"Now, if you will just sit back and relax in your Loungeabout for a few minutes, I'll check on your clothes. They should have been here by now. And perhaps I'll bring along another new outfit to show you. The new tri-sex style might suit you nicely."

"Don't bother," the man sighed, leaning back all the way in the chair, then pulling it up smartly to its upright position. No point in getting too comfortable.

He only wanted to get back to his cabin, to his old overstuffed chair and his simple life. At home, he didn't even have a radio, much less a 3-dimensional super-living-color quadraphonic-sound television set, or whatever they were calling them nowadays. For nearly ten years, he had been living in quiet solitude, alone, away from the pressures to accumulate a lot of useless merchandise. Since he seldom read the newspapers (there were only a few worthwhile papers left these days, anyway) he hadn't realized just how different the world had become. Somehow, he had thought that as long as he paid his taxes and stayed out of the hustle-and-bustle consumer world, they would leave him be.

He should have known better, though; should have realized it was inevitable. Even when he had been living in the city, years before, his friends had often looked at him accusingly when they saw that he wasn't buying any new furniture or appliances or entertainment devices for his tiny walk-up apartment. They all made little jokes about their accumulations of goods and their corresponding debts, protesting as though they truly wished to be free and clear. But they didn't; not really. And they had resented him for being debt-free all his life.

The snide comments about "fitting in" and "living a responsible life" had grown increasingly hostile. Their definition of responsibility seemed to consist of accumulating more and more debts, becoming part of the system by virtue of owing more and more to it.

Well, that kind of life, living from paycheck to paycheck, wasn't for him, and he had often told them so. He was proud of the fact that he owed nothing to anyone, like his father before him. And he couldn't see why he should be apologetic about it.

Finally, the only alternative seemed to be a move out of the urban rat-race completely, to his secluded cabin in the woods, surrounded by birds and deer rather than over-striving humans. Since his needs were so modest, he got along very well for all those ten years, living like a modern-day Thoreau. His garden supplied most of his food, and he managed to earn a few dollars through temporary jobs in town from time to time. Best of all, his cabin had been bought and paid for in cash, years before, so the only real housing expense was the still-modest property tax.

Even when the township had put through an assessment on all the property in the area, he managed to come up with the cash by working a double-shift in the service station fifteen miles away. The assessor had said he was the only resident who paid the full amount in cash; everyone else had taken the easy-payment route.

Still, he should have recognized how much the world had been changing all along. Whenever he went to the general store nearby, he had to be sure to bring the correct amount in cash, as they seldom had enough change. Almost no one paid his bills in cash any more, or even carried ordinary small change. Even the public telephones were gradually being set up to accept credit cards. And he had even seen some soda-pop vending machines that worked with a charge card.

All told, though, his life had been good and pleasant. Until he received the summons, from the Benevolent Debt Counselors.

Perhaps he should have ignored it, torn it up and forgotten about it. That had been his first impulse. But they would have gotten to him eventually, somehow. He knew that now. At the time, he had been certain that it was some sort of ridiculous mistake, the kind those computers were always making; that they really wanted someone else.

And how could a debt counselor, whatever that was, send out a summons anyway? It appeared completely legal, the same kind of summons which a court would send to a prospective witness in a big criminal case.

Well, he had been due for a short trip to the city to purchase a few small items – books and teas and such – so he would take a few minutes to go to this debt counselor and clear up the matter.

They had been friendly at first, suggesting that he make himself comfortable in one of the unoccupied offices while they checked his file. A younger version of Jeppson had talked about trivial matters while they waited. But gradually, subtly, the conversation had taken a turn. The young counselor began to ask pointed questions about financial responsibility, about advertising, about the free enterprise system. He made increasingly derisive comments about people who attempted to avoid their true responsibilities to the world around them, who were trying to tear down the business system with their hedonistic lifestyles.

Finally the man could listen to no more. "Wait a minute," he cautioned. "What do you think you're doing, accusing me?"

"Subversion," the young counselor had sneered. "Out and out subversion, if you ask me. Oh, the other counselors think I go too far, but if it was up to me, I'd lock up all the counterproductive riffraff like you and throw away the key. One of these days it will happen, mark my words. You anti-progress freaks will be dismissed permanently." His voice had grown angry and taut, his face contorted with subdued rage.

"Oh relax, Wilson," laughed the older man as he entered the office. "You'll have to ignore Wilson," he added, turning to the waiting man, "he does get carried away at times." Dismissing the younger man with a wave of his hand, he said, "I'll take over now."

"My name is Jeppson," he explained, seating himself behind the desk in the chair vacated by the younger counselor, who had now left the room. "Why don't you tell me a little about yourself."

The man had stirred in his comfortable reclining chair. "This is a mistake. I don't owe you anything. I don't owe *anyone* anything."

"Of course you don't; no doubt about it. But I'm a little confused, and perhaps you can enlighten me. I've been going over your file, and I can't quite understand how you manage to live, with an almost nonexistent income and no credit record at all. Frankly, nobody can live on what he earns these days. Everyone, and I mean everyone, has to take on at least a little debt of credit purchasing to get by, to acquire the basic necessities. And for a few of the finer things in this life, well, to be quite honest, a goodly amount of borrowing is absolutely essential."

"Not for me," the man had responded. "I live a simple life, bought and paid for. I have no debts to you or anyone else, so unless you have something specific to ask me about, I'll be leaving."

"I'm afraid not, son. Not just yet. The door is locked, so you'll have to stay with us a little longer."

"You can't do that. This is a free country."

"Oh, nothing is free, son," Jeppson had laughed. "Pardon the awful pun, a little debtor's joke. I know what you mean. But we counselors do have the power to summon and detain people when necessary. Within reason, of course."

"Detain them for what?" the man had asked, wary now, his apprehension growing.

"Just a bit of consultation. It won't hurt a bit, I can assure you. So relax in that Loungeabout chair – comfortable, isn't it? – and we'll carry on. If you want anything – a drink, a cigar, lunch – just push the button on the chair. I'll be seeing you again a little later."

After Jeppson had gone, a large screen lowered its way across the far wall and the room light was turned off. The images on the screen were pleasant at first, an ephemeral little story about a boy and a girl finding each other after a lengthy separation. The episodes had been interrupted by commercials, the same sort of commercials the man remembered from the time when he had been an occasional television viewer, years back. But these commercials were much more glaring, more intense, certainly more colorful and bold in their brazen suggestions of eroticism and youthful beauty.

More frequent, too. The episodes of the story seemed to get shorter and shorter, the commercial breaks longer and even more forceful.

Finally, the story had ceased altogether and the screen displayed a continual succession of advertising messages. The conventional screen had taken on a 3-dimensional effect, like the 3-D television sets he had noticed in the store windows in the downtown area. Totally nude young ladies romped with similarly denuded and handsome young men, verbally attributing their successes to one or another face cream or deodorant, which they practically thrust out of the screen at regular intervals. The commercials for the new automobiles (which looked surprisingly similar to the automobiles of ten years before) featured debonair, elegantly-dressed men picking up voluptuous, scantily-clad girls at every street corner. The girls became ecstatic as they pawed the car's upholstery and, finally, the driver.

It was more than visual, too. The man could almost smell the girls' perfumes, practically taste the lipsticks they taunted him with, nearly feel the smooth skin they displayed unashamedly as they writhed on the latest all-weather imitation leopard-skin carpeting offered on easier-than-ever terms.

Prices were seldom mentioned at all. Instead, the only suggestions of monetary transactions were the sleek, gleaming pens which seemed to be proffered from the screen every few moments. One could almost grab the pen and easily sign the clearly-printed dotted line that filled the screen.

Eventually, the screen was raised into the ceiling, and the live performance began. One by one, a handsome and suave salesman had brought his wares into the office and gone into an elaborate sales presentation. Exhortations to sign for an air-powered window washer (inside and outside, guaranteed to reach the third floor) and a 15-speed (forward, reverse and sideways) combination lawnmower/vacuum cleaner/snow blower/driveway cleaner were followed by a well-rounded lady's appeals on behalf of a matched his-and-hers set of Great Classic Books. Each of the salespeople held a pen in hand, along with a contract on which was printed no more than a dozen large, easy-to-read words.

Over and over, the man had resisted, answered "No!" in a tone ranging from annoyance to rage, until finally he burst into tears. The salesperson in the room at that moment – an Amazonian woman whose lewd suggestions for use of the low-energy-consumption motorized massage couch she had dragged in were lost on the man's fatigued brain, departed in haste.

The man had fallen back in his chair, in the full reclining position, depleted. Sleep had come easily.

Jeppson was back, carrying the man's old suit, holding it away from his body as though it were contaminated. In his other hand was a hanger which held an iridescent mass of blue-green fabric, so bright that it was difficult to determine its shape, except that it appeared to have short pants.

"Here's your old suit, son," Jeppson smiled. "And a shiny new tri-sex outfit. Hardly possible to compare them, is it? Notice the inward-turned lapels, the 10-button closure. Quite a piece of goods, wouldn't you say?"

"The old suit, please," the man said in a tired voice.

Jeppson hesitated, then handed him the rumpled, old-fashioned vested suit. "The underwear and socks are in the shopping bag." He looked longingly at the tri-sex suit, shaking his head. "Pity. Such a lovely shade of shimmer-blue."

"Can I leave now?" the man asked, putting on his old clothes as rapidly as possible.

"Soon," Jeppson answered with his usual smile. "Very soon. Just a few more details to cover. Take a seat, please."

The man, now fully dressed in his comfortable old suit, ignored the Loungeabout recliner and sat on the straight-backed wooden chair in the corner. Jeppson frowned slightly, but shrugged and took his position in the plush high-armed oversized chair behind his desk, folding his hands in front of him.

"Well now, I don't mind admitting that yours is one of the toughest cases I've come across in all my years here. Maybe even *the* toughest; a true challenge, you might say. Frankly, I've done my job very thoroughly, far more thoroughly than normal, and still we are at a stalemate. I can't really understand it, but you've managed to resist, even scoff at, every appeal we've made to you. We've shown you every imaginable time-saving, effort-saving, pleasure-giving device which our great nation has to offer. Devices that kings and heads of state and the super-rich wouldn't have even dreamed of just a few short years ago, and they could all be yours in a moment. But still you resist.

"So let's get down to basics. What is it that you want?" The man could barely contain himself, could hardly keep from laughing. "I want to go home. Haven't I told you enough times? I want to go home and be left alone."

"Yes, of course," Jeppson sighed. "But I mean really, what do you really want? I warn you, we could have found out ourselves. A short while ago, you accused us of hypnotizing you, or drugging you. A false accusation; but believe me, if we had wanted to, we could have done it easily. And we could have found out without any doubt what it is that you really, truly want, deep down. We could have done that, but I chose not to. I much prefer our clients to deal with us honestly, to tell us what they truly desire and allow us to fulfill those dreams in the easiest possible way. The law, as I have told you, is on our side. Determining a client's dreams and aspirations by, uh, irregular means, is quite permissible in special cases.

"In short, then, we can compel you to reveal your innermost desires by chemical or other methods, if you don't do so on your own. But I'm still in favor of playing it straight, giving you every opportunity to be honest with us. Quite frankly, causing you to join our credit system under duress is repugnant to me, and would not look good on my record, either. We want a nation of voluntary consumers, not a mass of forced debtors. And that's exactly what we have. You're the last of your breed, young man, and there's little reason for you to resist any longer.

"So I'll put my final cards on the table, so to speak. We've offered you everything possible in the legitimate sense. Now I will move on to the illegitimate. I am prepared to offer you anything whatsoever that you desire, whether legal, moral, ethical or otherwise. So what will it be? A slave? A harem of willing, or unwilling, twelve-year-olds? A lifetime supply of illicit drugs? A license to kill?"

"What?" the man asked with a start.

"A license to kill," Jeppson repeated. "It's not a commodity I offer lightly. Believe me, I would much prefer that you accept a less extreme item. But I mention it only to illustrate that anything at all is within your grasp, and requires nothing more than your signature.

"This hasn't been publicized, but you may have heard the

rumors that conventional charge cards could be used for illicit services: paying for a prostitute, buying narcotics, hiring a killer, that sort of thing. It's not true just yet, but a program is in the works and it's only a matter of time."

The man grinned, looked more relaxed now than he had since his ordeal began. "That last one, the license to kill, is tempting. Especially if I can have you as my first victim."

Jeppson was not smiling. "This is no joke, son."

"I'm not joking. But I'll resist the temptation. I understand what you're saying, but I'm going to tell you just one more time. There is nothing that I want, nothing at all. I am entirely satisfied with my life. Or I was, until you dragged me into your monstrous scheme. I want nothing more than to go home and stay out of your precious consumer system."

"I see," Jeppson said, leaning back in his chair. "Then that is what you will get."

"Huh?"

"Release. Freedom, if you will. That is also a commodity I am prepared to offer you. But you will have to sign for it, naturally. And the price is not low, I'm afraid."

"Price for what? What are you talking about now?"

"Son, I'm afraid I will have to place you under arrest. I don't like it, but I have no choice. Therefore, as an officer of this state, I hereby arrest you for violation of the Economic Treason Act."

Jeppson fumbled around in his top desk drawer. "I have a card in here somewhere, to inform you of your rights. This is my first experience along this line, so I'm not entirely familiar with the details. Ah, here it is. You have the right to remain silent, the right to counsel, the right to confront your accuser. Pretty standard up to there. But here's the important part: you have the right to dismiss the action against you at any time, by simply signing an agreement to pay all the fines and penalties assessed. Needless to say, such fines and penalties need not be paid in cash, all at once. We will supply you with an appropriate charge card to handle it, whenever you so request."

The man stared at Jeppson. "You're serious."

"Absolutely," Jeppson affirmed. "There will be a trial in a reasonable time, though it may be a while as the Act is something new. We don't really have any precedents for its use, but it is definitely legal and approved by the government as well as the C.U., Consumers Unanimous. However, I am empowered to make any out-of-court settlement that might be appropriate, to assess your fine and your intention for paying it off."

Jeppson reached for his intercom. "I'll call our security officer now and we'll have you settled in before evening. For the time being, you won't have to be placed in the regular prison cells. We have a special security room for extraordinary cases."

"Wait a minute," the man yelled. "You're actually going to put me in jail? For not agreeing to buy anything on time?"

"I'm afraid so. Until you're ready to discuss your payment program."

Jeppson turned to the intercom. "Hendricks, please come into my office. You'll be escorting a prisoner to the solitude room."

He turned to the man. "He'll be here in a moment. Normally, you would be allowed a televiewer call, but I understand that you have no close relatives, so ...."

"I'll call a lawyer, then. I don't know any, but there must be some kind of lawyer's referral service."

"Oh, not for cases of this sort," Jeppson protested. "Not yet. Plenty of time for lawyers later on."

He looked at his watch, pressing a tiny button on its side. A monotone voice proclaimed: "Three thirty-one and forty seconds."

"Very good," Jeppson said. "You'll be settled in just in time for the dinner hour. Since the Prison Reform Acts, you'll be pleased to learn that the food in our penitential system is superb. And your quarters will have a full- dimensional, supra-sound television screen, so you'll be able to keep up with world events. And with the messages for our latest products. Unfortunately, you won't be able to turn the set off; it's on a timer arrangement to ensure complete coverage of each day's merchandising program."

"Wonderful," said the man, slumping down into his chair. "I suppose it has a fancy chair and bed, too."

"Absolutely, my boy. Nothing but the best. I suppose you are not entirely aware of the advances made in penology in recent years. Ever since we began to treat each offender as a fallen-away consumer, providing even former thieves and pickpockets with a substantial line of credit, we've had remarkable success in rehabilitation. Unfortunately, the problem of personal, violent crime is still with us. But before long, crime for personal gain will be a relic of the past. Why rob and steal when you can simply obtain every necessity, along with most luxuries, by simply making use of one's charge cards."

"But the stuff still has to be paid for," the man protested. "You can give a thief all the credit you want to, but he still has to pay for his purchases. By additional crimes, no doubt."

"Yes, that's true," Jeppson admitted. "But we are working on means to permit everyone to earn a sufficient amount to pay for their purchases. In the case of the criminal, we can channel his talents into crimes that are beneficial to society. The need for industrial spies, factory demolition experts, political assassins and the like is increasing every day. Eventually, all former criminals will be doing their duty as productive citizens, one way or another. And the only real crime left will be the one for which you are being held: non-participation in the society. Frankly, we don't expect many offenders when that day comes.

"You can go with Hendricks now. And whenever you would like to talk, just press the button over your bed. I'll be available during regular office hours, 10 until 2. Enjoy your telescreen."

The room was brightly lit, gaudily furnished in shimmering shades of white, lavender, and coral. The screen covered the entire wall, and a continual stream of commercial messages emanated from it, each one in blazing color and accompanied by loud, grating audio inducements.

A boatload of laughing, beautifully tanned Adonises invited the man on a cruise around the world, pointing out the adventures and dangers that would be his if he would only sign his name. A businesslike government official offered him a once-in-a-lifetime opportunity to accompany the astronauts on the first manned Mars landing; he would even receive official recognition as one of the first men to step on that planet. For a substantial extra fee, he could even be listed as the first.

Every imaginable type of everyday merchandise was hawked, from marijuana-flavored chewing gum (guaranteed to produce a true "high" with no aftertaste) to frozen giraffe meat ("a new tall taste for the aspiring gourmet") to a monarch-sized bed which rocked back and forth to simulate the rolling motion of an 18th-century sailing ship ("the excitement of sailing with Magellan with none of the unpleasant risks, for a thrilling night's sleep every night").

Occasionally, a more basic appeal would be presented. Like the blatant offers made by an incredibly beautiful, perfectly-formed, nude young woman who lay expectantly in a four-poster bed, surrounded by equally-unclad girls-in-waiting. "A night of delirious sensuality," she promised, "to please the most discriminating erotic palate."

The man had to keep telling himself that she wasn't real. But she looked so fleshlike that he was almost sure that she would actually leap out of the screen at him, as she suggested orally. "No messy, dirty cash," she proclaimed at the end of her segment. "Only bank cards accepted."

The room had no windows, but the time of day flashed on the

screen periodically (courtesy of "Perfectron Audible Watches, guaranteed to lose less than a second in a century").

An hour passed, then two, then three. A tray was pushed into the room through a slot in the door. Reluctantly, the man raised its cover and saw what must have been a twelve-course meal: golden lobster tails, twice-baked potatoes, escargot, spinach souffle, trifles, three old bottles of wine. Alongside this feast was a familiar-looking charge slip.

He returned to his constantly-vibrating bed and lay atop the plush, silky, flesh-colored spread, trying to ignore his rumbling stomach. A little later, the meal was withdrawn and a substitute repast of beans in runny tomato sauce and hard white bread appeared in its place. There was no charge slip with this one, so he ate quickly, washing down the tasteless food with bitter coffee.

He tried in vain to sleep, but the penetrating sound of the televised enticements would not allow a moment's peace. A day passed, two days. More meals of beans and bread were consumed, after he was treated to the sight and smell of a succession of banquets which would have pleased the most demanding big-city gourmet.

It was four days before he pressed the button.

His simply-furnished, unpretentious cabin was no longer so spartan. During his absence, several loads of the latest convenience appliances and entertainment units had been delivered, unpacked and spread all over the house.

He didn't know whether the deliverymen had obtained the house key legitimately, broken in, or what; but it didn't really matter. The various items had been sent on an approval basis: no payments until they had been tried out and enjoyed for specific trial periods. Apparently, this was part of the new economic laws, too. In the past, purveyors of consumer goods had to send slick, full-color broadsides describing their merchandise. Now, they sent the merchandise itself, and it was up to you to return it if you didn't want it. And if you weren't present when the goods were delivered, they had the right to leave them on your premises.

The mailbox, too, was packed tightly with direct-mail advertisements, samples, appeals of every kind. In fact, the mailman had somehow gained entry too and left a pile of earlier mail in the center of the room. Since the man had never before bought anything on credit, he had received very few ads in the mail; now they were making up for that omission.

He sat down cautiously in the brand-new Rocker/Recliner/Sleeper Relaxer Chair, still covered in plastic wrap. He didn't bother to remove the wrapper; he was too exhausted from his ordeal. The sight of all the objects in the room, the pile of mail on the floor, made him queasy. He didn't want to think about it, wished it would all disappear, but knew he would eventually examine and read everything.

Jeppson had explained the terms of his fine carefully. With interest accumulating at 3 percent a month, it would take every spare cent he could earn to simply keep the fine at its original figure; reducing the total would be impossible.

Still, Jeppson had been unhappy. He had explained that use of the new Treason Law was a last resort, that he would have been far happier if the man had acquiesced voluntarily. The fine, in that case, would have been nominal, even nonexistent. Friendly persuasion, he had explained, was the way in which Jeppson, and his superiors, wanted the last holdouts to be brought into the system. Compulsion was an abhorrent, if necessary, final choice.

There was only one way to reduce the fine. To voluntarily select an item – an orchestral-quality music system, an electronic orgy simulator, adventurous luxury getaway at a resort in the Alaskan war zone, the services of a seemingly almost prepubescent lady of the evening, anything – and sign the credit agreement for its purchase.

The Last (Debt-) Free Man

He sighed in dismay, settling back finally into his (actually, the company's) Relaxer Chair. As he glanced down at the piles on the floor, an ordinary-looking brochure caught his eye and he leaned forward to pick it up.

The cover was printed in soft, non-fluorescent colors. A serene scene of uninhabited forest land with birds and animals and fish leaping up from a swift-flowing river. It was the kind of scene he hadn't observed in years, even in his own sparsely-populated region. Visions of his boyhood, fishing trips with his father, camping excursions with the Boy Scouts filled his mind as he turned the page to the solicitation inside.

"Tired of the routine of city life?" it read. "Try a week at Primeval Acres. No television, no televiewers, no modern conveniences. Just rolling rivers, little-traveled hiking paths, primitive accommodations, and guaranteed solitude for the weary worker." The price for the vacation package was outrageous. But the familiar words were given on the back page: "No Money Down – No Payments Until Next Year." The combination application form and credit application was printed in plain black-and-white ink.

On the table next to his chair was a cheap, old-fashioned ballpoint pen. He picked it up, hesitated just a moment, and began to write his signature in a firm, bold stroke.

26

Slow Getaway

They caught up with me just outside of Milwaukee. Which was really the last place I expected to be arrested in; it's a city I've always liked. Liked so much, in fact, that I've pulled off some of my sweetest jobs in its outlying areas.

My untimely capture wouldn't have happened at all if I'd left the driving to Greyhound. But no – I had to make my getaway in my tired old car. Seemed like a fine idea at the time, a perfectly reasonable method of escape from the scene of the crime, you know? But if I had it to do over again, I think I'd rely on public transportation.

The job itself went off without a hitch – a piece of cake, as they say on the TV. As usual, I had picked out a small bank in an older suburb, one that hadn't been hit since the Dillinger days, if ever.

Naturally, the proceeds wouldn't exactly be enough to retire on, but I've managed to pursue my profession for more than a dozen years now without a bust, simply by not being too greedy. Two or three jobs a year, planned carefully to give me the best possible chance for a safe getaway; that's the way I operate.

Those two or three heists bring in maybe fifteen or twenty thousand a year. As I say, not a princely sum, but plenty for Hazel and me to live on comfortably. I even pay my taxes on most of it - I'm listed in the IRS records as an independent marketing consultant – so I don't court trouble from the Feds.

Did I say that I'd never had a bust? Well, that's not strictly true. I did spend a year-and-a-half in Joliet some time back, but that stretch wasn't for a bank job, so I don't count it in my won-and-lost record. The time was for driving a stolen car and, believe it or not, I didn't even know it was hot.

That was the first time I'd gone on a job with a partner, a liquor store holdup. Going double definitely wasn't my style, but at the time I was pretty low on funds, and I was assured that the chance of failure was practically zilch. You know how it is, when you're broke you sometimes take risks you wouldn't consider when you're flush.

But they didn't get me for the holdup, only for the car. Idiot that I was, I hadn't even asked Eddie – he's my wife's cousin – if the car was his, I just assumed it was. I mean, we weren't going to drive up to the liquor store in the car. We were planning to park it down the street, so why should I think we needed a stolen car? Honestly, it didn't even occur to me.

Anyway, we got stopped before we even got to the store. Before we reached the suburb in which it was located, to tell you the truth, pulled over by a highway cop who must have been studying the hot-car sheet right at that moment, and spotted us passing him. Sheer luck, it was – the bad kind. He said later that we were speeding, and that's how we drew his attention. But I don't think I was going over the limit, I always drive very carefully.

I should have realized long ago, though, that cars were my downfall, and changed my *modus operandi*, so to speak. Even as a teenager, cars were always the thing that brought about my unpleasant contacts with the law. And I was a pretty cautious driver as a kid, too. Some people shouldn't ever get behind the wheel, I guess – it only brings bad luck or something.

Well, that was then and this is now. This time, the whole operation had gone smoothly. Within seconds after I walked out of the bank, I was on my way out of town, having been noticed by no one except the teller. That's one of my trade secrets. I'm a very ordinary-looking guy and I dress as commonly as possible, drive a nondescript car, strictly anonymous in every way. Even when I'm observed in the act – don't mess with complicated disguises – people have a terrible time giving a physical description of me. I know, because I've read some of them in the newspapers afterwards, and I could hardly believe they were talking about me.

Just a week before, I'd had the Ford tuned up and George, the head mechanic at the dealership, said he'd looked it over personally and it was in top running shape. I didn't really believe him. I'd been hanging around the shop waiting for the car and, as far as I could see, the new kid was the only one who'd worked on it. But the engine did sound A-1, and on the drive home the car seemed to have a lot more pep, so I was satisfied.

Until today. Until I was maybe four miles away from the bank, in the next suburb down the line, and it stops dead. I still don't know what happened; the engine just quit while I was rolling along at forty miles an hour. Fortunately, I was able to steer it off the road and into a big parking lot, almost coasting into a legal parking place before it stopped completely. That was about the only piece of good luck I had, as it turned out.

At the time, though, I didn't let myself get too upset. Actually, it had happened at an excellent spot – an uncrowded shopping center – and the incident hadn't drawn much attention from the few passersby, even though I'd had to push the car by hand for the last few feet into the parking slot. When you look ordinary enough, hardly anybody notices you even when you're doing something not ordinary at all, like pushing a car. Believe me, it's true.

So there I was, suddenly without wheels, and with an attaché case full of money to be dealt with. I hadn't even checked the case to see how much I'd gotten away with; that would come much later.

I sat in the car for a minute or so, pondering my next move. As far as I could tell, nobody on the street had paid any attention to me when I drove away from the bank. I was almost certain that I hadn't been followed, and I'd been watching the rear-view mirror mighty carefully. So I should still be in the clear if I could only get the car out of the lot before any store cops realized that it had been parked for a suspiciously long time.

All I had to do was get home fairly rapidly, borrow our neighbor's car for a few hours to drive back here and arrange for the towing, and nobody would be the wiser. By that time, the cops wouldn't be looking for me this close to the bank.

Home was only a hundred and fifty miles away. I could get there by three in the afternoon, and be back to the parking lot before dark.

At that point, I thought seriously about hopping on a bus, getting out of the neighborhood as fast as possible. Several elderly women were waiting at what appeared to be a bus stop – probably for one of those buses that hits a number of shopping centers and winds up downtown, where I could catch a long-distance bus for home. The cops certainly wouldn't expect me to be sitting on a slow-moving bus with the bank money.

But then I thought about this movie I'd seen on TV, where a bunch of bank robbers made their getaway on an interstate bus. As I remembered it, the job had been very well planned, too, but still they got caught. It doesn't make sense, I know, basing my decision on a story from the TV. But I guess I'm superstitious, and I suddenly didn't care for the idea of being trapped in a bus if there should be a roadblock or something.

Yeah, I know, roadblocks aren't your everyday occurrence, even after a big bank robbery, and this was a minor-league heist. In fact, I had never seen a roadblock in my life – not in real life, only on the tube.

Still, I had funny feelings about it and, in any case. I didn't know where the bus would go, so I vetoed the idea. I figured it wouldn't be a problem to rent a car, and I walked over to a public telephone to call one of the smaller rental agencies. On the commercials they say they'll even come out and pick you up, and handle the rental papers on the spot.

Sure enough, the girl merely asked where I was, and said they would send a car over right away, since the shopping center was pretty close to the city airport: Looking back on it now, I probably should have taken a plane instead.

Anyway, after five minutes or so this guy shows up with last year's Ford and hops out, keys dangling from his hand.

"Mister Corey?" he asked. That's the name I had given to the girl, though it's not my own. However, I've got a driver's license in that name – cost me fifty bucks – just for problems of this kind.

"Yes," I smiled. "This is the car?"

"Right. Just a little paperwork and you can go on your way. If you're headed south, maybe you could drop me back at the office?"

"Sure thing," I agreed. A couple of minutes wouldn't matter that much. So I pulled out the driver's license and handed it to him as he filled out the form, using the car's fender as a desk.

"And how long will you be wanting the car, sir?" he asked.

I knew it would only be a few hours, but wanted to play it safe. "Oh, a day or two; maybe longer." Actually, it might be less suspicious if I kept it for a couple of days.

"Very good, sir. Now if you'll show me your credit card?"

"Credit card? No, I'll pay cash." I had a couple of cards in my wallet, but naturally they were in my own name.

He frowned, didn't seem to know quite what to say. "Uh, I'm afraid we can't take cash, sir. Credit cards only."

"But I'll pay the deposit. However much you like." I had over six hundred dollars in my wallet, for emergencies. Obviously, I wouldn't use the bank money for travel expenses.

"I'm very sorry, sir," he said, shaking his head sadly. "It's company policy. No cash, only credit cards. We accept any of the major cards – American Express, Visa, ..."

"I don't have any cards," I protested. "What is this? I've rented cars lots of times, always paid cash for the deposit."

"Well, I understand the company – all the rental companies –

have gotten stuck quite a few times. You know, people paying a fifty- or hundred-dollar deposit, then damaging the car. Or keeping it much longer than they had agreed to. And we've had a hard time trying to collect the balance. So it's all credit now, sir. You don't have any cards at all?"

I was furious. What's going on anyway, I thought. Cash is no good anymore?

"No, no cards. There's no way?"

"No, sir, I'm afraid not. Perhaps if you'd like to take one of the credit application forms – I have several here – you can send it in. Then next time ...."

"I need the car now, not next time!"

He looked pained, anxious to leave. A couple of people were watching us now.

"It's okay," I consoled. "I should have realized."

Now he smiled a little. "I'm really sorry, sir. Don't hesitate to call on us the next time you need a car. Can I drop you somewhere?"

"No, no. You go ahead. I should have known."

I just stood there, unbelieving, as he drove away. Here I was standing with who knows how many thousands of dollars in cash – including six bills in good money in my wallet – and I couldn't even rent a lousy car to get it all home. Well, I thought, it's a good thing I didn't pursue the matter any further, ask to talk to his superior or some such foolishness. After all, I was hardly in a position to want to draw attention to myself.

So what next? The obvious. If you can't rent a car, buying one is the only reasonable alternative. As luck would have it, I spotted a big used-car dealership a block or so away. If I could pick up a run-down transportation car for a few hundred, something good enough to get me home, I'd be in good shape. Later, I could sell the car quietly. Or abandon it. No, that would attract attention in itself. Maybe I could drive it to a junkyard somewhere, sell it for scrap.

Wait a minute, I told myself, let's not get ahead of ourselves. Get the car first and deliver this attaché case into the safety of my den, for a leisurely accounting. Hazel would be getting anxious if I didn't get home at the time I'd specified. I picked up the case and started off toward the car dealer.

Glancing quickly over the offerings at the front of the lot, I didn't see anything appropriate. Maybe in the back row there would be a few junkers for sale.

I'd almost reached the sales office when the siren started blaring. I must have jumped a foot, nearly dropping the case. Then the spotlights came on, giving off a blinding beam even though it was broad daylight outside. What in the world, I thought, couldn't they simply grab me by the arms, read me my rights, and haul me off to the slammer? What was all this hoopla?

"Here he is," a voice shouted. "Number ten thousand. Bring the cameras over this way, let's go there."

A fat middle-aged man, wearing a garish green leisure suit, waddled toward me holding a microphone. "And your name, sir?" he asked with a silly grin, waving the microphone into my face.

"Ummm," I answered. I wasn't sure which name to give him. To be honest, for a second or two, I wasn't exactly certain what my real name was. That happens once in a while when you're using an alias, especially when you don't often have to actually say your name out loud.

"Come, come, sir," he prodded, "Nothing to be afraid of here. All we need is your name and you're the proud owner of a brand-new color TV set. And there's a twenty-percent discount on the car of your choice, too."

I'd been concentrating on the salesman so closely that I hadn't noticed the others. There must have been a dozen of them, some holding cameras or lights, some just standing there smiling inanely.

"What is this," I blurted out. "What do you want?"

"Smiling Jack's Ten-Thousandth Customer Extravaganza," he

replied with a full mouthful of teeth showing. Undoubtedly, this guy was Jack. "And you're the lucky number, our ten-thousandth valued patron. Now if you'll step over this way ...."

Obviously, I should have gone along with the whole business, accepted the prize graciously, and left. But the lights and cameras brought back memories of that one time in stir, and I must have gone crazy for a minute. I turned and walked – no, ran – toward the street.

"Wait a minute!" the fan man yelled. "Where are you going?"

I ran at least two blocks before I turned and looked back. A few pedestrians were staring at me strangely, but no one had followed me. I sure didn't like the idea of my face appearing on film, or TV, or whatever the cameras were for, but maybe they hadn't been turned on yet. And I definitely shouldn't have made such a silly fool of myself. But nothing could be done about it now; I still had the problem of getting home.

Oddly enough, there was another car dealer across the street from where I was standing, still puffing from my exertion. I'm not in the best physical shape anymore, as Hazel keeps reminding me. This was a much smaller dealer, and there was no sign of any special festivities, so I squeezed the handle of my attaché case and strolled across the highway.

This salesman was not the gregarious type at all. He didn't even seem very interested in selling anything. I picked out an eight-year-old Chevrolet from the back row and asked the price.

"Nine hundred," he stated nonchalantly.

"How does it run?" I asked. If it started and moved, I was ready to buy it, but I wanted to make the purchase appear normal.

"Not bad," he shrugged. "Want to take it for a ride?"

"No, I'll take your word for it. Don't know that much about cars anyway." I grinned. "The running of 'em, I mean."

I pulled a stack of fifty-dollar bills out of my wallet as I started for the office.

The salesman didn't move. He stood right in my path, a wary look on his face. "You're going to pay cash?"

"Cash, right. Five hundred, you said?"

"Well, yeah. That's our asking price."

"Good enough for me. Do you have the title ready? I'm in a bit of a hurry."

"Hold on a second," he warned. "We're not accustomed to taking payment in cash. You see the sign out front, easy payments? That's the way we prefer to work it. We can give you an outstanding credit deal, no problem there, so long as you've been on the job for a while."

I sighed. The last time I had bought a car, the dealer was ecstatic about the fact that I was willing to pay cash. He told me a whole series of stories about people who'd skipped out on their payments over the years. He didn't even handle the credit stuff himself anymore, simply sold the contracts to a finance company.

"Ah, I think I see the problem," I suggested. "The five hundred is your time payment price, or the trade-in price, or something. You make your profit on the payments, right?"

"Well ...."

"So what's the cash price? Now, right this minute."

"Listen, it's not that simple. We're not set up for cash deals, that's all there is to it. The boss doesn't like to have cash around the office; too many robberies. Anyway, you couldn't take the car with you now. We have to apply for license plates, state inspection."

"I can take care of all that myself. That's what I've always done."

"Oh no," he said emphatically, "we can't allow that. The state raises a big fuss nowadays if we let a car out without making absolutely sure that the paperwork is handled just so, for sales tax and all. However, I can let you have the car tomorrow. I'll take care of everything this afternoon, take the cash right to the bank. You can pick up the car first thing in the morning."

I was about to break into tears. Here I was supposed to be making my getaway from a major felony, and I'm standing and arguing with a lousy salesman, trying to force him to sell me a car. The world's gone crazy, I realized. Me too.

"No, that won't quite do," I said. "I'll stop back again."

"Well listen, give me a call first – here's my card – and we can take care of everything in a couple of hours. Or if you'd prefer a newer model, we can take your credit information over the phone. Takes only a half hour or so to get it approved."

Wonderful, I thought. It's quicker to buy the darned car on time than to pay cash.

"I'll think about it," I said, turning away. "Thanks a lot."

"We have a full selection of later models ...."

If he only knew. If I could have afforded a later model, I would have bought one before the job. Then I wouldn't be going through all this nonsense. But Hazel and I had never had enough ready cash to go into a late-model car. Like I said, crime pays; but it doesn't pay quite enough for all of the luxuries.

Over an hour had passed since I pushed the Ford into its current resting place, and I wasn't any further along than before. But I still wasn't worried. At least there hadn't been any police cars racing around, no sign of any problem in that area.

Naturally, you're wondering why I didn't take direct action – steal a car and take off right away. The fact is, I don't know the first thing about stealing cars. I'm a bank robber, nothing more. I don't know any more than the average person about other kinds of crimes, don't hang around with criminals or that sort of thing. Except for Eddie, who I try to avoid as much as possible since that botched job that earned me the prison time. According to the papers, practically every punk kid in the country must have the skills to steal the car of his choice at any moment, but I wouldn't know the first step.

Keys, I thought suddenly. Even I could steal a car if someone left their ignition key in it. They're always warning people about taking their keys with them, but I know for a fact that a lot of drivers don't. Sometimes, I forget about it myself when I'm only going to be parked for a few minutes.

I walked quickly back toward the parking lot. Halfway there, I stopped abruptly. I couldn't steal a car from the same place where I'd left my own. Wow, that would be asking for it. Good thing I thought of the risk. I turned around and headed back the other way, reaching another shopping center – a smaller one – after three blocks.

It took only a couple of minutes of strolling among the cars before I discovered the right one. An older, nondescript sedan, dented and rusty but not enough to stand out. The kind of second car a lower-income housewife would drive to the supermarket. As a matter of fact, I had seen it pull into the lot, driven by precisely that type of housewife. Better yet, she'd had a couple of screaming kids with her, so it would take her a while to finish her shopping. By that time, I could be miles away. I could drive most of the way home, ditch the car on a side street, then take the city bus the rest of the way.

Yes, the key was in the ignition. Amazing. The engine started up instantly, and I pulled out of the lot without looking back. Actually, the rearview mirror was broken, so I couldn't very well look back even if I wanted to. It was running beautifully, a little noisy but smooth and powerful, once I'd gotten it onto the Interstate.

The cops pulled me over after less than ten miles. Not regular cops, but the pollution control division.

That old car was operating well enough, but apparently it was also throwing out a cloud of oil smoke behind it. Recently, they've been getting tough about air pollution, stopping cars that smoke and making the drivers arrange to have their cars towed to a garage for immediate repairs. I didn't know that before; they told me about it after they discovered that I couldn't produce ownership papers for the car and called in the license plate number. Which, of course, wasn't registered to me.

Moreover, they knew all about the bank robbery and were very interested in the attaché case next to me on the seat, since it was the type a bank patron had described as belonging to the thief.

Later on, at the station, the regular cops told me that my haul had amounted to over thirty thousand dollars – my biggest ever, by far. Hazel and I could have finally afforded that vacation in Hawaii that she's been pestering me about.

I've got a lot of time on my hands now, a minimum of five years unless the parole board comes through. I'm getting a lot of exercise, though. Hazel will be pleased with my physical condition when I'm released.

Yesterday, a fellow came around to talk to me about taking vocational training classes. He showed me a long list of courses they offer to inmates, to prepare them for straight jobs on the outside. It didn't take me long to decide. I'm going to put in for Auto Mechanics.

27

Guzzler Gulch

James Bond was just slipping into the driver's seat of his gadget-equipped Aston-Martin on the screen for the final scene when Mr. and Mrs. Blick climbed into the back seat of their own car. A few hesitant kisses and gropings while in the front, coupled with some eye-opening views of bikini-clad beauties on the huge drive-in screen ahead, had roused both Blicks. A session in the rear seemed irresistible, inevitable.

They were not alone. No heads could be seen in the cars on either side, but an occasional sigh or muttering, a minute fluttering of the car's body, left little doubt that most patrons had their attention glued to each other rather than on the fuzzy, multi-spliced old film.

After a few minutes of grappling and fondling, Fred raised his head and sat back against the seat, regaining his breath. "This is nice, Doris, but I'd like a little more."

"Fred!"

"Huh? Aw no, no," Fred soothed, well aware of her shyness even after a dozen years of blissful marriage. "I mean with the car. Sitting here just reminds me how it used to be when I was a kid. Can you believe I once owned one of these guzzlers? A Pontiac GTO, just like this one. Black, though. Four-barrel carb, floor shifter. Hundred-twenty miles an hour that rattler would go."

"I know it, Fred. You've told me a thousand times."

Fred shifted his eyes to the left, sighing heavily. "And look at that Cougar. My buddy Tom had one of them. Jeez, my heart starts thumping just thinking about it, actually being out on the road in something like that, middle of the night, just me and the highway, barreling around curves."

Doris chose not to look at the Cougar, preferring not to see what might be taking place behind the steamy windows. Hardly a customer in the movie was under forty, she knew, but the place was well known for its scandalous behavior. Fornicating in the back seats, tossing plastic beer cans out the window, screaming and yelling like a bunch of teenagers in those old beach movies they showed every August.

"Forget it, Fred," she cautioned. "We go through this same scene every time we come here. You can't drive that way anymore, and that's all there is to it. Maybe we shouldn't come here at all, you get so upset."

"Well, it's fun anyway. But I wish you could let loose a little more." He chuckled, grinning so Doris wouldn't be offended or shocked. "You know, maybe go all the way, like they used to say."

Doris smiled in spite of herself, having tried to prepare herself for that eventuality, the last couple of times they'd gone to the movies. "Fat chance, you beast," she said with mock fierceness. "No tubby 48-year-old is going to get into my pants. Or get them off. Now that fellow playing James Bond, maybe he'd have a chance."

"In the back seat?"

"Sure, why not?" Doris knew Fred wasn't really disappointed, just suffering from nostalgia. Their marital life, including the physical side, had always been great. She just wasn't ready to go public, no matter how intent the other patrons were on their own debaucheries. This obsession with the cars, though, was getting to be a problem.

The movie credits were beginning to roll and, as usual, the Blicks had missed the ending. Fortunately, they had seen the film before, and would be able to describe it in detail to the children in the morning, at breakfast.

Before the credits ended, most of the patrons had left their cars, emerging slowly from the driver's and passenger's seats, obviously reluctant to slam the doors and walk away. But they all did, Fred and Doris included, some heading for the rail stop at the rear of the theater, an elite few moving toward the tiny parking lot a half-mile beyond.

The Blicks were among the elite, reaching the lot after the usual trek through undergrowth in the dark, tripping every few steps. "They could at least set up a few lights," Fred complained, "even if they don't want to spend the money chopping away this jungle. Gosh, sometimes I'm almost sorry we bought the car."

"Sorry? You? After fighting for years trying to save the money? Fine time to tell me."

Fred opened the driver's door, letting Doris fend for herself on the other side, and crunched himself into the tiny seat. Before Doris's door was closed, he'd already entered the code numbers and punched the GO button more roughly than necessary. Seconds later, the vehicle was moving slowly out of the lot, its dim lights barely able to see the potholes that seemed to increase in both size and number without letup.

Out on the road, he opened it up to its maximum speed of 25 miles an hour and settled back for the two-hour drive home.

The GTO, the Cougar, the dozens of Mustangs, Marlins and Eldorados remained behind, immobile, permanently facing the movie screen and awaiting the next group of customers. Never again would they move out to the road, feel the jab of an adrenaline-enriched driver's foot on the accelerator, snarl their twin exhaust pipes in defiance. They served no purpose other than providing seating space for those dwindling numbers of middle-aged men and women who couldn't forget what it had been like to drive through the windswept night, who needed to be reminded of drive-in movie nights of their youth, who felt at home in the tattering vinyl seats of automobiles that had long ago become museum pieces.

Guzzler Gulch

More than a dozen years had passed since the last "guzzler" – last gasoline-powered vehicle of any kind – was pulled off the road. Top-level government and industry experts had known for years that estimates of oil reserves had been grossly exaggerated, that the end of the internal combustion engine was coming far sooner than any but the most pessimistic scientists had predicted. In fear of social upheaval, they held off letting this knowledge be made public. Instead, they frantically searched for ways to speed up the development of solar and electric vehicles that could replace the millions of gas and diesel autos on the road.

They had succeeded only partially. By the time the Gas Vehicle Requisition Act was passed, giving car owners sixty days to dispose of their cars or make them permanently immobile, production of non-oil-using vehicles was still far behind the need. And with their 25 miles-an-hour top speeds and snail-like acceleration, the new solar electrics were not well received. Not until motorists finally realized that this was all there would ever be, at least in their lifetimes.

While it had long been proven possible to make fuel-free vehicles that promised acceptable speeds, the mass-produced versions simply could not make the grade. A handful of rich folks could afford the prototypes that almost approached the old 55-mph limit and accelerated with a bit of zip, but even those sluggish and tiny vehicles were priced well beyond the reach of most. The Blicks had scrimped for half a dozen years to purchase theirs. Since the government made every effort to discourage use of private cars, the electrics could only be bought for cash.

Although a bonus had been paid to owners of gasoline autos who agreed to destroy them, several million still existed. Owners of cars from the Eighties, and even Seventies, usually accepted the liberal amount with some satisfaction. They knew the old bus would no longer be of any use anyway. But those possessing older autos, from the Sixties and before – the ones with monster engines, flashy paint jobs and glittering chrome – tended to resist.

At first, the officials were satisfied when owners turned in their ignition distributors or carburetors. The sale of auto parts had been halted completely, so replacements would be impossible to obtain. Besides, a jail sentence awaited any speculator caught with a spare part of any kind.

Before long, though, the ingenuity of backyard machinists was producing a supply, small but dangerous, of hand-fabricated components to fit the old engines. This led to the Crankshaft Law, intended to be the final solution. No one, it was assumed, would be able to fabricate a precision-machined metal object weighing a hundred pounds or more without attracting attention. Besides, the authorities were ruthless in rounding up all the old cranks (both metallic and human).

Naturally, though, there is always some clever machinist who can devise anything out of scrap iron, or somehow renew a seemingly demolished crankshaft.

At his office the next morning, Fred couldn't get those old cars out of his mind. It happened every time he and Doris went to the flicks at that old drive-in. He grew irritated by the fact that they still called it a drive-in, even though nobody had driven in for years. And he would wind up daydreaming about GTOs and Trans Ams for days afterward.

Watching out of the corner of his eye so old man Barnes wouldn't catch him, Fred spent the better part of the morning doodling vague sketches of old automobiles on his display screen. Fortunately, he had a corner work station, so fellow workers couldn't spy on his forbidden artistic creations. Even so, he kept one finger poised near the Erase button, another ready to call up an instant budget report, should anyone come near.

Fred was so caught up in designing a teardrop-shaped fender, though, that he almost missed Barnes' approach. Detecting the scent of the supervisor's cheap cologne just in time, Fred managed to get a sales forecast for the new line of Executive Dolls onto the screen as Barnes' weasel face came into view.

"Busy, Blick?"

The voice was even whinier than usual. Fred instantly brought his cooperative smile into place, hiding the loathing he felt for the snoopy supervisor. "Yes sir. Absolutely. Just going over the forecasts for the Executive models. The female versions should be a hot item, sir."

"Good boy, Blick. Keep me posted."

Fred almost stuck out his tongue at Barnes' retreating backside, but restrained himself. "Boy!" he thought. For crying out loud, I'm ten years older than that moron, and he calls me Boy. Sometimes, he would even give Fred a patronizing pat on the head. It was bad enough to be kept at the same boring job for half a dozen years, without having to take guff from some snot-nosed kid supervisor.

Flicking the report off the screen, Fred went back to his designer daydreams, lazily tapping out the names of some of the old cars he loved. Camaro, Porsche Turbo, Duesenberg. Jeez, what he wouldn't give to get behind the wheel of one of those ancient masterpieces, with a ten-foot hood stretched ahead of him.

As usual, Fred had finished his paid-for work in the first twenty minutes of the morning. Everyone else in the office always seemed so busy, but Fred never seemed to have anything to do. He suspected that they, too, were faking it, immersed in their own daydreams. But no one ever spoke about the amount of time their jobs actually required, so he could never really be sure. And he was too frightened to ask, fearing that someone would discover he had virtually nothing to do each day, and boot him out onto the street. This job wasn't much, but it paid for his modest family needs – and for the Volta sedan.

At lunchtime, Fred ate hurriedly and wandered over to the plant area. Hanging around the few remaining production workers, he'd heard vague rumors, hints, about some gas-powered cars. One of the guys had even spoken about some kind of clandestine race, but he'd shut up immediately upon realizing that Fred was nearby. Fred had heard other bits of gossip about such races, too, using not only the spirited little cars of the Eighties – the last of the breed – but even some of his favorites, the muscular brutes of the Sixties and Seventies.

He was in luck. The fellow who'd spoken about the races was alone at his machine, nobody in easy listening distance. Fred had never talked to him, but recalled his name was Mac.

Fred had no real business in the production area, but sales analysts did go down there on occasion, so his presence would not be considered unusual. He strolled casually up to the quietly-running machine, watching its operation for a few seconds before the operator turned around. "Hey Mac, how's it going?" he said cheerfully.

"Mel."

"Huh?"

"My name's Mel. Do I know you?"

"Mel, sure. Sorry. No, not exactly. I'm from up in sales."

"So what do you need?" Mel's voice was calm and controlled, with just a trace of suspicion evident.

"Oh, nothing really. I was just…." He realized instantly that this wouldn't do, he'd have to get to the point right away.

"Listen," Fred said, "I don't know how to get into this, so I'll just say it straight out. If you don't want to say anything about it, that's okay."

A slight grin was forming at the corners of Mel's mouth, almost hidden by his bushy mustache. "Okay. Go ahead."

"It's about cars. Races, or something like that. I hate to admit it, but I heard you saying something about it once or twice." Fred gazed up at the ceiling, not wishing to see the response on Mel's face.

"Yeah, I've seen you around. Heard about you, even. You like the cars, eh?"

Fred knew his face had turned bright red, as though they were discussing the price of a teenage prostitute. Which, considering the compelling urges he regularly felt deep in his groin when imagining himself behind the wheel again, wasn't so far from the truth.

"Yes. I do. And I thought you might know, uh, might be able to tell me, uh – "

"It'll cost you."

"Cost? Really?" Fred wasn't so surprised by the need to pay for such illicit information, but by the ease with which it might be elicited. "Okay, sure. How much?"

"Fifty. Cash."

Glancing around the shop, certain that their remarks were being overheard, that police informants were waiting to pounce on him for even seeking out such information, Fred lowered his voice to a whisper. "Uh, how do I know – "

"That it's straight scoop? You don't. They're against the law, you know." Mel turned back to his machine, ready to flip the On switch, before Fred grabbed his arm.

"Okay." Fred reached into his pocket and fumbled through a small sheaf of bills he'd placed there, just in case this encounter would prove fruitful. Without looking down, he pulled out several of the bills. "Fifty bucks."

Mel's face seemed to have grown an evil smirk. Or perhaps Fred just imagined it did, based on his guilty feelings.

"Here, I'll write it down for you," Mel said after pocketing the money in a flash. He grabbed Fred's pen from his pocket and quickly wrote out a few lines on a scrap of newspaper he picked up from the waste bin. "Have a good time," he said with a laugh, handing Fred the paper.

"Thanks. Jeez, thanks a lot. Will I see you – "

"Could be," Mel interrupted, turning abruptly back to his machine, the transaction completed. "I like 'em too."

The train seemed to take forever getting out to the fringe suburbs. Fred had left the office at noon on this Friday, as was his custom. He preferred that his 25-hour weekly work schedule be spread over five days, giving him every afternoon free.

His wallet contained five hundred dollars in crisp bills, drawn out of the joint account early that morning. Taking a withdrawal in cash drew attention, Fred knew; but he'd taken pains to look nonchalant in front of the teller camera. Doris would probably be furious when she discovered the withdrawal, but he'd handle that later. After all, illicit fun was expensive, and he was entitled to a little of it.

The brief, yet detailed, scribbled instructions had told him how much money to bring along, and where to leave the train, along with a vague map of the subsequent hike. Fred got off at the indicated station – one stop before the end of the line – along with half a dozen other well-dressed men who paid no attention to him as they walked hurriedly out to the pathway.

Fred lagged behind, looking for the narrow side path that was shown on the map. He found it easily, noting that it was filled with footprints that looked recent.

The walk took well over an hour, veering off onto several small roads and byways before Fred came to the base of a steep hill. Practically a mountain, though he hadn't really seen a mountain since he was a kid. Funny, he'd never known it was so hilly out in this area; must have been years since he'd last been around here.

He checked the instructions one more time, shrugged, and began the upward trudge. The path veered well away from the road. Fred had not seen a single vehicle since leaving the train station. Tense at first, he now breathed easier, seeing that the trek took him far away from possible traffic. The police weren't likely to pop out from behind bushes on a steep hillside path, but could turn up at any moment out on the potholed two-lane highway that could be seen in the distance through the trees.

Guzzler Gulch

Halfway up, Fred was exhausted. He wanted to sit and rest, but it was growing late. Besides, his excitement was barely controllable now. He almost felt like he was already in the driver's seat, tooling around pairs of tight S-curves and graveled grades – race courses that had grown ever more real in his imagination during the plodding trek. He plodded onward, amazed that the path had suddenly grown considerably wider, and was filled with beer cans, food wrappings, and miscellaneous litter.

Minutes later, the trees cleared a wider expanse and Fred came upon a small shack. Several men milled around the area, wearing faded STP caps and worn-out racing gloves. One had a battered crash helmet on his head, with speckled remnants of automotive decals clinging to the dingy white structure.

Fred had worried about seeking out an illegal event. He'd heard rumors of people being jailed for simply firing up a gas engine. Not only rumors; the news reports carried occasional bulletins of mass roundups of auto owners. Lately, though, the reports had become rare, as though the officials didn't want to draw attention to such activities. But when Fred spotted several uniformed policemen in the crowd behind the shack, including the chief of police from a nearby town – one who'd been on the news several times claiming that no more cars existed in his domain – Fred took his first deep breath since leaving home.

Of course, he realized, how could they get away with it unless some cops were involved too. It was logical. Cops, even more than the general public, had to miss the feel of power beneath them. They sure didn't get much of it from their bicycles and horses, nor from their electric squad cars, which were only slightly more energetic than the standard models.

"Hey you," yelled a bearded fellow, not moving from his position leaning against a tree but casting a suspicious glare at Fred. "Whatya want?"

"Uh, I heard, uh, cars ...." Fred could barely get the word out.

"Two hunnerd to get in, two more to roll."

Fred tried to feign shock at the amount, but instead slipped four fifty-dollar bills out of his pocket. They were limp with sweat from his eager hands, wrinkled from incessant handling during the long walk. He held the bills out toward the beard, who snapped them up in a single sweeping motion. "I'll decide later."

Fred followed the other man's pointing finger, stepping over a rope and into the entrance of a cave. Inside, it was cool, dank. But instead of the expected darkness, Fred was amazed to find bright lights aimed downward from the cave roof. Half a dozen cars stood silently in rank, every graceful metal contour illuminated by the overhead lamps. Men stood quietly in shadows beyond the cars, speaking in whispers.

Easing into position near a group of three, Fred stood patiently, waiting, waiting. Until the silence was shattered by a blast of unmuffled exhaust from somewhere beyond. The snarling notes lasted only a moment, then died away, resonating through the tight space like a legion of artillery fire. Fred's heart was pounding hard as the sound faded, and he noticed smiles breaking out on all the nearby faces.

"That be old Rusty," said one of the men. "Good ol' GTO she goes like a sonabitch."

Other men had wandered to the center, and began to open some of the car hoods. Fred strolled casually over, peeking down at the dual four-barrel carburetors of a Buick GS455, then a full-race Mustang Mach I, with outside exhaust pipes uncapped. Alongside sat a V-12 Jaguar coupe, a Porsche model Fred didn't even remember from his study of the picture books, a Corvair Spyder that he did. A pair of low-slung Corvettes stood aimed at the back end of the cave, men sitting in each driver's seat. There was even an antique supercharged Studebaker, tailfins soaring – one of the luscious old Hawk coupes from the Fifties that had disappeared even before the "muscle car" got going.

Fred stood transfixed as, one by one, the cars fired up, each driven off with a burning of rubber on the wet ground, a snarl of defiant exhaust. Instead of driving out the entrance through which Fred had arrived, they roared toward the back, out a barely visible square cut into the cave wall. Good Lord, Fred realized, that's the race course right out there.

Almost shaking in anticipation, Fred returned to the entrance, easing alongside a roughly dressed man who seemed to be in charge. "Uh, say, the guy outside said – "

"Road or drag?"

"Huh?"

"You wanna go around the road course or drag straight out?"

"Hmmm. Well, road I guess."

"Race or alone?"

Fred didn't have to think. "Alone. This time. Just to see how it is, you know?"

The new batch of fifties was pocketed as quickly as the first. "Buick," the man said. Palms sweating mightily, hands trembling, Fred reentered the cave, ambled over to the GS Buick with its rear end jacked up and twin pipes waiting, and slipped into the driver's seat. An instant's twitch of the ignition key, and the massive V-8 sprang to life with a roar. And died again before the tachometer had a chance to respond beyond a single motion of the needle.

Next time, Fred punched the accelerator pedal before trying the starter, and the engine mercifully took hold. Slipping the pedal, he knew the others were gazing enviously in his direction. The thought of killing the engine a second time drove him nearly crazy. So he let it idle for several seconds while he wiped the sweat from his brow. He was almost faint from the excitement, heart racing, breaths arriving in heavy gasps.

Nudging the accelerator until the tachometer read halfway up the scale, he felt a surge of adrenaline comparable in intensity to the powerful throb of the motor. He stepped down on the clutch, moved the long shift lever into first gear. Strange, he thought, that he remembered how to do it, considering how many years had passed since the last time. Feeling totally in control now, Fred revved the motor and let out the clutch – and the engine died in an instant. He'd popped the clutch too fast, though trying so hard to let it out gradually.

"Hey, move it!" yelled the custodian. Onlookers had turned, and were grumbling, muttering. "Jerk."

Fred turned toward the crowd and tried to apologize with an unconcerned shrug; but he knew a sheepish look gave him away. He hoped no one could see his hands shaking, his head twitching. Once again, without delay, he fired up the engine. This time, he let the clutch out ever so slowly. The powerful car moved off toward the cave entrance, without a wheel-spinning exit to call attention to Fred's motion.

As Fred maneuvered past the entrance, the custodian called out: "Just follow the signs. One time around, that's all. It's a measured mile. We'll clock ya if you want."

"No thanks," Fred replied. "I'll take care of it."

The ride was like a dream, over in practically a flash. He'd gotten the speedometer up to 85, well under its peak, but the curves on the mountain road were treacherous and he was, well, scared. But eager for more.

"Listen," he said upon returning, "how about a race?"

"Two hunnerd."

"Well, I've only got $100 left. But I can – "

"Ah what the hell, gimme the hunnerd. Have a good time. Hey Charlie, this guy wants to go around with you."

Charlie left his perch on an old stump and hopped right into the Studebaker. Fred almost laughed, certain he would beat that one. But Charlie was a comparative youngster, no more than thirty, and he handled the ancient coupe with startling skill, exiting from the cave.

At the Start line, a flagman gave them a bored GO sign, and they raced off, neck and neck. Seconds later, Fred nearly sailed off the mountain's edge, hit the dirt several times, and was beaten by many lengths by the Studebaker.

The experience was expensive, Fred thought. Dangerous. But worth it. He would be back.

28

Crazyhouse

As the attendant turned the lever, an icy spray of piercing waterdrops assaulted my skin, each one stabbing the surface like a frozen needle. For me, it was tantamount to torture – though persons accustomed to cold showers might not have minded the liquid attack.

Even they, on the other hand, might have objected to the indignity of the procedure. For a shy person such as myself, troubled by the sight of his own body, standing naked in the presence of a bored orderly – after being ushered abruptly into the shower stall – evoked images of past humiliations that stemmed from public nakedness.

Swimming class in high school, for instance. Young people today can barely believe it, but in the 1950s we had to learn the crawl and breaststroke while stark naked. No swimsuits allowed, ever. As a 12-year-old unmatured twerp in the presence of older boys with five o'clock shadows and threatening penises, swim class stretched beyond discomfort into an ordeal of uninterrupted distress.

Never did learn to swim in high school, though it's hard to say how much the lack of swimwear contributed to that failing. I hadn't learned at the YMCA, years earlier, either. We were naked there, too; but because we were all six or seven years old, it wasn't quite as embarrassing.

On this day, my first in the mental hospital, the orderly didn't seem to care about the size of my penis, or whether I had one at all.

He didn't care how frigid the rat-a-tat water droplets were, or whether I was comfortable or not. Neither was he interested in how thoroughly I washed, as long as my rapid actions qualified as an official shower.

As it turned out later, he was a pleasant enough fellow. On induction day, though, his orders were simple. Right to the point. Step by step. New patient equals shower. Clean up the new arrival.

Showering was among the final steps in the process, before being handed plain pajamas and a thin robe. That would be my total attire – augmented by soft slippers – for the next day and a half.

In the dayroom, I'd seen that nearly everyone wore street clothes. The only exception was a shaky middle-aged man who, I soon discovered, had been admitted only shortly before me. He was holding a cigarette as if trying to keep it from biting him: obviously eager for its nicotine-laden smoke, but barely able to hold the cylinder still enough to place it between his lips.

He was an advertising man, he later told me. Pretty big in that field, I gathered. Until he couldn't take it any more, and suffered what was euphemistically called a nervous breakdown in those days.

That was a catchall phrase for just about any kind of mental disturbance that prevented a person from carrying on with normal life. Some of those who broke down pulled out of it themselves, though God only knows how. Most of them had to seek professional help of some sort. Plus a cornucopia of allegedly helpful medications, of course – many with potentially worrisome side effects.

Arthur was definitely one of those who finally sought help: a voluntary patient like myself, not at all eager to get back into the dreaded outside world. Here, despite the occasional inappropriate yell or aberrant response by one or another of the patients, it was more peaceful. A lot more.

As for myself, I'd arrived armed with a referral from an outside psychiatrist. I'd only seen him a couple of times. We spent most of those sessions skimming through newspaper Help Wanted ads. Not because he believed getting yet another job would do me any good. He just urged me to try and get one so I might have medical insurance, which could pay for hospitalization. (Plenty of employers included insurance coverage in those days.) I knew that wasn't possible anymore, and told him so.

As an alternative, he recommended going to a new mental hospital, not far from downtown Chicago. Because it was a public, not private, facility, I might be accepted without having to pay. His parting thought was a prediction that I would be given shock treatments. Thankfully, the hospital's staff decided otherwise.

Following a brief interview and evaluation by an in-house psychiatrist, I was admitted on the spot. That interviewing psychiatrist became my doctor not only during my hospital stay, but for several years afterward.

After being shown to my room, I was told to go back to the dayroom as soon as I settled in, to join the other patients. Most rooms on this floor were doubles, so I would have a roommate. Not only had I never resided in a group setting of any kind, I had never had a roommate. Yet another reason to be uneasy on that first day. Only a few highly troubled folks got a single room, including one man in his twenties who was catatonic.

I quickly realized that the dayroom, across the hall from the nurse's station, was the center of daily life on the ninth floor. Unless they had specific activities or appointments elsewhere, patients were encouraged to make use of the couches and comfortable chairs. Socialization was a basic principle of treatment plans. That was fine for the more extroverted residents, but for shy introverts like myself, being required to chat and discuss with persons previously unknown to me was not a helpful remedy for my mental issues. Meeting people and coping had always been a stressful endeavor.

Loners were intensively discouraged throughout. Staying in your room during the day was forbidden unless you were ill or had a valid excuse for electing solitude over interaction.

Before long, though, even some of the most asocial patients often made friends with one or two others, who were already acquainted with a few people, allowing cliques to form. To my surprise, I soon found myself belonging to one, made up of both men and women. The dining area occupied one end of the dayroom and, as is typical in such situations, group members nearly always sat together.

Talk among the patients seldom got into world events, focused instead on pragmatic issues related to ninth-floor life. A bit of gossip about certain patients turned up, too. So did complaints about specific staff members. No surprise there. Each day was like living in a cocoon, almost wholly separated from the outside world, unconcerned about what was going on out there. That world seemed awfully far away. We had enough to worry about, and deal with, on the ninth floor.

Angry outbursts occurred at times, but that was to be expected, considering the clientele. The ninth floor was generally considered to be a relatively quiet, easier-going place. Violent patients and others subject to troublesome behavior resided on other floors.

In large groups of many sorts, there's often one person who stands out as troublesome. One of them lived on the ninth floor. Rude, crude, ill-mannered, bigoted, angry – not unlike similar folks in the outside world, but hard to avoid here. Can't remember his name, but the ladies gave him a suitable nickname: Gip. Translation: the "backward pig."

Idle hours weren't considered a sound treatment policy for the mentally disturbed, so activities were abundant and encouraged. Once a week, a dance was held in a large activity space on the ground floor. For many, it was an hour or two of convivial pleasure with the opposite sex. For some, dance night was a time of anguish and avoidance, demonstrated on one occasion when a highly troubled young woman asked me to dance with her – and I refused.

Why would I do such a horrible thing? Because her particular form of illness made her rather childlike. Therefore, she stood out among the other patients – which meant I would be in the spotlight, too. The women at my table berated me soundly for my callous behavior. Fortunately, a better person than I agreed to dance with her, which essentially consisted of simply swaying back and forth in time with the music.

Games were popular, even though not everyone liked them, mentally troubled or otherwise. Contests and performances took place now and then. Good for extroverts, bad for those who preferred not to participate, and possibly for those who lost.

Most of us looked forward to movie nights. In addition to an hour or two of escapism, they occasionally served as opportunities for stolen kisses. I'm embarrassed to report that once or twice, I was one of those who took advantage of the darkness.

Not long after my entry into one of the dining-room groups, an awkward element of such residential accommodations came to light: patient-patient romances. Though not exactly common, they were certainly not rare. Mine might never have happened if one member – an 18-year-old girl with a lively nature – asked each of us who they were most attracted to in the group. Well, one member in particular had caught my eye, despite my usual difficulty in meeting and becoming acquainted with women. I could hardly believe that this particular woman pointed to me as her chosen special friend.

Obviously, there were limitations to any budding male-female friendship. The staff wasn't about to allow intimacies to develop among the residents. Especially if someone involved was married or otherwise attached to a non-resident on the outside. In my case, the woman was indeed married – as well as eight years older than I was. So, except for movie night and a quick but passionate kiss when we managed to get onto an elevator alone, our newfound relationship was limited to quiet talks at the end of the ninth-floor corridor.

That relationship was firmly hobbled when our psychiatrist (we shared the same fellow) got wind of our forbidden behavior, warning that it set a bad example, especially for the younger patients. I agreed to steer clear of her, but knew I wouldn't be able to comply for long. Such is the way of illicit pairings, I'm afraid.

Nearly everyone seemed to be on medication. Most likely, several. During my 3.5-month residence, I was given just about every tranquilizer known to mankind – often in heavy doses. Antidepressants, too. Thorazine, Stellazine, Librium, Mellaril, Elavil. Did they help? Not enough to notice, unless the dosage was high enough to make me drowsy.

Though I was psychoneurotic, at the most, I was prescribed some tranks that were normally given to the seriously psychotic. At the time, tranquilizers were comparatively new, and doctors quickly learned to rely on them and prescribe them excessively. That's what I think, anyway.

Did people improve as time passed? Were the anxious, the fearful, getting better?

Many were. Every few days, it seemed, someone on our floor announced that he or she would be leaving shortly.

Traditional psychotherapy, as expected, was a primary part of the recovery process. It works for some fearful people, but not for all. Reaching meaningfully past fears, fantasies, or agitation often winds up being a do-it-yourself venture, at least in part.

One person appeared to improve instantly, for unknown reasons. That young fellow who had a single room walked into the corridor one morning, looking and acting like an entirely different person. No longer silent and trapped within himself, he was suddenly talkative and friendly. For the rest of my time on the ninth floor, his catatonic symptoms never seemed to recur.

Visitors were among the few elements of residential life to look forward to – unless they triggered unwanted thoughts or behavior. In addition to my mother, two or three of my male friends visited me weekly. None of them ever seemed to acknowledge that we were sitting in the small café within a mental institution.

Conversations differed little from those we had regularly during sessions at late-night Chicago restaurants that catered to night owls.

For involuntary patients, in particular, the prospect of escape – whether temporary or permanent – was inevitably an element of quiet chats. My own lady friend planned one, and I wound up helping her carry it out, including recommending a hotel to head for once she reached the outside world.

One day, following a session in the outdoor activity area, she managed to stay behind after the others were on their way back to the ninth floor. How she managed to scale that chain-link fence, topped by barbed wire, remains a mystery. She was a small woman, wearing a long skirt. Evidently, the need to get away exceeded her ability to think about the obstacles involved.

Because I was permitted to have an occasional day in the outside world, shortly after her escape, I met her in that recommended hotel. Shameful, I know.

More than halfway through my residence at the Institute, I considered applying for a short-term, seasonal job as a delivery truck driver, which I'd had a year earlier. If it were available again this year, maybe I'd be able to handle it, helped by the knowledge that it would only be for a couple of weeks. The staff encouraged this choice. So, one day I left the hospital and took a bus to the North Side of Chicago, to look into it. Surprisingly, I was hired.

A day later, I left the Institute carrying a lunch packed by the food service folks and took that same bus to the truck terminal. Three hours later, I was headed back to the hospital again. At some early point on my route, all the mental symptoms leaped back into play. Suddenly, I couldn't go on. I was panicking heavily, just like I'd experienced so many times before, when I had to quit a job – or just walked away, unable even to explain that I was quitting.

Somehow, I managed to drive the truck back to the terminal, quickly tell them I couldn't continue, and with great difficulty ride that bus back to the Institute. Obviously, I was not ready for real life. Not yet. Maybe never. A job I'd been able to handle for three weeks a year before was now proven impossible by lunchtime.

At some point, voluntary patients like myself would start to transition from wanting to remain indefinitely, where life was comparatively safe, to a desire to re-enter the world. Not unlike prisoners plotting (or fantasizing about) getting out. For more than two months, my worry was about being ejected too soon. Now, I began to wonder about the possibility of release. Some of my recently-made friends were already gone, replaced by new patients who didn't appear to be so friendly.

After three months, I felt better than when I'd been admitted and departure was tempting, but I remained hesitant about returning to normal society. All the more so, after that temp-job debacle. Far too much fear and anxiety, tension and obsessions, doubtless still lurked beneath the surface of consciousness. On the whole, though, it seemed like time to go, and the staff agreed.

At the time of my residence, in the early Sixties, the Illinois State Psychiatric Institute was practically brand-new. A showplace of mental health treatment, more like a luxury hotel than the stereotype of a mental institution. Public, too, which meant I was paying nothing.

Who would have guessed it was already antiquated. On the way to that sad state, at any rate. It's gone now. Gone for years, in fact, as outpatient treatment facilities overtook and eradicated the traditional mental hospitals: the better ones, along with the "snake pit" variety. Which showed how much the government appeared to care, in the end, about doing much of anything, the right thing, for the long-term mentally ill. That's how I see it, anyway. No doubt, experts disagree.

29

A Bad Time for Crime

The clock in the barber shop window showed nearly 2:00 a.m. as the girl walked rapidly down the deserted downtown street. Her footsteps echoed loudly in her ears as she raced along, moving as fast as she could comfortably travel on her clumsy platform shoes. This part of the city was no place for a lone woman to be walking at night, and she knew it. And if there had been a cab available, she wouldn't be here at all, but safe at home in her own bed.

She crossed one of the seemingly endless business streets against the traffic light; not a car or person could be seen. As she scurried along the new block, her steps sounded even louder than before. It was then that she realized she was not alone in the street.

Heart suddenly pounding, her breath coming in quick gasps, she tried to walk faster yet, nearly running, not daring to turn around. The extra set of footsteps, matching her own in tempo, louder and faster, became a sickening roar in her head. Finally, she had to give in to impulse and turn to face her pursuer. The last thing she saw was a glimmering flash of steel, a knife, as it hurtled toward her precious body.

The ornate grandfather's clock struck 6:00 p.m. as Henry strolled slowly into the crowded meeting room. He walked with a slight limp, aided by a beautifully-carved cane. Impeccably dressed and immaculately groomed, his bright eyes and contour-trimmed goatee belied his seventy-one years.

As he stepped to the front of the room, edging in behind a desk that stood slightly above the floor like a lectern, he surveyed the group carefully. More than thirty men were seated haphazardly on overstuffed chairs and long couches. They were dressed in a variety of styles, from traditional to the very latest fashions, with a few in jeans and work clothes. Though they varied in age, with a couple of senior citizens who appeared even older than Henry, there were no young men at all; the youngest was at least thirty-five.

Nodding his satisfaction, Henry cleared his throat and rapped on the desk top to gain their attention.

"Gentlemen," he said in a rich baritone, "this meeting of the organization is now in session. I think we all know why we're here, but I'll let George Harvey give us a quick rundown. George?"

A fiftyish man wearing a slightly antiquated vested suit strode to the front and turned toward the audience, a serious expression on his weathered face.

"Thanks, Hank. Last night, a young woman was attacked and murdered down on Olvera Street. She was no one special, and you might not have seen the report in the paper this morning. So it's not this particular crime that brings us here tonight. To put it simply, this is just one more in a long series of killings and almost-killings which we've been faced with in this city during the last few years. And we're here to do something about it.

"It's really a crime," he continued, "what's going on in the street today."

Several of the listeners laughed out loud. One of them, a lanky forty-year-old wearing wrinkled jeans and a work jacket, said, "That's a funny thing to say, coming from one of the best heist men in the business."

George grinned just a bit, tapping his fingers anxiously on the desk as he spoke again. "Not funny at all. No, that's the whole point, there's nothing funny about it. All of us in this room are criminals, that's for sure. And we're some of the best criminals in the country, in my opinion. So we can't be accused of being opposed to crime.

"But lately, the whole idea of crime has taken a disgusting turn.

Instead of a way of making a pretty easy living, which is what it's been for most of us, crime has become a way for some really sick people to take out their sicknesses and hostilities on the rest of the world. The psychopaths and crazies have practically taken over."

George's face was turning red as he said, "They've taken one of the oldest occupations in the world, one that's been almost respectable in a way, and turned it into something dirty. And I don't mean to be cute when I say that.

"You take this killing last night. Some of us here have wasted people, that's true. But a young girl walking on a dark street? A stranger? And for no apparent reason? She couldn't have had more than two or three dollars on her.

"And that beating of the old guy on Hibbard last week. That was for money, so it might be understandable. But did they have to hit him with a chain and nearly kill him? Hit him 10 or 12 times at that, so he'll be in the hospital for weeks. Would you have done that, Billy, in your jackrolling days?"

Little Billy Weston shook his head as he answered. "Not me. Just take the money and run, that was my motto. One way or another, that's pretty much how all of us have lived our lives. We're no saints, but we never hurt anyone without a good reason. I get just as sick when I hear about these goings-on as you do, George."

"I quite agree." a quiet voice stated flatly. This was Jack Winterpoole, a thin, neatly-dressed sexagenarian who had spent his working life as a house burglar. "I never harmed anyone in my life. When someone would wake up and find me in their bedroom, I might have threatened a little. But never actually did anything. Don't think I ever would have, even if someone had tried to interfere. I never carried a weapon, you know."

"I think we all agree, then," George proclaimed from his post at the front, "that these boys have given crime a bad name. Every time one of them hits somebody over the head for a couple of dollars, it makes it tough for all of us. The public is getting awfully riled up about all the street crime that's going on, and in the end it's us, the old-fashioned kind of criminals, who suffer. As some of you know, who've been busted lately."

Murmurs of agreement could be heard throughout the room, as heads nodded and a couple of recently-released ex-cons stared down at the floor.

"The question, then, is what can we do about it. Or do we turn in our lockpicks and blowtorches and go straight?"

The murmurs were even more pronounced after this last statement. It was clear that such a course of action would not meet with approval from this audience.

George smiled. "I thought not. Well, some of us have hit upon a solution. Not a perfect solution, but a beginning. After all, the problem has been getting worse for quite a while now, so we can't expect overnight miracles.

"This might seem like a weird suggestion to some of you, but think about it before you vote on the proposal. To put it bluntly, we are planning to form a vigilante group for this city."

It was like an electric shock. Those few men in the back who weren't paying close attention were suddenly jolted upright. The looks on faces ranged from bewildered to angry.

"What do you mean, George?" Billy Weston asked, standing up so suddenly that his cigarette fell out of his mouth. "We're all going to turn pigeon? Turn in these creeps to the Law? Or just kill 'em like that Bronson guy in the movies? I mean, they're the scum, sure, but still ...."

"Like I said, Billy," George responded, "think about it before you get yourself all excited. No, we don't intend to turn anyone in. The way the courts are nowadays, they get off most of the time anyhow. Guys like us get the hard time, but the hit-on-the-head boys cop pleas and get that little slap on the wrist, or a couple of months in a nice school for boys. We all know that. It's obvious that the law either can't or won't do anything about these sicko amateurs, so it's up to us 'pros' to do the job. But we're not going to go and shoot them down in the street, either; that would make us as rotten as they are.

"Our idea is to give them a fair trial for their crimes, but without the nonessentials. We'll even have a kind of judge, and all of us will act as a jury. Between us, we'll decide what should be done with each guy we nab.

"We're all aware that those Supreme Court decisions – Miranda and all that – are a good thing, giving everyone their rights. But the whole process has gotten perverted, and the scum gets off on what amounts to technicalities. It's gone way too far, everyone knows it has.

"Well, we'll be giving those boys their basic rights all right, but in a sensible way. Nobody is going to be railroaded here, no deals with lawyers like in the courts. Just straight justice, given equally and without mercy to the rats who don't deserve any."

"It's like in the movies, a court of crooks." It was Billy again, smiling now.

"Almost. But a lot more effective. The details will be worked out later, but we want to take a quick vote now, to see if your thinking is in line with ours. Incidentally, the credit for this idea goes to Jack Winterpoole. He's not as senile as he looks."

The mood had changed from gloom to good humor by the time the roll call was completed.

Neon signs were everywhere, beckoning the unwary and the jaded into every sort of pleasure palace:

THE HOT ONE MASSAGE PARLOR
ERNIE'S XXXX-RATED READING ROOM
BLACK HOLE BAR – LIVE NUDE ENTERTAINMENT

The two well-dressed, portly men strolling along the edge of the curb looked as though they had sampled each business enterprise, and not found them lacking in satisfaction.

"What a night." the taller man sighed. "Those girls ...."

"Can't take it, huh?" leered his companion, with just a touch of drunken slur in his speech. "Maybe you'd rather be back home with Betty."

"Arrgghh! Cold, hard Betty? After that dark little girl with the big body? You kidding? I'm just looking forward to tomorrow night. More of the same for me, I'll tell you."

"One more night, Fred, then it's back to business."

Neither spoke again as they approached the end of the Strip area, where gaudy neon gave way to the dimly-lit, modest homes of the city's permanent residents. Few of them ever bothered to enter the adjoining entertainment area; that was for the tourists. And the muggers.

As the men crossed the dark alleyway, heading for their car, a voice startled them into sudden alertness.

"Where you goin', man? Where's my money?"

Fred's hands began to sweat as he turned to face the threatening voice. Relaxation came as suddenly as the terror when he recognized the man by his shoulder-length blond hair.

"Aw, it's just the guy who introduced us to those Oriental girls. Boy, they were really something; everything you said."

His words ceased in an instant as a hand slapped him across the face, knocking him back against a parked car.

"You didn't pay me for that chick, man. Let's have it."

Fred cringed in pain from the blow, gingerly touching his cheek. "What do you mean? You said she was a friend of yours. You didn't say anything about money. And I gave her twenty dollars anyway, I don't owe you anything."

"Twenty bucks?" the intruder scoffed. "That chick's worth a hundred. And she says you got a lot more than a hundred in that fat poke of yours. So hand it over and you can run home to mama."

The hand struck again, sending Fred against a lamp post. His friend stood transfixed, unbelieving, trying to look the other way.

"Hey Gene." called the assaulter, "this dude don't want to pay up. What do we do with dudes that don't pay up?"

His partner, silent until now in the shadows against the wall, giggled. "We does away with 'em. With this here steel. And it's my turn to do the doing."

A flash of metal leaped to his hand and he ambled slowly out of the shadows into the scene of the confrontation.

"I'll give you the money." Fred screamed. "Let us go, and you can have it all. I don't need it. Take it all."

"Too late now, man." the giggling Gene smirked. "Too late. Looks like you two boys is done for." The knife was pointed at Fred's stomach, its wielder quiet now as he slowly began to press it into the flabby flesh.

"No!" Fred moaned. "Please, please ...."

A dull thump was heard, and the assassin suddenly slumped to the ground. Another thump.

Fred looked up, dazed, at two unfamiliar figures. Both of his attackers were lying on the ground, silent. His friend was still standing immobile, seemingly unaware of what was happening.

A harsh, yet quiet voice said, "Get out of here, you two. We'll take care of this."

Fred could barely make out the features of the newcomers, who stood back away from the glare of the streetlight. There were two of them, dark and motionless.

"Are you cops?" Fred asked. "Those guys were trying to kill us."

"Just get out of here now," the voice requested again.

"But I'm bleeding," Fred protested. The knife had actually penetrated the skin of his abdomen, and a trickle of blood was running down his pants.

"Then go to a doctor. But get out of this area. Be thankful you're alive."

Fred turned to his companion, grabbed him by the arm and pulled him along, away from the scene. After they had gone, the newcomers bent down and began to drag the two crumpled bodies into the alley.

The meeting room was quiet, somber, almost dignified. Henry was sitting at his familiar desk, holding a small gavel in his hand. Two youngish men were tied to straight-backed wooden chairs with heavy rope, one man on each side of the desk.

"This session will come to order," Henry proclaimed, tapping his gavel as he spoke. "We have three cases to be heard tonight, so let's get on with it."

George Harvey stepped up to the desk, followed closely by Billy Weston. "I'll be prosecuting these cases," George explained, "and Billy will be defending. Henry will act as the judge.

"The first case is Gene Brady and Phil Perkins. Mugging two men in the entertainment district, after providing them with the services of some young ladies. Attempted mugging, I should add, and attempted murder, too. Two of our guys put the sap to them before they could finish their work."

He went on to relate the facts in the case, which were then corroborated by the two spectators who had actually watched Gene and Phil in the act and brought them in.

"Both you and Will saw the whole thing, then?" George asked. "There's no doubt as to their identity, or the facts I've described?"

"None at all," answered Adam Quince, one of the men who had stood in the shadows watching the crime take place. "Will and I slugged them just in time; that knife was already on its way into the victim's gut. And we dragged these two guys away from the scene and brought them here, so there's no doubt that they're the ones."

Henry, the judge in the case, cleared his throat. "Any comment from the defense?"

Billy Weston turned to the two defendants, who had been sitting silently through the recitation of the evening's events, their faces sometimes sullen, sometimes sneering.

"Yeah, I got a comment," replied the blond assailant. "What do you old jerks think you're doing, anyway? You can't pull this kind of stuff."

"Just answer one question." George said. "Do you deny the facts in the case? Do you deny that you assaulted and tried to kill two men on Higgins Street earlier this evening?"

"I ain't talking" was the reply. "None of us is talking."

"Well, men." the judge declared. "That's their right, they don't have to talk if they don't want to. They don't have to incriminate themselves. Is that your answer, you two?"

"Yeah," sneered the blond. "No incriminatin'."

"Then the jury's duty should be easy," stated the judge. "No need for all the formalities, retiring to a jury room and all that nonsense. And I don't think we need to hear any more from the defendants or their, ah, lawyer. The facts seem quite clear, that these two men did assault two pedestrians earlier tonight and demand money from them. And further, that they attempted to stab one of them to death.

"Remember, this is no kangaroo court. We offered these two an opportunity to present their case. The fact that they chose not to permit Billy to offer any opposing facts is their decision, their problem. If no one has any further objections, then, I'll turn the case over to the jury, which is all of us. Okay with you, Billy?"

"Definitely." Billy answered. "As far as I'm concerned, they've been given their chance for a fair hearing. And I know a little about trials myself. Just went through one a couple of months ago."

George laughed out loud. "And you got off too, Billy."

"That I did. And to tell you the truth, I shouldn't have, I was guilty as hell. But the cops had flubbed the case and they had to let me off. Anyway, this court might not be as fancy as the ones downtown, but I don't think these guys have any complaint coming."

"All right then." the judge said, leaning back in his chair. "We'll take a secret vote, and the majority rules here."

The group required only a few minutes to complete its vote.

"Unanimous." declared the judge after counting the slips of paper. "Guilty as charged, no recommendation for mercy.

"Now let's get to the next cases. We'll have the sentencing after we hear all of them."

The following case was a particularly brutal rape, observed by two old-time armed robbers who had been patrolling the slum area of the city. A 19-year-old girl had been assaulted at knifepoint, stabbed and molested. The observers had heard her cries for help but had been too far away to stop the crime, arriving on the scene when the attacker was in the midst of his vicious act.

"We couldn't get there in time." one of them testified, a tear running down his face. "But as we were running up we could hear this creep laughing as he did it to her, sticking at her with that knife as he, uh, you know. ..."

This defendant attempted to deny his crime, but the blood on his jacket and the unwavering testimony of his apprehenders convinced the jury otherwise.

"Guilty," ruled the judge again. "No mercy. The defendant shows no remorse for his filthy crime, and there's no evidence of mental disturbance."

George, the prosecutor, stood up. "It's obvious that he knew perfectly well what he was doing and, as far as I'm concerned, he should get the most severe penalty. One more thing. I didn't mention this during the testimony so it wouldn't prejudice your decision, but this young fellow has been assaulting ladies for a long time. He's been in court at least four or five times for his efforts, but got off every time because he's so young and innocent-looking. I called a policeman friend of mine and he told me all about this man, so you can be pleased with your guilty verdict.

"No telling how many young girls will be safer with him out of the way."

The final case was different. A 30-year-old man had been

brought in after a pair of observers had seen him hit an older man with a bottle, then run away.

The defendant was frightened, but told his story with what seemed to be total sincerity.

"This might sound crazy," he admitted, "but that old guy was trying to rob me: Not the other way around. We were both sitting on the curb, drinking wine. I'd just met him an hour or two before, didn't know anything about him. When you're on the bum, you pick up companions wherever they happen to be.

"Anyway, I was getting pretty drunk, even drunker than usual, and I suddenly felt this guy's hand in my pocket. Well, I may look pretty much down-and-out right now, but I had at least twenty bucks in that pocket from a day-labor job I had last week. And I wasn't going to let it go without a fight, drunk or not.

"I don't know exactly what happened, but we were struggling and I had the bottle in my hand, so I guess I hit him on the head with it. Then I didn't know what to do, so I just up and ran. Until I got hit on the head myself. That's the truth, I swear: I've never been a thief. A bum, yes, but not a thief."

He was sober now, and sat with his head facing the floor as he spoke. His words had a sobering effect on the audience as well, and they brought in an almost-unanimous "not guilty" verdict.

Before letting him go, the judge cautioned him: "It would be best if you don't tell anyone exactly what happened to you here. I'm sure you understand that we are most effective when we operate as a kind of secret organization."

"No, no, I won't say a word. I just want to get away."

After the innocent bottle-wielder had been escorted outside, Billy Weston asked: "Was that wise, Henry? Wouldn't it be better if the word got out about what we're doing? So the creeps will think twice about working the street?"

Judge Henry smiled menacingly. "They'll find out, all right. That young man will talk, no matter what he says now. Some of the street people will believe him, some won't. But it won't matter, we have another way of spreading the word. So let's get on with the sentencing."

The "convicted" rapist was brought up to the desk first. He said nothing, but displayed a good deal more fear than he had shown during his hearing.

Henry pondered a minute before speaking. "Deciding on an appropriate sentence is not an easy matter. Obviously, we can't send anyone to prison, and wouldn't want to even if we could. And we don't want to sink down to the level of the street criminals and simply kill them. Though we have several members here who would be happy to do exactly that. They have the experience, too.

"No, I think an entirely different approach is needed, kind of an 'eye for an eye' method, the only kind that might do some good."

He turned to one of the spectators. "Jack, do you still see that guy who beat the molestation rap a few months ago? The one who likes young men?"

"Occasionally," was the answer. "He's a disgusting person, but he plays a fine game of pinochle."

"Good," said the judge. "Get ahold of him and tell him we have a little job for him. I imagine he wouldn't mind an opportunity to befriend a nice-looking young fellow like this one."

"He'd love it. Especially if one or two of us went along, to be sure this gentleman wouldn't resist Charlie's advances."

The judge smiled grimly. "The sentence of this court is that, for your crime of raping and stabbing a young girl, you yourself will be, uh, dealt with by a certain well-known deviant. And I understand this Charlie knows a few tricks that would surprise the Marquis de Sade. I'm sure he'll have some special plans in mind, just for you.

"It might happen in your home, or maybe on the street. You'll never know when. But we'll find you, Charlie will find you, you can count on that. As often as Charlie is in the mood, or until we decide you might be ready to change your ways. Let him go now."

The pair of muggers came to the desk next, still sneering and diffident.

"As for you two," the judge continued, "for your crime of assault and attempted robbery and murder, you will have your status changed from perpetrator to victim. In this room are at least a half-dozen professional thugs, mostly retired now, but their skills make you two look like beginners. Several of them are experts with the brass knuckles and other interesting instruments, great at dealing with squealers and other undesirable characters. They'll especially enjoy practicing their old talents on both of you.

"You can go now, but you had better be watching behind you from now on. Our men will be out on the street watching you, ready to attack you whenever they feel like it, or whenever they think you might have a few dollars on you. Believe me, you won't be able to resist; they're pros, not knock-on-the-head creeps like you. What they want, they'll take. And if they suspect that you've been getting your money by more muggings or other unpleasant activities, they'll be ten times as tough on you. So if you value your good looks, you might consider earning your money at a straight job."

Henry leaned back in his chair as the muggers were being led out the door. "Of course, whatever you men take off those two in cash will be turned in to our operating fund. Who knows, if we get a few more cases like this, we might be able to make a profit with this court."

30

Sunday Morning Blues

Five a.m. No one else on the street. Frank walked slowly, aimlessly, averting his eyes from each streetlight. Years had passed since he'd had any place to go.

He sifted through the change in his pocket. Ninety-two cents. Hardly enough for a flop, but okay for a breakfast at Tony's. Or a couple of shots. Frank knew he would choose the latter. He would be needing, craving them soon.

Seven long, painful hours to wait until the taverns opened. Damn Sunday mornings! Keeping all the bars closed so the family fools wouldn't be tempted on their way to church. If only he'd had enough for a bottle before they shut the doors.

Looking down an alley, he saw a group of three, huddled together, passing around a pint of muscatel. He hesitated for a moment, recognizing one of the rumpled men, then picked up his pace, turning his head toward the street.

No, he wouldn't join them. That was going too low. Whiskey and beer, yes, but not that rotten wine. Frank still placed a small value on his intestinal system. Not all that much, considering the brands of whiskey he drank, but enough to keep away from the raunchy sweetness of port and muscatel.

With the dehydration rising in his mouth now, he suddenly decided to splurge and spend a fourth of his fortune on coffee. Maybe he would see someone he knew, borrow a dollar or even a half, giving him enough to get by nicely until Monday. Then down to Ready-Worker early in the morning. With luck, he might get in a full eight hours of work. That would last him the week, if he got a few breaks and found a free place to sleep.

On most of his recent visits to the agency, though, the answer had been the same: "Nothing today." He couldn't even recall the last time he'd put in a full day. Even though he hated the thought of begging, it was tempting after a lengthy series of rejections for even the daily-pay jobs.

A couple of times he had succumbed, given it a try, following the lead of some experienced street beggars he'd run into. But he'd never managed to take in more than a dollar or two after a whole day – an endless, soul-destroying day – working the sidewalks. And had to drink up the earnings immediately to get the taste of humiliation out of his mind. Asking friends, acquaintances for coins was one thing; strangers quite another.

The cafeteria was warm, a welcome relief from the chilly early morning air. Frank ordered his coffee, heavy on cream, and sat at a table next to the window to load it with sugar. From there he could watch the street, see if anyone he knew came by. Someone to help him out with a little loan. Only till Monday. Or point him toward some kind of job, anything, a chance to get from this day, this hour, to the next.

He hated the thought of working out of that lousy agency, though. The damned employers they sent you to were so supercilious. And the permanent employees were worse, believing themselves miles above the daily-pay men. Fools. They think they're really living because they have a steady job. And condemn those who can't, or won't, live that way.

The coffee was hot, good. It took the dry, rancid whiskey taste from Frank's mouth. It seemed like he would never get used to the taste of whiskey. But he had to have the stuff. To remember. To forget. To live.

Frank was arrested in his somber thoughts by the appearance of the girl. She entered the cafeteria, looked around, then stepped to the counter.

Strangely attractive even in her torn and fading blue wool coat, white cotton socks and plastic loafers, one sole flapping with each step, she turned several male heads in her wake. Her red hair shone as a smoky yet brilliant flame, a forceful beacon overseeing the grayness of the room and its occupants, as she ran a gritty hand through the tangled strands. Purplish lipstick looked odd on her unlined, youthful face, dirt-spotted on cheeks and forehead, as though the mouth belonged to someone else.

It had been some time since Frank had thought much about women. Though he had been married to Alice for nearly ten years before hitting bottom, she seldom entered his mind for more than a fleeting moment. Most of his cronies took on one of the many fleabags on the street when the need became overwhelming, but Frank would not stoop to that. Better to abstain entirely than take a chance on catching heaven-knows-what from a two-buck whore.

Besides, the whiskey blunted those urges quite nicely, thank you.

Watching the girl as she picked up and paid for a coffee, rummaging through a raggedy coin purse to find the correct sum, Frank found himself almost wishing she would come and sit at his table. But that could never happen. What woman, except one of the wine-soaked, varicose-veined, flabby one-time women of the street would ever choose to come his way. For he really looked the part of the bum he was, with his week's growth of stubble, unruly and greasy long hair, clothes last washed and mended weeks, months earlier.

His once-white shirt, now the color of slightly-rusted steel, boasted only two buttons. Trousers torn down one leg, frayed at the cuffs, grease-spotted in an amorphous pattern of browns and grays to brighten the indiscernible color of the original, now-faded fabric.

Last month's newspaper in his shoes, remnants of last week's skimpy meals still stuck in his teeth, last night's cheap bourbon clogging his brain. No. It would be a good long while before Frank would be accepted by anyone, especially a young female, as a nearly-human being.

But she was walking toward his table. Not even hesitating in her step, gazing right into his eyes for a moment. Instantly, Frank became flushed, trembling, embarrassed now to be seen by her in this condition, up close. There would be no getting away.

She was actually going to sit with him.

No words were spoken as she did so. She sat quietly, sipping at her hot coffee, seemingly enjoying its fragrance for what seemed an eternity before she spoke.

"Lousy Sunday mornings," she said, an initial frown turning into a slight smile. A pretty smile, but with mouth closed, as though she were reluctant to show her teeth.

Frank grinned shyly, cleared his throat. "Just what I was thinking. Rough night."

"Rough world. Rough life. All the nights are the same." Her voice was softer than her words, with a trace of huskiness that seemed out of place.

"I haven't seen you in the neighborhood before."

She sighed, "Haven't been here long. Just made it in from St. Louis the other day."

"St. Louis, there's a dead town," Frank reminisced. It had been years since he'd been there. Or anywhere, for that matter. And he didn't really remember, couldn't separate the exciting places from the duds. He had been young then, seeking adventure, youngman thrills. That was before he'd discovered how much easier it was, how strangely comfortable, to remain oblivious.

"It's not a bad place if you know where to go."

"That's true anywhere," Frank nodded. "Frisco, L.A., New York. They're all the same when you know the ropes."

"Yeah," she agreed, glancing up at the ceiling, "doesn't matter much where you are, I guess."

She looked directly at Frank for a moment, then shifted her eyes slightly to the side. "Say, you don't happen to have a little change to spare? About took my last coin for this cup of black."

"Afraid not. I'm down to zero this time. Sorry."

"Don't be. No problem. I'll find some straight dude this afternoon, get enough for three, four squares anyway. You got a pad?"

"Bounced out three days ago. You?"

"No, man," she replied. "And I am yearning for a soft Sealy for my aching back. I'll tell you, I'm going to make sure of the quality of the mattress before I take on anybody today. Listen, I have to clean up a little. There a ladies' john here?"

"Straight back, to the right," Frank directed, pointing a quivering finger toward the rear of the cafeteria.

The girl drank down the last of her coffee and walked quickly to the back, leaving Frank alone again with his thoughts. Such a pretty girl. Looking so beat, dragged out. But like she hadn't been in the life for very long, like fresh-scrubbed girlhood must be a recent memory.

God, he thought, she couldn't be more than twenty. Maybe less. But everyone has his problems, and Frank had more than his share. Work problems, eat problems, drink problems, what-comes-tomorrow problems. He had no time, no taste, to be concerned with anyone else's troubles.

She did intrigue him, though. So young, more like a college co-ed than a cheap hooker. The life pulls them down from every kind of upbringing, all the social strata. It drags down the unemployed dishwasher to drink sneaky pete with the millionaire's scion. The ex-debutante to compete with the daughter of welfare, each vying to sell her body to a passing ugly, disheveled, perverted half-man for the price of a rotten meal. Or a drink, a quick shot, a snort.

Some stay for a few months, a few years; most are resigned to a lifetime in the life.

All classes are represented down here. All drink together. All sleep together. Join shaky hands to put up a feeble resistance to society's demands. Join bodies to comfort one another when the pain is too great, reality too pressing.

There is nothing a man cannot do in this free society if he sets his mind to it, including refusing to do anything. He may be scorned, abused, pitied. Still he fights for his shabby slice of existence, sees up from the bottom of the well, cannot look down any farther, knows and sees life as it has shattered its incomplete recipients.

The neighborhoods are fast disappearing, victims of the wrecker's ball, the urban planners. The people, the walking victims, are still here. Spread out now, more than they used to be, but still visible below the surface of the unswept streets. Buildings may go, but Skid Row is always left behind, nearby.

The Sunday dawn crowd now nearly filled the cafeteria, a popular resting place. Groups of four and five alkies, sharing a single doughnut or order of toast, dropping their nickels and pennies into a common wine fund. A few junkies in the back, far away from the wide grimy window with its smearily-painted announcements of edible bargains – consoling, plotting, conniving, recalling yesterday's fixes.

Prostitute, derelict, day worker, neverworker. Even an occasional descendant of the hoboes of an earlier age, thought to be extinct but still traveling the country much as his predecessors had done. And often enough a few students, sociology majors, sit taking notes in a corner, laughing among themselves, pointing well-trimmed fingernails, despised by all. So high and mighty in their Brooks Brothers vested suits, sighting down at the unwashed, unshaved, unalive.

Frank couldn't keep the girl from his mind. He imagined her lying at his side in a massive bed, covered with sparkling white, soft, fluffy sheets, repeating – and meaning – those near-forgotten lovewords. To embrace, to comfort; yes, to satisfy.

It was futile, of course, to suppose that any joy could come of it. But fantasies were fun, a rare commodity, and Frank had long ago resolved to always let the chips fall as they chose. One never can know – nor should know – what pleasures, what new misery, tomorrow might bring as an unsought surprise.

He feared his luck was running out now, though. And almost dared to hope that she could somehow renew it.

There were signs, like last week's missed Daily Double. The half-dollar bet could have brought in twenty, and the second horse loses in the photo. Perhaps a change was imminent. Frank decided he would bet the first money he could lay his hands on, on another Double. Numbers two and eight. Always lucky before, they would be again. The luck would return, like in the old days, when he'd made his living on the ponies. For two years. Golf in the morning and the track in the afternoon. Living in the finest hotels, the best entertainment, good food and better drinks.

But his luck had run out then, too. Suddenly, without warning, it had stopped. Never another winner.

The girl returned from the ladies' room looking a lot cleaner, but still so ragged. "What I need, man," she announced eagerly, "is some new clothes. Had to leave everything behind in St. Louis. Find me a good old sugar daddy one of these days and get set up again."

"What are you going to do now? I mean, you can't find anybody at this hour."

"Anything in mind?" she asked with a smile. "If only you had a room. I'm tired as hell. How about you?"

"Slept a couple of hours in a parking lot, but they chased me out too quick."

"For real now, how much gold are you holding?"

Frank counted his fortune again. It didn't take long. "Exactly seventy-one cents. And no more where that came from."

"Don't worry about where the next comes from," she cautioned. "Let's just concentrate on getting set now. Once I score, we'll be sailing easy street."

"What do you mean, we?" Frank wondered. "Where do I fit in?"

"I picked you out, man. It's the way I operate. You take it easy, I make the arrangements, and we both live high while we can. Unless you've got objections."

"No objections," Frank assured her. "No. But I don't get it, how you can expect me to take advantage of you. You don't even know me. Do I look like some kind of pimp?"

"Please, man, no talk like that. It's the way I work, that's all, take it or leave it. What have you got to lose?"

"You're right there." Frank scratched his head, nodded. "Okay, why not? You are on. So what happens now?"

"I'm carrying a fin, my emergency fund; so we have five seventy-one. Where do we find a room for under five? Something pretty nice, though, and no questions asked."

Frank thought for a moment. "The Westmont Hotel. It's out of this crummy section, but we can walk it. Four bucks fifty a day, and the rooms aren't bad. Of course, it's been a while since I've paid that much."

"Well, maybe things are looking up, friend. I feel lucky today. By the way, my name's Sandra. Sandra Wolfe. It's real."

Frank extended his hand, only momentarily ashamed of the grimy fingernails. "A pleasure, Sandra. Frank's mine. Frank Wilson. It's my real name, too."

"Let's make it to this hotel now, man. I need a few hours sleep before I get to work."

They left the restaurant and headed north, away from the section. Away from the stench of unclean bodies, of uncollected garbage, of consumed and unconsumed alcohol. Walking toward a neighborhood of slightly better liquor, a little less stink.

Toward a new life, new hope? Frank entertained the thought with some pleasure. He had been waiting for a change, for a few breaks. Nothing like this had ever happened to him before, but who knows, maybe this could be it.

Probably not, but he would string along anyway. As she had so aptly put it, he had nothing to lose.

The Sunday morning sun was rising over the buildings now, announcing the new day. A day, for most, no different from the one before. For some, another day of sadness. Others, a day of joy, surprise.

A laboring man rises from his bed, caressing his again-pregnant wife, wishing for the day when his big break will come. Maybe today. Until it does, he struggles on, supporting too many mouths. In the church he will pray to God for the strength to keep going. For the courage to remain at his work, accept the abuse, not yielding to the temptations of the street.

The nonworkers, Frank's kinsmen, found their courage not in the cathedral, but in the bottle. Or the needle. Or for some, within their own twisted, ugly minds. The black-overcoated man, wearing false cuffs and collar, taking his pleasure in the squeals and screams of little children as he reveals his atrophied manhood. The ancient vagrant sitting on a curb, caressing a black silk garter, reminder of long-past happy days. The homely, pockmarked old lover, searching for a day's romance with one of his own, one not too fastidious.

For three long years, Frank had dwelled in the midst of the forgotten, the lost, the misunderstood. Those whom the middle-world thought had disappeared with the crumbling buildings. Some hoped to find their peace once again; most were content to live out their futile lives as best they could, away from public view.

Still-dark doorways and corridors housed the men possessed of nothing save the vestiges, the remembrances of days, weeks, years gone by. Without even the price of a bowl of red, a half-warm spot to sleep. Sad times had passed before, would surely return again.

As Frank watched the girl now in the morning's light, he reveled in her tender beauty, unmarred by false adornment. Eyes that have seen too much of life for one so young, so vital. A mouth, lips now devoid of that foolish coloring, waiting in expectation of better days to come, maybe today. Her walk, that of a tiny girl, contrasting with the strong body, the clenched fists, of a desiring and desired woman.

Neither spoke as they reached the periphery of the section, the lowest of the low, and walked on where now and then a tree, a bush, stood against the cracked pavement. To Frank's amazement, Sandra paused to pick a flower, one of the first of the oncoming spring, one of the few city growths to be found in any season. Sniffed it, put it in her hair, for all to see and sense its freshness.

WESTMONT HOTEL
Transients Welcome

A residence scorned by those of the middleworld, but admired and coveted by one up for the day from the dregs.

Frank and Sandra entered the once-shining portal of the now-deteriorating vestibule and strode up to the desk, looking as though they had the world by the tail. And Frank, to his surprise, almost believed it. For a few seconds, at least.

The bored, tired night clerk roused himself from dozing and presented the register for Frank to sign. Long before, he and his predecessors had tried to accept only a better class of clientele. He no longer cared, no longer asked for marriage licenses or stories. Just a name. Any name would do. Accompanied by cash, in advance.

The room was small, with a double bed topped by a colorless spread, a rickety dresser below a cracked mirror. One kitchen chair, plastic seat peeling, spotted with paint, sat facing the dirt-encrusted window, open to a dark airshaft – and to darker encounters past the windows on the opposite wall, should anyone care to raise the ripped yellow shade and observe.

Compared to the resting places Frank was accustomed to, it might have been a castle, a Rockefeller mansion.

They slept until almost noon. Sandra was already up and dressed for action, somehow looking astonishingly neat in the same raggedy outfit, when Frank awoke.

"You can stay here and sleep a little longer," she said gently. "But be out of here by two. I should have something lined up by then."

"How long should I stay out?"

"Three, four hours. Knock when you come back. I should be free by then, but you never can tell."

She kissed him on the forehead. "See you tonight then."

After she had gone, Frank got up quickly. He dressed and left the hotel, walking back toward his regular haunts. What kind of deal is this, he thought. What kind of man does she think I am.

He didn't understand what she wanted from him. Why she would seek out another man, maybe many men, in order to take care of him. Something was wrong. This was screwy, something out of storybooks. She would probably never be back.

Still, what else could he do. What else did he want to do.

He had no money, nowhere to go. It would really be an easy go, all right.

Such a nice, pretty girl, though. He hadn't laid a hand on her during their nap, but her closeness had stirred up a lot of almost-forgotten feelings. Nice feelings.

Frank walked aimlessly again, caring little where he was headed. Paying no attention to time. He had walked clear through the Skid Row section and its adjoining slums before making up his mind. Yes, he would call his brother Eddie.

His younger brother would get him a job. Ed had always gotten him jobs, given him a few dollars – along with the usual lecture about how he was pissing away his life.

But could he do it? During these past three years, he had never worked at anything for more than a week. Seldom that long. What was he capable of anyway? He couldn't go back to the office, the white collar. Not after what he had been through.

What difference did it make, though, what he did, what kind of job he could get. As long as he had a reason to start again, it didn't matter.

He caught himself. What reason, he thought. My God, you'd think I was some kind of schoolkid in the middle of an infatuation. What is she to me? Some little hustler I've known for a few hours.

But it didn't seem to matter. Frank felt a change in his bones. So strange. He really wanted to be a part of the world again. Maybe he couldn't do it, but he would give it a try. No matter what the reason.

Stepping into an outdoor phone booth, avoiding the clutter of broken glass and fast-food wrappers on its floor, he glanced at a clock across the crowd-infested street. Almost three. He'd been walking for nearly three hours. He inserted a dime in the slot and dialed the number he never quite forgot, even in the bleary haze of alcoholic oblivion.

"Hello, Ed? Frank. Your brother Frank. ... Yeah, it's been a long time. Listen, I'm looking for a job, can you help me out? ... I'm serious this time, really. ... Never mind why, I mean it. ... Tomorrow? Right. Thanks, Ed, I really appreciate it. You won't be sorry. So long."

Frank relaxed now. It was all set. He would be able to start on the loading dock at Ed's company on Tuesday. But a damned interview tomorrow, and him looking like a bum. No matter. He could go to Ed's tonight, or better yet in the morning after Ed had left; talk to Betty, wash up, borrow one of Ed's old suits. Betty wouldn't hassle him, make him feel like a beggar.

So many people were on the streets now. Going somewhere. All the working stiffs. Still, maybe they had reason.

Hundreds of children were playing in the park, ignoring the litter. On the slide, the swings, the teeter-totter. And off by themselves, small groups engaged in games unknown to any grownup.

Frank had always wanted, enjoyed children. Perhaps. ...

Within an hour he was back at the hotel, in front of the door. He wondered if a man was in the room. Reaching for the doorknob, key in hand, he stopped, turned abruptly, walked down the stairs again. No. She was no good. He was no good.

Frank sat on the bottom step, head in hands. The day clerk was dozing just as peacefully as the night clerk had been.

Thinking over the day's events, he pictured Sandra's slim, vibrant body – unseen but wildly imagined – recalled her tender kiss. Could it work out? In only a few hours she had caused him to want to do something, to take a positive step. What could she do for him in a few days? More important, he knew, or at least felt, he could do something for her.

Frank walked up the stairs a second time, more confident now. Banging on the door, he stood, feet apart, hands on hips.

When she opened it, he pushed past her, not saying a word. A fat man lay on the bed, clad only in boxer shorts.

"Get out!" Frank screamed, handing the man his pants.

"Hey, what the hell," was the reply, but no one came to the man's aid. "Listen, I give her ten bucks."

"Give it back, Sandra."

She didn't move.

"Give it back, I said." Frank's fists were clenched, his face red with rage.

Sandra slowly paced to the dresser, extracted a single bill from a drawer. Frank grabbed it and shoved it at the man, who was hurriedly putting on his coat.

"Out! Out!" Frank pushed him, sending him stumbling out the door, shoes in hand, and slammed it shut.

They stared at each other for several moments. Then Sandra turned away slowly, nonchalantly wrapping her partly-exposed body in her coat.

"What's with you, man? What did you go and do that for?"

"You don't have to give yourself away any more," Frank answered quietly.

She laughed abruptly, with a snort. "Give away? That's not what I had in mind, fool. Anyway, maybe I like it. Ever think of that?"

"Do you?"

"No, not all that much. But it's okay for now, it's no fate worse than death, you know. So if you think I'm going to fall down on my knees, bawl like a baby thanking you for taking me away from all this, you're nuts. No sir."

"But I only – "

"Listen," she interrupted angrily, "you come up with this lovey-dovey business on your own, you don't ask me what I want. And I'm not ready to play house with you or anybody. I just like having a guy around, that's all; a guy who won't beat me up or make trouble, who's a few laughs, a little fun sometimes.

"You seem like a nice enough guy, I'd like to hang with you for a while, see what happens, but you're no kind of white knight, buddy, rescuing some princess. I don't need you or anybody else to take care of me."

Frank was stunned, listening solemnly while sitting on the tip-edge of the bed, staring in disbelief. She was right, of course. He'd been thinking only of his own changes, assuming she'd follow along eagerly, thinking every woman, even a hustler, really wanted a man all the way.

He tried hard to hold back the urge toward self-pity, from being told he wasn't a knight in shining armor. And that was exactly what he'd expected, that she would see him as some kind of crazy saint out of the gutter. Christ, a couple of hours ago he was just another bum, now he's seeing himself as a saint.

Sandra looked directly at him, a softening evident in her mouth and face, fumbling at her coat collar. "I mean, I don't want to holler, I don't know, maybe it might even work out into some kind of regular twosome, you know? But for now, it's take it or leave it. All that matters is now."

He took a deep breath, not knowing whether to laugh or cry. Good God, this is the kind of offer men dream about, but hardly anyone ever gets even once. And you're about to turn it down because of some Sunday School notion that a real man doesn't live off a woman, never mind asking her what she thinks.

"Sure. Sure thing," Frank said gently. "We'll just see what happens. Listen, I've got something going tomorrow, I'll probably have a little money. A job."

"Don't matter. You want a job, get one. If you don't, forget it. I can make plenty when I get going. No problem."

"Well, too bad I shoved that ten bucks out the door so fast. Because I'm hungry." And he was, not having eaten since early morning, and only a donut at that.

"Yeah, me too," she said, standing and stretching. "Tired too. Anyway, finding another trick on Sunday night isn't so easy."

"Well, we've got the room until morning. That's a start. Tomorrow we can eat, but today – "

Sandra laughed, letting her coat fall away. "Sure, why not. I guess we can figure out a way to pass the time until then."

31

Our Biggest Job Yet

Traffic was heavy in the downtown area as he crossed the wide boulevard. It was almost noon, and the workers were beginning to pour into the streets from the myriad of office buildings.

He stretched his neck skyward, toward the peak of the gleaming new skyscraper, gradually moving his eyes down to the giant nameplate – Imperial Business Equipment, Inc. Several people glanced at him as he made his way through the revolving door, into the crowded lobby.

His suit was a conservative blue pin-stripe, in excellent press but a bit old-fashioned against the current vogue of narrow-trousered, cuffless models. He was not old, yet not young, and his full beard lent a vague air of authority, or perhaps gentle non-conformity. But the office employees passed by without a second glance, hurrying out to their lunches.

The elevator zoomed upward, each occupant staring stonily ahead. He stepped off on the 17th floor, going directly to the single, plainly marked door:

Alfred Brown
Vice President
Customer Service

Entering quickly, he set down his briefcase and handed a card to the receptionist.

"Oh, yes," she said. "Mr. Brown is expecting you." She snapped on the intercom. "Mr. J. Christ to see you, sir."

After a short pause, a voice responded. "Send him right in, Miss Alexis."

Miss Alexis smiled and pointed to the walnut-paneled door. "Right through this door, Mr. Christ."

He picked up his briefcase and walked in. The suite was huge, with floor-to-ceiling windows overlooking the traffic and offices below. One wall was lined with photographs of the company's data processing equipment in use. He glanced at the photos, then turned to Mr. Brown, who looked up and rose quickly, extending his hand.

"Mr. Christ, come in. You don't know what a pleasure it is for me to meet you."

"My pleasure, Mr. Brown. I was admiring your office. The view is superb."

"Isn't it, though," Brown said, smiling broadly. "I noticed you were looking at the pictures of our machines, too. You know, we have installations in almost every country in the world. Afghanistan to Zanzibar, as we say."

Mr. Christ smiled courteously. "I have heard, Mr. Brown. I must say I chose your organization because it is probably the only one that could even approach our problem."

Mr. Brown pulled out a chair for his visitor and sat down himself behind the expansive oak desk.

"Yes, I think we can handle it," he said. "Certainly be a big job, though. The biggest we've had, by all means. But we're glad to have a crack at it. You can imagine the prestige this will give us if we succeed. The other firms might just as well fold up."

Mr. Christ frowned. "Well, I don't believe I would like to see that."

"Oh, just a figure of speech," Brown interrupted. We realize full well your position, sir. It's just that your account will be a real feather in our cap."

"I see. Well, can we get down to business, then. I have here the general outline of our problems; and, of course, our contract. We will have to come to some mutual understanding."

"Of course," Brown said, his smile wider than before. "Now let's take a little look at it. You gave me a pretty rough idea over the phone."

"Yes, Mr. Brown. Well, in short, the progress humanity has made in the past hundred years .... Oh, Mr. Brown, you are familiar with our operation. ...."

"Oh, certainly," Brown laughed. "In a very general way, of course. Your operations aren't exactly in the public eye."

"True, but just so you can realize the scope of the situation. We're really quite like any ordinary nation, you know. You do handle the accounts of entire governments, do you not?"

"Yes, indeed," Brown replied, taking a cigar from the gold box on his desk. Our machines are handling everything from Cold War strategy to family planning for the biggest nations in the world. *This* world."

"Very good, Mr. Brown. Our problems are much the same, but on a far larger scale, of course. In short, technological progress has made each mortal endeavor so complex that we are having a terrible time keeping things in order. With all the new developments that have been put into effect, any course we plan may be made obsolete overnight.

"Simply put, our unworldly presence has not kept pace with the startling leaps ahead in technology. Especially with your digital world, your computing devices. We have found it increasingly difficult to keep track of it all, much less devise tactics to smooth out the worst of the world's transgressions. As incomprehensible as it sounds, we are compelled to seek assistance from the ranks of the technologists, the mortal experts.

"I am afraid you would find our present strategical methods quite primitive. They worked so well for thousands of years, but now ...."

His voice trailed off, as if from exhaustion. He slowly rose and walked to the bar, pouring a glass of water from the decanter.

"You must excuse me, Mr. Brown. I have been working so much overtime trying to keep conditions in hand, much less searching for solutions. Even we have a breaking point, you know."

"Oh, I can understand that," Brown said, looking at the briefcase on the floor. "You said you had the outline here."

"Yes," Mr. Christ said, pulling a thick sheaf of papers from the briefcase. "And we shall need your very best programmers and technicians. I have attempted to phrase the problems such that they need not know the precise details of our situation, but I'm sure you can improve on my presentation. You realize that it just wouldn't do for too many people to be aware of our transaction."

"Everything is confidential here, Mr. Christ. I will personally go over each detail, to ensure absolute secrecy."

Brown leafed through the papers quickly, then set them on his desk.

"Now as to the, uh, contract," he said, grinning slightly.

"Oh, yes. I am sure you realize I cannot offer you terms similar to those sometimes offered by our, uh, competitor. You know, everlasting life, wealth, and so forth."

"No, certainly not," Brown exclaimed. "Nothing for myself."

"What then, Mr. Brown?"

Mr. Brown shuffled in his seat, his fingers drumming on the desk in a staccato rhythm.

"Simply this," he said. "We want to be present when you put our system to use."

"We?"

"Uh, yes. The board here at Imperial. And myself."

"But I understood no one was to know the exact details."

"Oh, not the employees," Brown interrupted. "Not the programmers and clerks. They'll each have only a small part, with no idea of the whole. But the rest of us, we're all pretty good programmers, too, and we'll be coordinating all the work. We think it's only fair that we be given a chance to witness its success. After all, it is by far the biggest job we've undertaken. Incomparable."

"It is somewhat irregular, Mr. Brown. I thought the entire process could be handled from here. Ordinarily, one does not enter the kingdom – our establishment – until, well, later."

"I understand that, sir," Brown said, soothingly. "But it will also make the final adjustments far easier if we can be present to see just how it's put into effect."

Mr. Christ frowned. "Do you mean it may not work properly?"

"Oh, we're almost sure it will work. Ninety-nine point nine percent. Still, no program is perfect. Particularly so, when the overall scheme is bound to be vague, at best. There will always be bugs, and the only way to get them out is to see what's happening at the source."

"I have tried my best to present the entire situation to you, Mr. Brown. A good deal of effort has been spent on this, by a large part of our staff. I don't feel our board will be anxious to handle it quite this way. As you know, we have been conducting our own affairs in our own way for a good while. Very well, I might add."

Brown smiled and looked directly at the visitor. "But not any longer."

Mr. Christ made no reply, but turned his eyes to the floor, away from Brown's penetrating stare.

"I'm afraid that is our proposition," Brown said. "Thousands of man-hours will be spent on this job, and we feel this isn't too much to ask in return."

The visitor looked around, tapping the chair arm with his hand. After a few seconds, he slowly looked up.

"Very well, Mr. Brown. It shall be done."

"Fine, fine. Now, we'll be in touch with you regularly. Oh, how can we reach you with any questions?"

"Perhaps I can call in each day?"

'Yes, yes. Every other day will do, I think. Try to make it around 2:00 or so."

Mr. Christ rose from his seat, picking up the now-empty briefcase.

"How much time do you imagine the entire preparation will require?" he asked.

"Well, it's hard to say, offhand," Brown replied, smiling again. "Six months would be a good guess, from what you've told me. But we'll let you know."

"I shall return at that time, Mr. Brown. Until our next meeting, then?"

"Yes, indeed. Again, I must say what a pleasure it has been to meet you." He laughed. "And to do business. We'll let you know how we're progressing then."

"Goodbye, Mr. Brown."

After the visitor had left, Brown walked to the portable bar and poured himself a stiff bourbon. When the intercom buzzed, he strolled casually to the desk and pushed the button.

"Brown here."

"We saw him leave," came a voice from the speaker. "Is it set up?"

Brown smiled and sipped his drink. "Perfectly."

Cold November winds blew hats and papers through the busy streets when the visitor entered the towering office building for the second time, accompanied by two clean-shaven men with cherubic faces. All three wore shiny topcoats, unusually light for such a wintry day.

As the elevator let them off at the top floor, they entered the office and a middle-aged, cigar-smoking man scurried into the inner office, pointing the way. The secretary was nowhere to be seen, but it was after five and she may have left for the day.

Half a dozen men stood in the office as they entered, and Brown stepped up quickly, hand extended.

"Mr. Christ, come in, come in. We've been waiting."

"Good evening, Mr. Brown. I assume these are the men we spoke of?"

"Yes indeed," Brown replied. "And we've got your program fully set up. As best we can, at any rate. All we need to do is try it out."

As Brown introduced the other men, Mr. Christ moved slowly from one to the other, peering solemnly into each man's eyes as he shook hands. He did not attempt to introduce his companions, and was not asked to do so.

The introductions completed, Brown came forward again. "Uh, shall we get to the business at hand, then?"

"Indeed, Mr. Brown. Won't you all be seated. I am sorry I cannot explain the details of what will happen, but I am certain you all understand. It will be but a moment."

An intense light poured into the room from seemingly every direction, pounding shut the eyes of the six men. After an indeterminate time, they were able to open their eyes again, and gradually became aware of their surroundings.

They seemed to be in a large room, but one with no visible walls. Everything appeared to blend together, with no separation between objects, or between nearness and distance. They became quickly aware, as well, that there seemed to be no ceiling to the room. And no floor. Yet, it was a room, an unlimited room.

All was silent, but a vague melodic chant could be felt in the distance. Or nearness. Unidentifiable aromas and sensations pervaded the very air, which was warm and humid, yet pleasant.

The man with the cigar sank to his knees, retching, his face almost white. He was in tears. The others stood silently, blank faces staring ahead, unmoving. Christ spoke.

"As you no doubt realize, we are now ready to observe ... well, you need not concern yourselves, for you shall see no more. If you would look to the right, please."

As they turned, a giant metallic device emerged from the walls, or non-walls. It looked like the 9106 computer they had in the home office, a nearly silent, immovable electronic monument. A stack of data cards and several reels of magnetic tape lay idle in the console area.

The men were regaining their composure somewhat, except for the cigar-smoker, whose face remained pale and whose hands still trembled – almost in time with the vague murmur of the machine's tape reels.

"Which of you will operate the machine?" Mr. Christ asked.

Brown answered for the group, drumming his fingers on the console desk, his glance moving from the machine to the group. "We have decided that Mr. Atkins, our president, should have that honor."

Atkins was the most confident-appearing of the six, clad in a green sport jacket with Ascot, quite unlike his followers in their somber business attire. His blond crew cut and leather boots gave him the appearance of a wealthy sportsman, rather than a leader in science. Only a trace of fear could be detected in his schoolboy expression as he strode majestically to the console, seating himself with a flourish.

The other men stood to his rear, with Mr. Christ and his companions behind them. All eyes were on Mr. Atkins as he switched on the input system and thumbed through the cards.

"Uh, Mr. Christ, is there some way we can tell if the thing is working properly? Like, if we put through the material on war, how do we know if it's go or not? If it's fully accurate?"

"You shall know," Mr. Christ said, his hands folded, eyes moving from Atkins to the machine. "You shall know."

"Well, all set, then," Atkins said, smiling, as he inserted the cards into the collator. The cards were sorted in seconds, and almost instantly the men became aware of what was happening. They could not really see, but they knew. It was as though some sort of movie screen were placed everywhere around them, a screen that showed not single scenes, but everything – people, buildings, feelings, sounds. They could experience everything at once, it seemed.

The cigar smoker retched again, his head almost to the floor. He screamed.

Atkins whirled in his chair and stood up. "Feinberg, for chrissake, stop acting like a little kid. Whatsa' matter with you anyway?"

Christ and his two companions stepped back from the console area as Atkins and the others concentrated on the newly-found sensations. "Hey, Frank," Atkins yelled. "Did you see that?"

"No" was the reply from a young, bespectacled man, who stood fidgeting with his pipe. "I don't see a thing."

"What the hell," Atkins screamed. "Look around you, will you? We're seeing history here, for chrissake! The rest of you see it?"

"Yes, yes, Bill," they answered in chorus.

"Maybe we all have to concentrate on one thing at a time," Brown offered, haltingly.

"Yeah, yeah," Atkins replied. "Now, this first part is supposed to be about the poverty problem."

The six men stared straight ahead, concentrating on poverty. "Here's the situation in India," Atkins said. "Everybody see it now?"

They nodded as Atkins turned to adjust a dial. "Who handled this part?" he asked.

"I did," answered the pipe smoker, engrossed now in what he saw and felt. "This will be taken care of by a state-provided birth-control program and an improved agricultural policy. In general, of course. Plus some adjustment in religious beliefs," he added, turning to Mr. Christ, who was standing some distance away, stroking his beard.

Gradually they had the feeling that the people they saw were becoming better dressed and appeared healthier.

"I'll be damned," Brown exclaimed. "Will you look at that."

"It's working fine," Atkins yelled. "Look, you don't even see the beggars around any more. Say, let's try it with something else. Just to make sure."

"How about Viet Nam, Bill?" asked the man who had been ill, now apparently fully recovered from the ordeal.

Atkins searched through the stacks of cards. "That's under war, isn't it?" he asked. "Yes, here it is, War and Communism." He inserted the proper cards and twisted the input dial.

Involuntarily, Brown jumped back as he became aware of shooting all around him. Bombs could be felt coming from overhead, and the men were tempted to run for cover, but there was none.

"My God," Brown screamed as he felt the impact of a nearby explosion, "it must be getting worse."

The pipe-smoking young man stood calmly, a sly grin on his face. "Relax, Al," he said. "It'll be all over in no time. A couple well-placed hydrogen bombs and there won't be a Communist problem any more. I put them early in the program so we won't lose too many men needlessly."

Atkins leaned back in his chair, oblivious to the sights and sounds surrounding him. "How will it happen, Frank?" he asked.

"Oh, it'll appear accidental. But by that time there will have been a breakdown in the Democratic party and nobody will know just what happened. They'll just know that the problem of war with the Commies will be eliminated."

"Just like the Civil Rights issue," Atkins laughed. "Eliminated the easy way."

Atkins turned back to the dials as the others continued to watch the progress of the war, unconcerned now as the tracer bullets whizzed by.

Mr. Christ turned to his companions, nodded, and they walked quickly away.

Atkins sat hunched over the machine, adjusting the keys with a small, oddly-shaped tool. He grunted, then turned to the group behind him.

"This will never work," he said.

"Of course it will," Brown assured him. "It has to work. Think of the good it will do for science. Calculating the path of approaching asteroids, predicting economic recessions, weeding out poor political candidates. Maybe even forecasting the weather precisely. Why, just imagine the uses business will probably find for it."

"Don't forget war strategy, too," added another man, standing near the back of the room.

"Certainly," Brown said. "Keep working on it."

Brown smoothed his waistcoat and turned to the others, stroking his luxuriant beard, his eyes reflecting the doubt felt by each man.

"What do you think?" he asked the younger man with wire-rimmed spectacles, who stood holding his long-stemmed pipe at a jaunty angle.

"I don't know, sir," he replied. "Perhaps we're intruding in an area better left untouched. It sounds good, but maybe we aren't meant to learn so much. Maybe we were better off with the abacus, with using our own minds."

Atkins continued to adjust his machine, his grunts becoming more and more frequent.

32

Score One

I first met Charlie in the unemployment office. I was there to apply for benefits for the second time that year.

First, I'd been laid off from a three-year job with a printing company, as a clerk in the office. Hundred and ten bucks a week for fondling a few sheets of paper each day. Officially, they called me an assistant accounting clerk. In reality, I was one of the millions of paper shufflers who were being rapidly phased out by all the computer processing equipment the companies thought they couldn't do without.

My job was eventually taken over by a handful of transistors, I guess. They'd do everything I could do, and more, and never take an extra-long coffee break.

That had been my first experience as one of the unemployed, and it didn't last very long. They managed to find another niche for me, in another nearly-identical office – this time in a metal products company – after providing rocking-chair money for less than three weeks. Just when I was getting to like the idea of sleeping 'til noon every day, dropping in at the compensation office on Thursday afternoons for a chat with some numbered bureaucrat clerk, they tossed me back into the workaday world once again.

The metal products company was not as impressed by my performance as they had been by my application form. I had barely gotten the hang of shuffling those new papers (they were considerably larger than the ones I'd shuffled at the printing outfit and had a lot more numbers on them) when I received a little pink notice with my pay envelope. They hadn't even bothered to tell me anything by mouth; just some words on a piece of paper to let me know that my services were no longer required.

Just as well, though. I had been growing intrigued by all the numbers on all the papers that were flowing across my desk, spending the better part of each day playing little numerical games with them, for my own amusement. Not that I'd shirked my official duties. I had duly recorded the bits of information with which I had been entrusted, transferring the little numbers from one sheet of paper into a big ledger book on my desk. It had been fun in a way. I felt like a Dickens character dutifully copying figures with a quill pen. My own pen was a Bic 19-cent model, but the idea was the same.

Anyway, my loss of remunerative employment brought me once again to the unemployment office, where I was certain I would be greeted as a long-lost relative, returned once again to the fold. Not so, of course. Even the few faces I recognized from my earlier foray into the world of government benefits gave no indication of familiarity. For one thing, they had changed my reporting day from Thursday to Tuesday, so most of the faces in the lines were unfamiliar ones. The expressions on the faces were the same as before, but the specific features were different.

Charlie's was the only face that looked human. The others stared vacantly at the back of the person in front of them, giving no sign of life until they reached the head of the line and droned out a few words in response to the questions of the equally-bored clerk.

Charlie, on the other hand, kept up a steady patter of jokes and near-obscene references to the parentage of the officials who sat at desks behind glass-walled cubicles at the other end of the hall. His jokes and chatter were lost on most of the standees, but I could hardly keep myself from laughing out loud. Some of his comparisons to rabbits and gorillas were really funny. Offensive, but funny.

After a particularly outrageous story about a personnel manager in a house of ill repute, I could no longer hold back and emitted a loud, hoarse guffaw. The other faces in line took no notice of me (they would hardly have noticed an A-bomb going off at the end of the line). But Charlie looked over with a pleased smile on his handsome, full-bearded face.

"A connoisseur," he said. "How thrilling to find that the loss of employment has not brought about the loss of your discriminating taste, young man."

Even though he seemed to be little older than me (I'm thirty-two) there was something about his demeanor that did make him like an elder, with me as his pupil and follower. So I did not resent his condescending approach at all. As it turned out, Charlie was always the leader and I the follower, so this was simply a sign of things to come.

"I'm a newcomer here," I said to him. "Haven't lost my sense of humor yet, like these other fellows seem to have done."

"Sad but true," he replied. "Their minds have grown as dull as their humdrum ambitions. It would seem that their total lives have been preparing them thoroughly for just this end. Through ardent preparation and planning, they have reached their ultimate goal: the unemployment line."

No one took offense at this unsubtle put-down. In fact, no one gave any indication that they were aware of Charlie's words at all. We may as well have been alone in the hall, instead of being surrounded by several hundred expressionless faces.

"For some of us, on the other hand," Charlie continued, "the unemployment line is merely a way-station, a point of respite on our way to loftier aspirations. Like you, my friend, I can see by your exquisite taste and manners that you are with us for only a momentary sojourn. I see great accomplishments ahead for you, as I do for myself."

Charlie always talked in that flowery way, like he was head and shoulders above the crowd. As a matter of fact, he had spent more time in the unemployment line during his adult life than he had in gainful employment. Me, I knew darned well that I was no better than the rest of the losers in line. But it was kind of nice to hear Charlie's enthusiasm and lusty attitude. When I got to the head of the line, I actually gave the bureaucrat a hearty smile rather than my usual scowl. He did not return the compliment, though. His frown was etched into his granite face for good. As I turned away from the counter and began my short walk to the outside world, Charlie came up behind me and grabbed my arm.

"Just down the block," he boomed, "is an entirely adequate lunch counter. Outstanding French Onion soup. Would you care to join me?"

Since my plans for the afternoon were rather hazy, actually non-existent, I agreed to accompany him. His company promised a few laughs, if nothing else. And I could use a few. The prospects for finding another job looked pretty bleak, and I hadn't received my first unemployment check yet. Worse yet, the old bank book showed a depressingly minuscule balance.

We were sitting at a table for two, right at the window. Charlie kept watching the people passing by outside, his eyes gazing intently into each face that came by our vantage point.

"All losers," he said with a shrug. "They've never been anything, and never will be. Satisfied to go home and stare at the boob tube every night with a six-pack in hand. What kind of life is that?"

I wasn't sure how to answer him. Lately, I'd been spending a lot of my own time staring at the uncritical face of the TV set myself. Sometimes with more than one six-pack on the floor.

"Well, what choice do they have?" I asked. "The big shots can have a good life, travel around, see a lot of things. The little guys, they can barely afford that six-pack and color TV set. If it gives them pleasure, what's the difference?"

"A big difference. They wouldn't take a better life if they had the chance. They're all in such a stupid rut that they don't even realize what's out in the world. So they settle for the safe way. Go to work every day, get that paycheck every Friday. Safe and easy."

"To tell you the truth," I admitted, "I wouldn't mind that regular paycheck so much. How long does it take before I get my first compensation check, anyway?"

"Piddling checks. Standing in that absurd line to collect a few measly dollars each week. Almost as bad as working. You should get your first one about four weeks after you first applied."

Our identical orders of the onion soup and cheeseburgers had arrived, and I had to admit that the soup was much better than expected.

"Of course it is," Charlie shrugged. "I know the specialties of the house at virtually every greasy lunch counter in the downtown area. Such knowledge may never find its way into Michelin's directory of the finest eateries in the world, but it comes in handy when one is strolling around the city. And when one is strapped for cash, which is my unfortunate predicament at the moment."

"Not for long, though," he added, glancing around to see that no one was paying attention to his words. "Believe me, I do not intend to spend the balance of my years in a frantic effort to survive on the good graces of the state."

"Have they found you another job?" I asked, "What kind of work do you do?"

"Job," he scoffed. "Who needs a job? I've had quite enough of the indignities suffered at the hands of minor-league tyrants. I have punched my last time clock, smoked my last harried cigarette huddled in the toilet, made my last excuse for taking a few much-needed hours off from some ridiculous employment. My friend, you will never amount to anything as a slave to the employing classes."

I sat staring down at the coffee cup, toying with its handle. This was getting to be one of those political speeches, the kind the Communists and Socialists used to give. Funny, though, you didn't hear those kinds of words very much anymore. It seemed as though all the left-wingers who used to stand on street corners harping about the great working class had gotten steady jobs or something.

"Am I boring you?" Charlie asked quietly.

"No, no. I was just thinking about the last time I heard anyone talking about the employing classes. Wage slavery and all that."

"Not many of us left," Charlie said. "All the old radicals of the 1960s, and the old-timers from before that, are living in the suburbs. Harassing their employees and fellow workers worse than the old bosses did.

"I've changed, too, since those days. The working class isn't worth worrying about; they deserve what they're getting. They voted in Nixon and that crowd, they can live with the consequences. There's no nobility in the working man. Or in work, for that matter."

"So what can you do?" I asked. "You have to earn a living somehow."

"Not at all. The answer is wealth. If you are wealthy, you never need to worry about having enough food and comfort."

"A great idea," I laughed. "Unfortunately, I picked the wrong parents. Mine never had a dollar to spare, from one paycheck to the next. When there was a paycheck."

"I, too, come from impoverished stock. One of the few latter-day radicals who did, as I eventually discovered.

"But there are additional ways to acquire wealth. Perhaps not the immense amounts of wealth that are possible to the fortunate heir, but a more modest level of financial assets – enough to carry on a comfortable and fruitful life. That much is indeed possible."

"How?" I asked. "By winning the state lottery? I've been buying a ticket every week for I-don't-know-how-many months, and never even got the five-dollar prize."

"Hardly," Charlie replied. "Obviously, one's chance of attaining one of the larger jackpots is minimal. No, I'm afraid that the one path open to those of us of modest backgrounds and minimal investment potential is a lawless one. The route of crime, my boy, is the golden road to independence, I am certain of that.

"Not that I am one of your born criminals, or anything of the sort. As a boy, a teenager, I was almost disgustingly law-abiding. The only crimes I have ever been involved in occurred during those troubled days of 1968 in Chicago, and I cannot very well interpret those as criminal in the true sense of the word. Most assuredly, I gained nothing in the way of financial stature by those vain acts.

"Today, however, I view the world in a considerably different light. Time has been passing. Before long I will be a middle-aged man, then an elderly one. Bad enough to be elderly at all, but I surely do not intend to become a *poor* elderly man."

"Well, I have to admit I've thought about crime once or twice myself," I admitted. "But I never did anything, or even thought seriously about it. I used to know a couple of guys who became criminals, guys from the old neighborhood. But they've both been in jail off and on for years, and I never had much desire to follow in their footsteps."

"Naturally not," Charlie said. "The food in prison is abhorrent, and the social intercourse quite limited. Obviously, I have no intention of paying the legal penalty for my imminent endeavors."

"I don't guess anyone does. Do you have something particular in mind? Or are you just talking hypothetically."

"Oh, I have some very definite plans," Charlie said, patting me on the hand as he drained the last of his coffee. "Like every successful criminal, I plan to make use of the talents and knowledge which I possess in the greatest quantity.

"Being a sedentary sort of person, most assuredly not a ruffian type, the physical forms of illicit behavior are out of the question. In any case, the thought of violence makes me ill. I've seen enough of it in the past to last several lifetimes.

"No, it is mandatory for someone of my particular personality to engage in the more cerebral criminal pastimes. And to take advantage of my abilities as an actor. I've performed in a number of minor dramatic productions. Nothing like Broadway, of course, or even off-Broadway. But my portrayals were deemed entirely adequate and convincing by scores of little-known critics."

I wasn't surprised. With Charlie's flair for fancy language and his continual change of facial expression, and his many gestures which he used to emphasize certain points in his discourse, what could he be but an actor? He even looked like one in a way with his heavy-lidded brown eyes that bored straight into you, plus his fashionably long, flowing dark hair and bushy, neatly-trimmed beard. Not your leading man type, but sort of a hairy version of one of the old character actors. George Sanders, maybe; or Sydney Greenstreet.

"In addition," he continued, "I have made a rather serious study of crime and the criminal modes of behavior during my frequent periods of unemployment. Believe me, there is nothing to replace intense study when one is embarking upon a new and promising career. I've covered just about every facet, too. Everything from the basic texts in criminology, the early theories of Lombroso and Sutherland, up to the daily reports on crime in the more scandalous of the daily and weekly newspapers.

"Besides that, I have read the fiction of crime ever since I was a boy. Holmes and Wolfe and McBain, as well as all the lesser-known stories and novels, by the major authors of detective and mystery fiction. I've even gone through old issues of the *Police Gazette*, and the lurid exposes in early issues of *True* magazine and similar publications.

"In short, I have done my homework. Only one basic aid is still lacking. For the best hope of success, I am compelled to enlist a confederate."

I should have expected Charlie was leading up to this, but I was momentarily stunned nonetheless.

"Well, I don't know," I stammered. "Anyway, why me? You don't know anything about me. I could be a cop, for all you know. Or someone who would want to turn in potential crooks."

Score One

Charlie smiled, sitting back in his straight-backed wooden chair, a toothpick making its way between his nearly-perfect set of teeth. "I pride myself on my ability to select people. Having done a bit of research already, I have little doubt that you will be an excellent choice. And I will do more, before providing you with any significant information on my plans. So far, as you can see, I have spoken only in vague generalities, not regarding a specific course of action."

He pulled a sheet of typewriter paper out of the pocket of his windbreaker, smoothing it out on the table between the depleted cups and plates.

"William Maris," he read. "229 Eastgate Avenue, which is a twenty-unit arrangement of furnished rooms, each renting for $140 per month. High school graduate, three years of college with no particular major field of studies, 18 months in the Army just before Viet Nam. Followed by a dozen jobs of various types, nothing of any consequence, the last one being a three-week stint as a clerk in a metal products company.

"There's more," he added, "but we'll leave it at that for now. At any rate, my information on you, coupled with my visceral feeling once I had looked you over, so to speak, have convinced me that you are my man. So what do you think?"

I sat back in my rickety chair, lighting a cigarette with clumsy fingers. My first impulse was to get up and leave, to say thanks but no thanks, to stick with my inconsequential but super-safe life for a while longer. My second impulse was the one that spoke.

"Sounds possible," I said. "I'm not saying anything for sure, but it's possible. Where do you get your information, anyway? You astonish me. Maybe you're the cop."

Charlie roared with laughter, drawing the attention of all the nearby eaters. His modest beer belly shook uncontrollably; his feet were stamping the floor.

"That's a good one," he snorted, still laughing. "You've got me there, William. A cop, that's a good one.

"No, I'm not a cop," he finally said. "No way. However, I do have a large number of acquaintances who can provide certain favors, and some of them are in positions of trust. Including some law officers, whom I met when I was doing research for some true-crime articles I wrote a few years ago. The articles never sold, but the contacts I made were worth the effort. They'll help me in the future, too, when we get down to cases."

I held up my hand. "Just understand this, first. I don't know anything about your plans yet, and if I don't like them, I'm out."

"Naturally," Charlie replied. "I wouldn't want you, or anyone, in it with me unless you felt as strongly as I do that the job is a reliable one, with every chance of success. You are of course free to withdraw at will, after I have given you the entire series of facts and plans.

"However, this is neither the time nor the place to go into such discreet discussions. And I have another appointment shortly, so perhaps we can get together again this evening. I would prefer to meet at my apartment, where I know we cannot be overheard. Agreed?"

"Sure," I said. "Why not?"

"Then here is the address," Charlie said, handing me a business card, which I glanced at quickly. "Eight o'clock would be an ideal time to commence negotiations."

"Wait a minute," I cautioned, "what's this business on the card? Charles Weston, Investigations? What do you investigate?"

"Not a thing as yet, William. The card comes in handy on occasion, though. I have other cards with other lines of endeavor printed on them, so you can overlook it. Nothing ominous, I assure you. Tonight then?"

"Yeah, tonight. I'll be there."

"Then I bid you farewell for the moment," he said with a wave of his hand, rising from his chair. "Eight o'clock."

He walked out with a flourish, like a king departing from a

meeting with his trusted, yet decidedly subordinate, advisors. Leaving me to ponder whether I really wanted to be one of those advisors, whether I wanted to begin a life of crime at the age of thirty-two.

I paid the check for both of us and walked out, not certain what to do.

The building was nothing special: a four-story walk-up like dozens, hundreds of others in the neighborhood. Squinting at the doorbells, I saw that Charlie's apartment was all the way up, 4C.

Thirteen steps to each floor, and I counted every one with an increasing wheeze. Exercise had never been my thing, at least anything more strenuous than elbow-bending at the corner tavern now and then. I knew I was in terrible shape physically; but since I led a pretty restricted life, I wasn't often reminded of it. My own apartment building had an elevator, so stairs were something I didn't confront very often.

I paused at the top landing, waiting patiently to catch my breath before knocking on 4C. The corridor was old-fashioned with fairly ornate woodwork and varnish, a little bit seedy but with a hint of its old elegance. At least it wasn't plastic and formica like the buildings in my own neighborhood, the new singles-type pads.

Charlie answered the door within a few seconds. He was wearing a garishly colored robe, holding a massive carved pipe in his hand.

"William," he said with a broad smile, "you're here. I have to admit that I had some reservations about your appearance here this evening. Come in, come in."

It was absolutely the most cluttered, crowded room I had ever seen. The walls were lined with bookshelves, each space filled tightly with books and magazines and papers. More printed materials were everywhere – on the big overstuffed chair that sat like a throne in the corner by the window, on the coffee table, piled on top of the antiquated television set, strewn all over the floor. Interspersed among the books and papers were coffee cups, dinner plates encrusted with half-eaten food, piles of ashes both in and out of impromptu ashtrays, and empty beer cans.

Beer cans of every brand, it seemed. There must have been hundreds of them, some upright, some lying on their sides, some crushed by someone's powerful hand.

"Neatness is not my forte, William," Charlie admitted as he swept the papers and plates from the couch onto the floor. "Orderliness of mind, in my view, must take precedence over neatness of one's surroundings. Take a seat, please. Have a beer? Or coffee?"

"Beer is fine," I said, easing myself into the space Charlie had made on the couch. He went into the little kitchen area, which looked even messier than the living room, and returned with a can of a brand of beer I had never heard of.

"Best Beer," he said. "That's its brand name, not a capsule description of its quality. Brewed in Chicago, I'm told. It may not be the king of beers, but the price is $1.09 a six-pack, so it does have a certain marked advantage over the better-known brews. A bit on the watery side, perhaps, but otherwise acceptable."

I snapped off the pull tab on the can and took a hesitant sip. "Not bad," I admitted. "Not bad at all. I'll keep it in mind for myself."

"Economizing on the essentials is absolutely mandatory, William. Beer happens to be at the very head of my list of basic necessities of life, so I must minimize my investment as much as possible. This allows sufficient quantities of cash for the luxuries."

A powerful knock could be heard, in some kind of code. Knock space – knock knock – space – knock. Charlie moved to the door with a broad grin. "I do believe this is one of those luxuries approaching at this very moment."

As Charlie opened the front door with a flourish, I could only come up with one word: Wow. She was a knockout. Not so young. Maybe twenty-six or -seven, but absolutely beautiful, with a full load of curves in all the right places. Obviously braless, wearing only a T-shirt and tight jeans under the fake fur coat she tossed onto the chair nearest the door.

With her physical attributes brazenly silhouetted in the light of the floor lamp, her presence roused several dormant thoughts in my low-alert brain. Mainly, that it had been a heck of a long time since I'd had anything like that. In fact, a long time since there had been a woman of any kind in my life. I'd almost forgotten about them, since the loss of my job and worries about earning money came up.

"William," Charlie said with a self-satisfied expression, "this is Marilyn. Marilyn, William. Marilyn is a very special friend. More than a friend, actually; a confidante, you might say."

"Hi," she said, settling herself onto the couch next to me. Not too close, but close enough so that I could feel her presence even if my eyes and ears were inoperative. She'd only said one word, one syllable, but the soft, well-modulated tone of her voice aroused some familiar yearnings within me.

Charlie interrupted the high-speed motion picture of sudden fantasy that was running through my thoughts. "Marilyn is here to learn about our plans tonight. Just as you are, William. Our undertaking will require three persons, at least. So if you will make yourselves entirely comfortable, I shall proceed with my discourse."

He opened the closet door and withdrew a sheaf of papers and a slide projector. Knocking several beer cans and a small stack of magazines onto the floor, he set the projector on the end table and pointed it at the front door. I hadn't noticed it before, but the door had a large sheet of white cardboard tacked onto it, evidently intended for use as a screen.

"Before we begin," Charlie said, "I will make one or two points perfectly clear to you about the project. First, in selecting a particular objective. a victim as it were, I made absolutely sure that the said objective would have a sufficient quantity of cash to make our efforts entirely worthwhile. Even though I have no intention of being apprehended during or after the event, I want to be certain that the reward is adequate for the minimal, but existent, risk involved.

"Secondly, I have no desire to bring harm to anyone, especially to the victim. Either physically or financially. The victim has a substantial fortune and can easily afford the loss of the amount we will be seeking. And with the Plan I have drawn up, there will be no need for physical violence beyond a very minimal level at the outset.

"However, we must be prepared for the unforeseen, so I will be equipped with a pistol and ammunition. The chance of having to make use of weaponry is less than one percent, but I want you to know that before you proceed. Neither of you will have to carry any sort of weapon, so if by some bizarre chance you are apprehended, the lack of such a weapon will be in your favor. That, and the fact that neither of you has any sort of criminal or illegal background."

He reached over and switched off the overhead light, turning on the projector with his other hand. A moment later the first slide appeared on the screen, a slightly fuzzy image of a middle-aged, well-dressed man. White, wearing a conservative suit, obviously a businessman of some kind.

"That, my friends," Charlie explained, "is Mister Frederick O'Toole. Age forty-six. Chairman of the Board of Hathaway Chemical Corporation, one of the larger manufacturers of industrial solvents. Income, sixty thousand dollars a year. Assets, approximately three million dollars, acquired largely through his marriage to the former Dolly Faber, heiress to an airline company."

An image of a rather stern, forbidding middle-aged woman replaced Mister O'Toole on the screen. "Age forty-nine, married to Mr. O'Toole for nine years, would have been an old maid (to use the ancient term) if he had not come along.

"Aside from her substantial financial assets, she had little to offer toward the romance, as you can easily see. But three million dollars can take the place of a great deal of physical beauty and similar traditional feminine attributes."

Score One

"As it happens, Mrs. O'Toole's rather hostile expression gives an excellent indication of her basic attitude toward Mr. O'Toole, and toward nearly everything else in this life. She is, to put it bluntly, a shrew, a harridan, who makes every effort to add unpleasantness to her husband's daily life. Not your storybook marriage by any means, but one that is hardly uncommon in this mercenary world."

Another flash on the screen, this time to a young boy, whose thick glasses and child-size vested suit made me think of Little Lord Fauntleroy. His facial expression was obviously inherited from the female side of the relationship.

"Young Frederick," Charlie said with a chuckle. "Approximately the sort of offspring one would expect from a loveless cohabitation – overprotected, spoiled, and generally unpleasant toward everyone around him. He attends one of those grossly overpriced private academies catering to the wealthy, who fear for the lives of their children and isolate them from any contact with the lower classes. His schoolmates do not hold him in high regard. Even when surrounded by a classroom of arrogant and unpleasant young boys, Master O'Toole stands above the rest in overall meanness.

"Interestingly enough, however, the elder O'Toole has great love for the boy, and hardly notices the fact that he is gradually turning out to be a model of snobbishness and haughtiness. Brought about, naturally, by the continual brainwashing from his mother. The boy, on the other hand, has developed quite a distaste for his father, barely tolerating him as a member of the household.

"In short, Mister O'Toole is inordinately fond of the youngster whether the feeling is reciprocated or not, and would not wish to lose him. However, these feelings are not held toward his wife at all."

Another flash, and a voluptuous bikini-clad young woman appeared on the screen, lying on an uncrowded beach, with a fuzzy male figure hovering in the background. If Mrs. O'Toole is on one end of the spectrum of feminine pulchritude, this specimen is clearly at the other extreme.

"And this, of course, is the obvious, and expected, reason. The cowering gentleman, in case you hadn't guessed, is Mr. O'Toole. And the young lady is Miss Elizabeth Barrett, currently employed as a typist in O'Toole's firm. She is, of course, something more than an employee, for reasons that are quite apparent.

"In fact, Mr. O'Toole would like nothing more than to spend the rest of his days with Miss Barrett. However, as is usually the case with such *ménage à trois* situations, the wife is a bit of a barrier. At this point, she is unaware of O'Toole's entanglement with the young lady, but it is only a matter of time before she learns the truth, if she doesn't already suspect."

Marilyn was gazing at the screen with unusual interest, a cute frown on her full, natural lips. Luscious as the girl in the picture was, I couldn't get my mind off of Marilyn. I wondered if she and Charlie were making it, or if this was strictly a business arrangement. Perhaps later I could bring up the subject discreetly, after she had left. If she did indeed leave.

I wasn't thinking much about the proposition Charlie had laid before me. The thought of getting involved in some kind of criminal activity brought a bad taste into my mouth. Still, I had nothing to lose by listening and the company was pleasant enough. Too pleasant, really.

"William?"

Charlie was looking at me quizzically.

"Are you still with us?"

"Uh, sure," I replied. "I guess I was concentrating on the pictures. Did you say something?"

He looked at me curiously. "No, I merely wanted to make sure you were paying attention. This is quite important, you know."

"Yes, I know. I'm sorry. That's quite a lovely young lady, though. Not hard to see why O'Toole is interested."

The next picture was a huge mansion, sort of a cross between the plantation South and California modern. Grecian porticos combined with immense picture windows and a full-width front porch. The lawn and hedges were obviously manicured professionally; hardly a blade of grass looked more than regulation length. In the driveway sat three cars: a Cadillac limousine, a Mercedes-Benz convertible, and a huge, elderly sedan, probably of 1930s vintage.

"O'Toole is a lover of mechanical devices," Charlie continued. "Cars, power tools, electronic gadgets, and so forth. The entire basement is given over to his workshop. Many of the solvents turned out by his company are designed right there, by him personally.

"The home was constructed just five years ago. Not to my taste at all – gaudy kitsch, in my opinion – but extremely expensive. In the back are an Olympic swimming pool and a double tennis court, neither of which is used with any frequency. Like most executives of his type, O'Toole's physical condition is less than perfect.

"His interest in mechanical matters is exceeded only by his interest in Miss Barrett. And she is the crux of our little plan. Without knowing that she is, of course. In arranging our scenario, I attempted to develop an acquaintance with the young lady, thinking that she might be induced to become a willing accomplice. However, it seems that she is genuinely infatuated with the gentleman, as I learned from a discreet conversation with one of her girlfriends.

"Naturally, I have considered a number of possibilities. A kidnapping, for example. Kidnapping of the wife is, of course, out of the question. O'Toole would probably prefer to pay us to keep her, rather than to get her back. And snatching the boy would be a headache I prefer to avoid. I am told that he is an absolute beast, and I doubt that we could keep him under control for the time needed. In any case, kidnapping carries extreme penalties, and the potential gain is simply not worth the risk.

"Outright theft, too, is a near-impossibility. To perform a burglary would necessitate the enlistment of a knowledgeable confederate from the professional criminal ranks, which I prefer to avoid. And it is unlikely that the family keeps any substantial amount of cash on hand. Besides, stealing merchandise, dealing with fences and the like, is gross. Which leaves one possibility, the one with the least potential for apprehension: Blackmail."

Charlie was ready for my objections.

"I know precisely what you are thinking, William. The term blackmail has some terribly unfortunate, tawdry connotations – visions of photographers peeking into transoms, crude meetings in dark alleys, destruction of families and careers."

"Well, yeah," I conceded. "That's about the way I see it. It's so – well, sneaky."

Marilyn spoke up for the first time. "I'm sure Charlie wouldn't do anything sneaky, or anything to harm the subject."

"Subject?" I asked. "He's not something to study, for God's sake. Isn't victim the more appropriate description?"

"Oh now, William," Charlie chuckled, "let's not allow the discussion to degenerate into mere semantics. Marilyn is correct, you know. We will bring no serious harm to either Mr. O'Toole or his family, nothing that cannot be undone with ease once we've achieved our monetary objective. You have my full assurance on this point."

"I'm not agreeing to anything yet." I didn't really want to get into this business. I'm not the criminal type at all. That was becoming more and more evident. The thought of doing something I'd later be ashamed of didn't appeal one bit. I was wishing I hadn't even come here, stayed at home in front of the TV as usual.

"Without a doubt," Charlie continued, "your conventional upbringing presents a barrier to rational speculation. But I can assure you that, once the endeavor is set on its course, you will see that we are treating no one with dastardly intent. The entire operation will be conducted as a business transaction, nothing more."

"I'll hear it out, but no guarantees. If I don't like it, I back out."

"Of course, William. If I may continue?"

I nodded, resignedly. Deep down, I knew I was expressing reluctance out of fear more than anything. Fear of getting caught.

Score One

I had no great love for big shots like O'Toole. Maybe he would be getting what he deserved for playing around, cheating on his wife. I didn't really have as many scruples as I made it appear. I knew that. And I was sure that Charlie knew it, too.

He was really a smart guy, I could see that. Not from his fancy talk and big words, but from the way he looked at me when I spoke, as if he could see right into my brain.

Charlie spent nearly an hour more outlining the plan, down to the most minute detail. I had to admit, he'd worked it out extremely carefully. If there was a flaw somewhere, I couldn't spot it.

When he finished, we shook hands on it, having settled on the following Thursday as the date for the procedure. Just four days off.

After what seemed like mere hours, the day of reckoning arrived. We were ready. As far as I could tell, at least, since I hadn't really absorbed quite all the details Charlie had explained.

Not that it mattered. By the time our D-Day arrived, Charlie and I were both behind bars. Can you believe it?

Marilyn, we soon learned, was not behind anything. She was free as the proverbial bird. Why? Because she'd turned us in to the police, who appeared to be trying to drum up some kind of conspiracy charge against us.

Since no crime of any kind had taken place, our conversations could be claimed as wholly fictional. Just a made-up story we told each other, about a *possible* crime that *somebody* might be able to undertake. A mental exercise. A game. Like trying to come up with a detective story, tossing out ideas about the crime and the criminals that popped into our minds.

They had us on tape, blabbing some stuff that didn't look good for either of us. Obviously, that was Marilyn's work, and she'd done it well. Still, why she wound up assigned to Charlie, embedded into our inevitably foolish little moneymaking plan, I can't imagine.

Despite all of his fancy, professorial words, his supreme

confidence, his impressive erudition, his carefully-constructed plans, Charlie – like so many male persons before him – had been sabotaged by a wily and clever woman. Looking back with a bit more clarity now, she was steadily and subtly using misdirection to keep his (and my) attention focused on her feminine attributes. So simple yet so effective, her subtly incisive performance prevented both of us from acknowledging any possibility that she was more than she appeared to be.

We'd been conned, in other words. For that failure to absorb what was happening, we deserved whatever punishment might be forthcoming.

33

The Courage of Kenneth

I've always been afraid. In the delivery room, thirty-five years ago, waiting to be extracted from my mother's womb, I was afraid. I know I was.

Far better to remain in the dark warmth of another's body than to face the callous worldlights outside. Lights that would never let up, never cease their aim at my attempts to hide and run.

They always managed to find me, illuminating my existence for the benefit of those critics who invariably stood to the side, ready to ask for what I could not, would not, give.

They say that everyone, deep down, is afraid (except for those psychopaths who cannot see the consequences of their moves). Perhaps. Only they don't know it; or if they do, always manage to find reasons and excuses for their avoidance of the difficult.

I gave that up long ago.

Why pretend that I am acting in a courageous manner when any fool can see the terror within. And without. Even during childhood, three or four years old, one's companions know immediately who is afraid and who is not. And gleefully devise methods to expose the culprit for what he is, pointing his flaws out to any who lack the perception to see for themselves.

I have no friends. I know a lot of people, always have; but no friend to whom I could express the frights that surround me during every waking moment – and rarely subside even during sleep.

My best friend was Jack. (We have no worthy word to express a friend who is not really friendly; acquaintance is hardly the term to describe the peers of one's childhood.) We met at the curb, right in front of our apartment building, as he tossed bits of branches and stones down the sewer grate, edging a little farther away each time in a test of skill. He lived in the side entrance on the third floor, I was in front on the first. I picked up some stones myself, following his lead, and tossed them all at once.

"That's not the way," he scoffed.

They've always scoffed. If not immediately, soon afterward.

"I can get every one down the hole from way back here," he proclaimed.

I didn't doubt it. Not wishing to test myself, I merely glanced around at him, with a silly grin on my face. (It's always been there on such occasions.) Knowing that my aim would only be adequate from a minimal distance, to be on the safe side, it would be prudent to toss at least three or four at a time, hoping one hit the mark.

"I don't want to play," I protested, leaning back with my head on the ground.

"It ain't playing," he countered. "Just throwing. Come on, take a few."

Accepting the proffered stones, I couldn't very well refuse to participate. Watching my inept prowess for a couple of minutes, Jack soon became bored, setting his handful of stones aside.

"Want to climb the mailbox?" he asked.

One of those large mail storage boxes – which had seemed mountain-like in childhood but would diminish to mundane size with the onset of adolescence – stood at the corner of the block, directly ahead of the corner of our building. I'd seen the kids climbing on it many times, watching out the window of our apartment. Sooner or later, I knew, if I spent any time out of doors, I would be expected – required – to follow suit.

For that reason, I chose to remain indoors for hours on end, tinkering with my battleships, until my mother insisted that I go out for some fresh air. Up to now, my presence had been overlooked by the others in their play and general roughhousing around the box. Each of them had taken his respective turn, standing back a dozen feet, running and making an enormous leap to the top of the box, then sitting atop it, face aglow, silently daring the next participant to risk the attempt.

Once, I had seen from my window the result of a missed attempt. Knocked unconscious as his head hit the edge of the box, William – who lived several buildings down the street – lay motionless on the sidewalk, blood oozing from his forehead. Within seconds, a group of mothers had arrived on the scene, wiping the blood away with their skirts and yelling for someone to call an ambulance. His own mother had not appeared, being one of the few who worked all day, leaving William on his own, with only a grandmother a couple of blocks away to care for emergencies.

Waiting for the ambulance, a lot of clucking had taken place among the mothers, deriding William's parent for leaving him alone. "Some people shouldn't have children," one of them insisted. "What's the matter with that woman, anyway?"

The mothers also had taken that opportunity to chide their own offspring for their carelessness and recklessness, and for being so foolish as to play around the mailbox that way.

"You see what happens?" one lady asked of her embarrassed son. "That could be you down there. What's the matter with you kids? Don't you care what happens to you?"

William came to before the ambulance arrived, awakening with a whimper that erupted quickly into an all-out yell. Seeing the other children surrounding the group, however, he made a heroic effort to control his screams, with only limited success.

Frightened as they had been at the sight of the blood, intensified by his unmoving form on the ground, the youngsters – boys and girls alike – had snickered, their knowing expressions noted and exchanged among the group. Secretly glad, though, that it was William down there and not one of them – but not letting on that they had any fear, or would in the future stay away from the box.

Jack had been among the group that day, seemingly pouting about the lost opportunity for challenging the box more times that afternoon, rather than demonstrating concern for William or displaying any hint of the terror that all of them must have felt to some degree.

I stayed inside throughout the episode, peeking from below the window shade so no one would know I had witnessed the event and mention it to me later. And vowing that nothing in the world could make me go anywhere near that box. As a matter of fact, for the next few weeks, I neatly circumvented the box when making my rounds in the area, taking a long route around it, walking on the grass and even out in the street rather than approaching too closely. And not going anywhere near when another kid was within sight.

On this fateful day, a week or so after the injurious incident, I knew I could no longer avoid the inevitable. Unless my parents could be persuaded to move out of the neighborhood in the next few minutes, I would have to take my turn. I was only thankful that Jack was the only one around: that the other kids were off doing who knew what.

Resigned to the task, knowing my fear would be obvious to Jack but that the challenge could no longer be put off, I glanced over at the military green behemoth. The feeling was a lot like what I would experience years later when, needing a job in a hurry, I foolishly agreed to serve as a house painter's helper (not thinking about the fact that he worked on buildings three and four stories high).

While pondering for the last time, I tossed a stone, missing the sewer hole for what must have been the twentieth time.

"Okay," I said in a whisper.

About the Author

James M. Flammang has been a journalist, writer, and editor for nearly his entire working life. Since the 1980s, he's covered the automobile business as an independent journalist. In addition to contributing product reviews and articles to such publications as autoMedia, Kelley Blue Book, CarsDirect, J.D. Power, cars.com, Consumer Guide, and the *Chicago Tribune*, Flammang has authored thirty books. Most were about automotive history, but he also has written six books for children. Flammang is a member of the Freelancers Union and the International Motor Press Association, and past president of the Midwest Automotive Media Association.

Lately, Flammang has eased away from cars to focus on books: mostly essays and memoirs, establishing TK Press to publish his work. *Mr. Maurice Knows It All* ... was the first. Next: the *Tirekicking Used Car Buyer's Guide*, followed by *Incompetent*. Coming soon: *Fraidy Cat*, to be followed by *Absurdities* and *Work Hurts*. In 2021, he wrote a history of the used car for his website, tirekick.com, which has been online since 1995. Born in Chicago, he lives just outside that city with his wife, advisor and editor, Marianne E. Flammang.

www.ingramcontent.com/pod-product-compliance
Lightning Source LLC
Chambersburg PA
CBHW070533010526
44118CB00012B/1117